JEST UPON JEST

JEST UPON JEST

A Selection from the Jestbooks
and Collections of Merry Tales published
from the Reign of Richard III
to George III

JOHN WARDROPER

ROUTLEDGE & KEGAN PAUL

LONDON

First published in 1970
by Routledge and Kegan Paul Ltd
Broadway House, 68–74 Carter Lane
London, E.C.4
Printed in Great Britain
by Western Printing Services Ltd, Bristol
© J. Wardroper 1970
No part of this book may be reproduced
in any form without permission from the
publisher, except for the quotation of
brief passages in criticism
ISBN 07100 6754 2

CONTENTS

		page
	Acknowledgements	vii
	Introduction	1
	Note on the text	26
1	Husbands, Wives and Wenches	28
2	Friars, Priests and Nuns	62
3	From Marcolf to Scoggin	74
4	Quips, Retorts, Tricks and Blunders	96
5	Men and Manners	116
	Sources	151
	Notes	156
	Appendix: Borde and Scoggin	198
	Bibliography	200
	Index	206

ACKNOWLEDGEMENTS

To the British Museum above all I extend my grateful thanks. Without its printed and manuscript treasures, and the efficient care with which they are made available, no book like this would be possible. My thanks for kind co-operation, and for permission to reproduce extracts, also go to:

Bodleian Library, Oxford; Cambridge University Library; Harvard College Library, Cambridge, Mass.; The Huntington Library, San Marino, California; Niedersächsische Staats- und Universitätsbibliothek, Göttingen, Lower Saxony.

INTRODUCTION

I

'I published this book to make men merry,' says Andrew Borde in his prologue to *The Jests of Scoggin*. That is also one of my aims, and readers are free to turn first of all to the jests and merry tales gathered here from the books of Borde and of many other men. Very little has been obscured with the passing of time. Indeed, these unfading stories from distant centuries could be the basis of a discussion on the essence of laughter. I shall try to leave such theorizing to others. I am, however, offering more than merriment. All the living, casual words that survive by happy chance (very often in single copies) are precious for our understanding of the past. Ancient ballads have been much valued; ancient jests are less well known, but can say more to us. They range comprehensively, with colloquial realism and gay fantasy, over the intimacies, disasters and delights of everyday life. They are material for the social history of England; and not only of England. A study of the sources takes us across boundaries, and far into the past.

The collection begins with England's first printer. At the end of his translation of Æsop, William Caxton gives some supplementary fables, followed by eleven stories of 'Poge the Florentyn' and two final stories evidently by Caxton himself. The date is 1484, and here are Caxton's closing words:

> And here with I fynysshe this book / translated & emprynted by me William Caxton at Westmynster in thabbey / And fynysshed the xxvi daye of Marche the yere of oure lord MCCCClxxxiiii / And the fyrst yere of the regne of kyng Rychard the thyrdde

INTRODUCTION

Caxton's printing shop in the precincts of Westminster Abbey had a good trade in religious works, and he had friends among the clergy, but he was not a prudish man, as the first two stories in the present collection will show. 'Poge the Florentyn' is worth some attention, as he is one of the notable Continental contributors to English merriment. He was Poggio Bracciolini (1380–1459), a humanist scholar who is now credited with having invented, as a young man, the early italic handwriting known as humanist script. It was a time when the Vatican valued classical learning, and Poggio served as secretary to a number of popes. But he had intervals of low fortune, for he was more than once a victim of the upheavals of the Papal Schism. When one of his masters, John XXIII, was deposed in 1415, Poggio travelled through Switzerland and Germany searching in monasteries for forgotten classical manuscripts. He rescued some of the works of Plautus, Cicero, Lucretius and others. In 1418 he came to England as the guest of the Bishop of Winchester but did not stay long; his beloved ancient authors were hardly known. About 1420 he was back in Rome, a papal secretary once more. Later he settled in Florence at the invitation of Cosimo de' Medici; had six children by a young wife (having had fourteen by a mistress); and wrote, among other works in Latin, his book of merry stories, *Liber facetiarum*.

Although the fifteenth-century Church was fairly tolerant (of ribaldry, but not of heresy), Poggio introduced his *facetiae* with some words of justification. 'I have read', he says, 'that our forefathers, men of the greatest discretion and learning, took delight in jests, jokes and tales, and for this they were not blamed, but praised. . . . It is, moreover, a worthy and indeed a necessary thing, commended by the philosophers, to comfort the mind when it is weighed down by troubles and study, and to restore its gaiety by means of light recreation.' He says further that in writing down these stories—which he and his friends exchanged in Italian —he wished to show that they could be put elegantly into Latin. Here he was no doubt being a little devious; men would accept in Latin what they might shy from seeing in the vernacular.

Poggio concludes by recalling the place where most of the stories were first told: a sort of club in the papal secretariat, a secluded room jokingly called the *bugiale* or lie-factory, 'where we collected the news of the day and conversed on various subjects, mostly for relaxation. . . . Nobody was spared. . . . Often the

Pope himself was the first subject of our criticism.' Now, years later (he is writing in 1451), the merry companions of his young days are all dead, and *tum temporem, tum hominum culpa, omnisque jocandi confabulandique consuetudo sublata* (whether the times are to blame, or men themselves, those merry confabulations have gone out of use).

Old men usually speak thus (although Poggio might well have sensed a change; Europe was preparing for Luther). Certainly his *Liber facetiarum* was instantly appreciated, and before he died he was able to record that manuscript copies had gone to most countries of western Europe, including England. From 1470 onwards it was printed in numerous editions. Partial translations began quite early. It is amusing to find that the first few Poggio stories to appear in French, at Lyons in the early 1480s, were translated by an Augustinian doctor of theology, Julien Macho. It was Macho's translation that Caxton put into English.

The uninhibited story of the bride misled by the donkey does not appear among the Poggio stories in later English collections. There is a good deal of Poggio in *Tales, and quicke answeres, very mery, and pleasant to rede* (about 1535), but it avoids his more indelicate passages. Even in the easygoing days of Henry VIII, the English tended to draw the line at some Italian bawdry. The translator of 1535 ignored, for example, Poggio's story of a preacher who was carried away in his denunciation of voluptuousness, and reviled husbands who *natibus uxoris pulvinum subjicerunt* (put pillows under their wives' buttocks), with the result that some in his congregation went home eager to try a refinement that had not occurred to them. (A moral tale with a lasting message.) Another suppressed story of a genial grossness tells of two friends, out for a walk, discussing whether coition or defecation affords the greater pleasure. They see a woman who has never been known to refuse a man. 'Let's ask her,' says one. 'She's an expert in both matters.' 'She's the last one to adjudicate,' says the other; '*multo enim futuit saepius quam cacavit*' ('she has made love far more often than she has defecated'—if one translates politely).

The earliest surviving full-length English jestbook has a true native flavour, although its sources are partly Continental. It is *A C Mery Talys* (A Hundred Merry Tales)—the book of which Beatrice speaks in *Much Ado About Nothing*, II, i: 'That I was disdainful,

INTRODUCTION

and that I had my good wit out of the Hundred Merry Tales—well, this was Signior Benedick that said so.' (The jibe was that she borrowed her wit, and from such an old book, dating from 1526; not that the book was poor.)

The man who printed the book, and very likely compiled it, is worth some notice. He was John Rastell (1475?–1536), a Coventry-born lawyer and an enterprising man of the English renaissance. He was a printer as early as 1512. In 1517 he set off on a voyage to the New World, but was foiled by a mutiny off Ireland. When he built a house in Finsbury in 1524, he added a stage and presented plays (near where Richard Burbage was to build his theatre more than fifty years later). He himself wrote some stage interludes. But it is above all the intellectual circle to which Rastell belonged that makes him historically interesting.

About 1504 he married Thomas More's sister Elizabeth; and about 1523 Rastell's daughter Joan married a friend of More's, John Heywood, the court wit, poet and playwright (so that Rastell was a great-grandfather of John Donne). It would be astonishing if More and Heywood, two notable jesters, did not contribute to Rastell's collection. I like to think that some of the misogynous jokes are More's, and that we hear his ironic voice in the moral of the two nuns who sinned: 'By this tale men may learn that a vicious act is more abominable in one person than in another, in one season than in another, and in one place than in another.'

A Hundred Merry Tales is strong in stories that turn on faults of the Church, and they are not there merely to make men merry. Thomas More, like his friend Erasmus, was a humanist who wished to reform the Church—not purge or overturn it, like Luther; and laughter rather than invective was a means of reform. When More later upheld papal authority against Henry's national reforms, he seemed to some of his friends to be betraying a cause. And John Rastell ended his life, indeed, at a far extreme from More—as an out-and-out reformist bitterly contesting a middle-of-the-road edict by Henry that confirmed ancient tithe rights in the City of London; and in 1535 when More was in the Tower waiting to die, his brother-in-law was also in prison and, as he wrote, 'brought to extreme misery'. In that misery he died, a year after the man whose merry table talk he had shared.

Laughmakers are not prudent men. In the traditional stories of

INTRODUCTION

many countries, jesters are sentenced to death for their impudent trickery—but then are reprieved by their wit. Life is not always like that. In 1549, thirteen years after Rastell, the author of another great English jestbook died in Fleet Prison. He was the Andrew Borde I have already mentioned, another many-sided man: failed monk, skilful physician, traveller, author and incontinent priest. Born about 1490 at Borde Hill, near Haywards Heath, Sussex, he was admitted to the Carthusian order, presumably in London, when still under age. Soon he was accused, not for the last time, of intercourse with women. Dispensed in 1521 from his monastic vows, he took up the study of medicine (though still formally a priest). He appears to have studied first at Oxford, and then in 1529 he went to the great University of Montpelier. If he was there in 1530-1, he probably encountered that other monk-turned-physician, his almost exact contemporary, François Rabelais. For Borde it was the first of at least four trips abroad. As well as studying at Montpelier, he performed some diplomatic missions for Thomas Cromwell, and he busily collected information. His *Introduction of Knowledge*, written 1542, published 1547, is one of the first English travel guides. In it he says, 'I have travelled . . . about Europe and part of Africa; as for Asia, I was never in.' He also records sadly that he once made a town-by-town directory for all Europe, giving routes, mileages and so forth, but 'one Thomas Cromwell had it of me. And because he had many matters to dispatch for all England, my book was lost.' (He is writing two years after Cromwell's execution.)

Another of his books, *A compendyous Regyment or a dyetary of Helth* (published 1542), a lively medical guide for the layman, is of particular interest here, for in its preface, addressed to the Duke of Norfolk, is a theme to which Borde returned many times:

> Divers time in my writings I do write words of mirth. Truly it is for no other intention but to make Your Grace merry—for mirth is one of the chiefest things of physic, the which doth advertise every man to be merry, and to beware of pensifulness.

In chapter viii of the book he says, 'To bedward be you merry, or have merry company about you, so that, to bedward, no anger nor heaviness, sorrow nor pensifulness, do trouble or disquiet you.' And his prologue to *The Jests of Scoggin* must now be given in full:

> There is nothing, beside the goodness of God, that preserves health so much as honest mirth, especially mirth used at dinner and supper, and mirth toward bed, as it doth plainly appear in the *Directions* [that is, Dyetary] *for Health*. Therefore considering this matter, that mirth is so necessary a thing for men, I published this book, named *The Jests of Scoggin*, to make men merry; for amongst divers other books of grave matters that I have made, my delight hath been to recreate my mind in making something merry. Wherefore I do advertise every man in avoiding pensiveness, or too much study or melancholy, to be merry with honesty in God, and for God, whom I humbly beseech to send us the mirth of heaven, Amen.

I discuss the book more fully in an appendix. Scoggin himself, John Scoggin, is stated to have been at court in the reign of Edward IV, who died in 1483, seven years before Borde was born. It would have been easy for Borde to hear tales of Scoggin from men who were young in Edward IV's time. Borde writes at the beginning of *The Jests of Scoggin*:

> I have heard say that Scoggin did come of an honest stock or kindred, and his friends did set him to school at Oxford, where he did continue until the time he was made Master of Art, when he made this jest:
>
> > A Master of Art is not worth a fart
> > Except he be in schools;
> > A Bachelor of Law is not worth a straw
> > Except he be among fools.

No doubt some of the seventy-six Scoggin stories are based on actual incidents; for example, the one I print about the herring bones. As my notes show, Borde brought in material from Continental sources, probably picked up on his travels. To enrich the story of a local hero in this way was common practice; in Germany, the same thing was done for Eulenspiegel. Whatever money Borde may have made by Scoggin and by his other books, he did not like people to think money was his object. In the preface to another book, *The Brevyary of Helth*, about 1547, he says:

> I do write this book for a common wealth, as God knoweth my pretence, not only in making this book, but all other books that I have made, that I did never look for no reward neither of lord, nor of printer, nor of no man living, nor I had never no reward, nor I will never have none as long as I do live, God helping me.

Perhaps he protests too much. He surely looked for some kind of reward, and probably got it, when he dedicated his *Dyetary* to the Duke of Norfolk and his *Introduction of Knowledge* to Henry VIII's daughter, Princess Mary. But in Borde's last years no powerful friend came forward to save him.

The evidence we have about his downfall seems to show that he did not follow the advice he himself gives in his *Brevyary* under the heading Priapismus:

> In English it is named an involuntary standing of a man's yard. . . . Let priests use fasting, watching, evil fare, hard lodging and great study, and flee from all manner of occasions of lechery, and let them smell to rue, vinegar and camphor.

Elsewhere in the book he advises as a cure for lust 'to leap into a great vessel of cold water, or to put nettles in the codpiece about the yard and stones'.

In 1547—the year that Henry VIII died and a Protestant faction came into power under the young Edward VI—Borde was living as a priest at Winchester. It was not a time when opponents of the Protestants, such as Stephen Gardiner, then Bishop of Winchester, could afford to deal leniently with scandals. The Borde scandal is recorded by John Ponet, a reforming (and married) churchman who replaced Gardiner. Writing in 1555 (*An Apologie fully answering . . . a blasphemose Book . . . against the godly mariadge of priests*, pages 48–49 in the 1556 edition), he says:

> And within this eight year was there not a holy man named Master Doctor Borde, a physician, that thrice in the week

would drink nothing but water; who under the colour of virginity kept three whores at once in his chamber at Winchester to serve not only himself but also to help the virgin priests about in the country, as it was proved, that they might with more ease and less pain keep their blessed virginity.

Ponet is engaged in demonstrating that the rule of celibacy entailed lechery and hypocrisy. (As an epigraph on his title page he has, 'It is a hard thing for thee to spurn against the prick.') Besides having his three days of water diet, Borde wore 'a shirt of hair', says Ponet, and hung 'his shroud . . . or burial-sheet at his bed's feet'. He confessed his sin before the Winchester justices 'of whom divers be yet living', and 'his shroud and shirt of hair were openly showed, and the harlots openly in the streets and great church of Winchester punished'. He was sent to Fleet Prison in London, and there in April 1549 he made his will; he left several houses. It was said that he died by taking poison.

Tales, and quicke answeres, the jestbook already mentioned on page 3, consists almost entirely, in its 1535 and its enlarged 1567 versions, of stories from Poggio and other Continental sources. It presents few problems. Nor does the next collection of note, *Wits, Fits and Fancies*, 1595, which is almost wholly a translation by Anthony Copley, a wandering English Catholic, of a Spanish book of jests and anecdotes, *La Floresta Española*, published in Toledo in 1574 by Melchor de Santa Cruz (1520–80). Copley dedicates the book to the 3rd Earl of Cumberland—who had distinguished himself in 1588 against the Spanish Armada, and who led later raiding expeditions against the Spaniards. The dedication says:

> . . . It seemeth that the Spaniard for his part (for so he was) did not basely conceit this matter [the book], that did dare direct it to so high a state as Don John of Austria, his liege's brother. . . . I did intend it to your late sea-voyage [against the Spaniards in 1593] to the end it might have pleased you to pass away therewith some unpleasant hours. But as it was not ripe enough for that season, so now I pray God it come in due season to your good liking. Divers of them are of mine own inserting, and that without injury, I hope, to my author:

INTRODUCTION

the which are easily to be discerned from his, for that they taste more Englishly.

In his book, Copley says, 'men may learn to jest without hurt, how to exercise wit without slander, and how to be harmlessly pleasant without ribaldry or the filth of unwashed words'. *La Floresta Española* is indeed a clean book, for censorship was strict in Spain. The few faintly bawdy touches in *Wits* (such as my Nos 22, 119 and 174) are Copley's additions. What is notable in *Floresta* is its black humour (for example, No. 173), and its terseness, which often causes Copley to inject whole phrases for fear that Englishmen will miss the point.

Wits was reissued, slightly expanded, in 1614. That seems to have been the last full reprint until 1755, when it reappeared under the title *The Laugher or the Art of Jesting*; but from 1595 onwards, many of its stories passed into general circulation.

Some *Wits* stories, and some from older sources, turn up in the best jestbook of the next generation, *A Banquet of Jests*. But there is a good deal of new material in this book, and the six editions with varying contents that were sold between 1630 and 1640 give a lively idea of the kind of joke enjoyed, and invented, by men of the world in Charles I's reign.

The first edition tells the reader:

> If any shall object and say . . . 'I know that, and this I have heard related,' those I thus answer: If many have heard some of them, but few or none (I dare presume) all. Besides, I do not challenge [claim] them for mine own, but gathered from the mouths of others; and what is stale to me may be to thee new. . . .

The anonymous editor (perhaps the publisher, Richard Royston) had trouble with the censor—possibly over stories touching on the court and the Church. He says, 'I must ingenuously confess unto you that had not the Licence curbed my liberty, the leaves of this book had been more in tale.'

In 1633 he added a large number of stories as 'The Second Part', and prefaced this with some verses addressed, not to some titled person, but to a man equally famous in those days: Archie

INTRODUCTION

Armstrong, who had been jester to James I, and kept the role under Charles. The book itself speaks:

> Must I that am a merry book,
> On whom my author pains hath took,
> Now in this witty age go look
>   And seek a patron?
>
> ... And I at length on one have light
> Who is a brave and worthy wight;
> Well guarded, though he be no knight;
>   A friend to Cupid.
>
> No doubt but I with him shall speed
> And we two shall be soon agreed,
> Because of me he'll stand in need
>   When he grows stupid.
>
> Go then, taunts, tales, you jests and jeers. . . .
>
> Go to thy patron and devote
> Thyself to him: he's one of note.
> Thou'lt know him by his velvet coat
>   That's so well guarded.
>
> If worthy Archie shall but deign
> To read thee o'er and o'er again
> (If he can read), for all thy pain
>   Th'art well rewarded. . . .

A 'guarded' coat is one faced with gold or silver lace. Archie did well by his jesting, and dressed like a courtier. In the time of James I, in 1618, the letter-writer John Chamberlain reports, 'Archie hath engrossed the making of tobacco-pipes to him, his deputies or assigns, which, though it seem a small matter, yet they say it concerns a number of poor men.' In other words, Archie had been rewarded for his fooling with a lucrative monopoly that robbed poor pipemakers of their livelihood—a royal practice that contributed eventually to the Civil War.

    I cannot find any good jests reliably credited to Archie. His talent seems to have been for horseplay and Scottish effrontery.

INTRODUCTION

Oddly enough, though, *A Banquet of Jests* has been attributed to him. I deal with the question on page 151.

Evidence that the *Banquet* stories were of the kind being told by gentlemen is clear enough in my next source, a manuscript collection entitled *Merry Passages and Jests*, made in the 1630s and 1640s by Sir Nicholas L'Estrange (1603–56) of the ancient family of Hunstanton, Norfolk. A dozen of his stories (including some of the best) also appear, in different words, in *A Banquet of Jests*. Now, L'Estrange records the name of the relation or friend who told him each of his stories. The dozen that are also in *Banquet* came from a dozen people, which indicates that they reached him independently, not from an owner of the book. The compiler of *Banquet of Jests*, I think, picked up many of his stories in circles that overlapped with those in which L'Estrange moved: lawyers, MPs and other men of affairs whose lives were divided between the country and London. It must never be thought that the people of Norfolk and Suffolk (or of more distant counties) lived isolated lives; certainly the great county families like the L'Estranges did not. When young, their men acquired law and some social graces at the Inns of Court. Later they often sat in Parliament. Sir Nicholas's brother-in-law, Sir William Spring, was MP for Bury St Edmunds during 1645–8, and for Suffolk in 1654. Those dates make another interesting point about the network of East Anglian landed gentry: they tended to be Parliament men, not Royalists. Sir Nicholas's young brother Roger (1616–1704) was a hotheaded exception when, early in the Civil War, he joined in a Royalist plot to capture King's Lynn—a plot that failed and sent him into exile. He is remembered as the Restoration wit, pamphleteer and translator, Sir Roger L'Estrange.

Some fame is due to Sir Nicholas as well. His manuscript collection contains just over six hundred items, of which I print thirty-one, most of them for the first time. No significant part of the collection has been printed since 1839, when William J. Thoms edited 141 items under the title *Anecdotes and Traditions Illustrative of Early English History and Literature*. 'The greater portion', he said, 'are unfit for publication.' But what more happily illustrative of English life than L'Estrange's stories of the doings of such men as Wiggett?

INTRODUCTION

A *Banquet of Jests* and L'Estrange lead naturally, in manner and in content, to Restoration collections such as *Coffee-House Jests*. Thereafter, as the decades pass to the eighteenth century, we find fewer and fewer new stories, barely visible among the constantly reprinted old favourites. Fashions had changed, and the talents that once created jestbooks were perhaps now busy with romantic and scurrilous novels, or bourgeois journalism.

Publishers, however, still devised new ways to vend old wares. There is no better example than a book whose name lives on—*Joe Miller's Jests*. On August 17, 1738, the *Daily Post* recorded, 'Yesterday morning died Joe Miller, comedian, of merry memory.' For many years he had been a star of the Drury Lane company. He was buried at St Clement Danes, and that would have been all, except in theatrical annals—but a hack writer named John Mottley (1692–1750), author of a few poor farces, in need of money, quickly put together a jestbook in Miller's name. It appeared in 1739 with this fanfare:

> *Joe Miller's Jests: or, the Wit's Vade-Mecum.* Being a collection of the most brilliant jests, the politest repartees, the most elegant bons mots and most pleasant short stories in the English language. First carefully collected in the company, and many of them transcribed from the mouth, of the facetious gentleman whose name they bear.

John Mottley used a pseudonym, Elijah Jenkins—and no wonder. Almost the entire 247 items in the book were lifted, with a change of phrase here and there, from two earlier books, *Pinkethman's Jests*, first published in 1720, and *Polly Peachum's Jests*, 1728. Those books were themselves largely re-workings of seventeenth-century collections, with catchpenny titles. Will Pinkethman, like Joe Miller, was a popular comic actor at Drury Lane; he died in 1725. The book in his name did not, at least, pretend to come from his mouth; it even admitted that some of its contents were 'taken out of other books of this kind'. *Polly Peachum's Jests* had nothing beyond its title to associate it with the heroine of John Gay's *Beggar's Opera*—except perhaps its sweeping social claim to comprise 'most of the witty apophthegms, diverting tales and smart repartees that have been used for many years last past, either at St James's or St Giles's: suited alike to the capacities of the

INTRODUCTION

peer and the porter'. It is remarkable that Mottley committed his thefts on such recent books (a fourth edition of *Pinkethman's Jests* had appeared only four years earlier) and apparently was not challenged. His book went through three editions in its first year, and there were five more, with various changes and additions, in the next six years.

No doubt the afterglow of Joe Miller's personality helped sales. He does seem to have been, as his gravestone said, 'a facetious companion'. Still, the book's great success is one of the mysteries of publishing. One important fact may be that the publisher was T. Read of Dogwell Court, off Fleet Street—not a fly-by-night firm, but one that was active over several decades. With each edition, too, he gave more value for money, so that by 1745 there were 587 items, plus twenty-three pages of moral sentences, sixty-eight pages of epigrams, and eighty-six pages of verse—some by Dryden, Congreve, Swift and Pope, as well as anonymous trifles, not all as neat as this:

> To a Sempstress
>
> Oh, what bosom but must yield
>   When, like Pallas, you advance
> With a thimble for your shield
>   And a needle for your lance?
>
> Fairest of the stitching train,
>   Ease my passion by your art,
> And in pity to my pain
>   Mend the hole that's in my heart.

The book was whimsically dedicated to a varying list of 'choice spirits of the age'. In 1742 these were 'His Majesty's poet, Mr Colley Cibber; His Holiness's poet, Mr Pope; Mr Orator Henley; Capt. Vinegar; the old Duchess of M[arlborough]; Mr Ancient Pistol; and Job Baker, the kettle-drummer.' The 'orator' was John Henley, an eccentric preacher.

Yet all this scarcely accounts for the triumphant longevity of Joe Miller. There were plenty of competing jestbooks in the later decades of the eighteenth century, some of them graced with the names of more notable actors: James Quin, Samuel Foote, David Garrick. They fade away, and Joe Miller goes on, changing with the times, swelling in 1832 to a collection of 1,546 items, *Joe Miller's Complete Jest Book*, and even surviving his emasculation in 1848 as *The Family Joe Miller*. In 1890 George Routledge published a sixpenny *Joe Miller Up to Date*, which I do not think contains one joke from the early days. It was probably compiled by a contributor to *Punch*: 'A little boy accosted his papa thus, "Papa, are you growing still?" "No, dear; what makes you think so?" "Because the top of your head is coming through your hair." '

II

Having arrived at the gentle humours of suburbia, it will be refreshing to turn to earlier times again—before Poggio, and even beyond Italy, to the farther shores of the Mediterranean. The journeying of jests across frontiers and across centuries is a process as worthy of study as the migration of folk-tales. Indeed, the study is all one, and folklorists have recognized this. Here I shall briefly discuss some forerunners and pioneers of European jesting.

The Englishman's common attitude to the people of the Moslem world is a mixture of amusement and scorn, tempered with uneasy respect. But in medieval times, before Western Europe had launched into the age of political and economic imperialism that is now fading, the Moslem world was Europe's equal—and Europe's teacher. It gave us chemistry, medicine, mathematics, philosophy—too much to list here. It also gave us stories. Many came to Spain during the long period of Moslem control. Traders brought them to Italy and France, and to all Europe. The process was not interrupted, but stimulated, by the Crusades, which were in part an expression of the Europeans' growing mobility and new thrusting outlook.

Among the Arabs and the peoples culturally close to them, one class of funny story collected long ago around two names: Si Djoh'a (Djih'a, Djeh'a, Jehā), who begins to be heard of in the eleventh century; and Nasreddin, known as Hodja (Hojja, Hajja, Cogia—an honorific title meaning scholar), who seems to date from the fourteenth century. But first a man must be mentioned of whom less is heard in the west: Ash'ab, a court entertainer at Medina, who is said to have died in A.D. 771. Some of the stories about him are later adopted for Hodja. Both men are tricksters who outwit themselves. For example, they start a story that the caliph is giving away money (or melons). People run off eagerly to share; they are away a long time; Ash'ab (or Hodja) thinks, 'It must be true,' and runs after them. Ash'ab is notable for greed and avarice. He says he has never seen a bride being led through the street to her bridegroom, without opening his door in the hope she would be led to him; and he has never looked at two people talking confidentially at a funeral without thinking that the dead man had left him something. When his girl asks him to give her a ring to remember him by, he says, 'No, remember that I refused it to you. I like that better.' (In Domenichi's sixteenth-century collection, a man asks what is the best way to be remembered after death. He is told, 'Leave many debts.')

If Hodja woes something to Ash'ab, he owes much more to Si Djoh'a. It seems, indeed, that Hodja Nasreddin's name was attached to the stories only when a Si Djoh'a collection was translated from Arabic into Turkish as late as the fifteenth or sixteenth century. Later the Turkish version, with additional stories, was retranslated into Arabic and into Persian and other tongues—long after Si Djoh'a had become known in Persia and even in Italy. Both collections have developed over the centuries; but the two characters are eternal. Both men (like Ash'ab) are at once wily and foolish, and subject to inspired flaws of logic. It is told of Si Djoh'a that a man carrying thirty eggs in his sleeves meets him and says, 'If you guess what I have here, I'll give you ten of them to make an omelette.' Si Djoh'a thinks hard and asks for a clue. He is told, 'They are white outside and yellow inside.' 'By God, I know!' he says. 'They're turnips hollowed out and stuffed with carrots.' Hodja is given the same joke in various forms. In one, he says to some children, 'Guess what I have in my sleeve, and to the correct guesser I shall give the largest apricot.' Both men are quick with answers in awkward situations. Hodja is caught up a tree, stealing fruit. 'Who's there?' shouts the owner. 'I am a nightingale,' says Hodja. He is told to prove it by singing. He tries, and makes a miserable sound. 'I am only a young nightingale,' he explains. 'I am still learning.'

In their comical idiocies, Djoh'a and Hodja are ancestors of our absentminded professor. One night Hodja thinks he sees a thief in his garden, although it is only a coat he has left hanging up there. He transfixes it with an arrow. When his wife laughs at him, he says, 'Thank your stars I wasn't in the coat, or you'd

INTRODUCTION

have been a widow now.' Another time, Hodja finds a mirror, but when he sees a face looking out of it he says, 'I beg your pardon, I didn't know it was your property,' and puts it down (or in another version, 'It's terribly ugly—no wonder someone threw it away'). Such stories were enjoyed by the Ancient Greeks, who told them of witless pedants. The way of thinking, and sometimes the actual jokes, were very likely passed on to the urbanized Arabs by the Greeks. In one old Greek story, a man buys a raven to find out by personal experiment whether it will live two hundred years. His intellectual process is like that of Djoh'a/Hodja, who shouts from the top of a tower, hurries down and runs off as fast as he can; he explains that he is trying to find out how far his voice carries. A Greek joke that is found among the Arabs (and in turn throughout Europe) is of a man who hears that one of a pair of twin brothers has died. When he meets the other twin, he asks, 'Was it you who died, or your brother?'

There was, indeed, an ancient and constantly refreshed Mediterranean joke pool, from which Western Europe drew what appealed to it. Whimsical-crazy stories seem to have travelled less well than comical-stupid stories, such as those outlined in the notes to No. 106. Europeans, and especially Italians, above the peasant level were fond of jokes that could be applied to stupid peasants. They were also fond of stories of a quite different category, owing nothing to Hodja but a great deal to the Arabs, and before them the Persians and Indians—I mean stories of faithless, deceitful and shrewish wives.

The man who did most to bring these stories to Europe in medieval times was not an Arab but a Jew, who in the year 1106, at the age of forty-four, was converted to Christianity in Spain and took the name Petrus Alfonsi. His *Disciplina Clericalis* is the earliest large written collection of eastern tales transmitted to the west. Although their justification was their moral purpose, they are, above all, entertaining. Often the only serious message they can claim is to warn men of the wiles of unchaste women. Some of the tales go back to a Sanskrit collection, *Hitopadesa* (Friendly Counsel). In one, a one-eyed husband arrives home from work unexpectedly when his wife is entertaining a lover. She hurries to meet him at the door and says she has dreamed that if she kisses his good eye, the sight of the other will be restored. She kisses; the lover slips out.

INTRODUCTION

Disciplina Clericalis quickly spread across Europe, and its stories were borrowed and adapted, in particular by Boccaccio and other Italians of the thirteenth and fourteenth centuries, and by the makers of verse *fabliaux* in France in the same period. A notable editor of the *fabliaux*, Courde de Montaiglon, makes a good point (*Recueil Général*, page xvii) about the role of Jews, and Petrus Alfonsi in particular, in the migration of such tales from India and Persia: 'The first [intermediaries] are the Arabs, but they would not have been enough; the second and true intermediaries are those cosmopolitans *par excellence* (and the only cosmopolitans of the Middle Ages): that is, the Jews, eastern themselves in spirit and tradition . . . who alone knew Arabic and who alone could translate it into Latin.'

Petrus Alfonsi introduced a note of urbanity into the literature of the western Church. In the following century there was a still more genial converted Jew who must be mentioned, if only to contrast him with the heretic-smiting bishops of the west. This was Bar-Hebraeus, born in Syria in 1226, the son of a Jewish physician. After conversion he rose rapidly in the Syrian branch of the Christian Church, and from 1264 to 1286 he was its head. He is notably tolerant and cosmopolitan. His collection (see bibliography) includes stories about Greek, Hebrew, Persian and Indian sages, Moslem rulers, and Christian and Arab ascetics. Some of his jokes are also in Hodja collections, which perhaps took them from Bar-Hebraeus. He tells some coarse stories, and says in justification, 'In the tabernacle of wisdom every kind of thing is necessary. Nothing whatsoever that in a natural way sharpens the intelligence, enlightens the understanding and comforts and rejoices the mind in its sorrow and suffering should ever be rejected.' (Even Poggio did not venture to make such a permissive declaration.) Bar-Hebraeus can laugh at his religion. He tells of a comedian in a cold winter in Sebastia (now Sivas) in the mountains of Turkey, who has a new tunic. A non-Christian asks him for it, saying, 'You will still have your cloak, and your Christ commanded you to give away both.' The comedian replies, 'This command may have been given to the people of Palestine in the summer, but it was not given to the people of Sebastia in the winter.' Another comedian hears a man advising a traveller to scare off wild dogs by shouting Psalm xxii, verse 20, 'Deliver my soul from the sword; my darling from the power of the dog'.

The comedian says, 'But let him take a stick in his hand too, for not all dogs understand the psalms, although there may be some who read them.'

Such things are far from the spirit of two western bishops who, a little earlier in the thirteenth century, had been developing the use of brief and often funny stories. Bar-Hebraeus's aim, as he says, was to sharpen the wits and to give pleasure. The western bishops, Jacques de Vitry and Etienne de Bourbon, had the sterner object of drawing the faithful to their sermons and driving home moral lessons. Their stories are known as exempla; when they are funny, it is for a didactic purpose. The technique of direct appeal to ordinary people was sharpened as a weapon in the Church's counter-attack against sceptics and heretics, and in France especially against the Albigensian movement that arose in the twelfth century. Jacques de Vitry (about 1180–1240) used his eloquence to preach the crusade launched against the Albigensians in 1209; joined in the cruel war against them; took part later in the disastrous Fifth Crusade in Egypt; and returned to preach once more against the stubborn Albigensians. Etienne de Bourbon (died 1261) was an early and potent member of the preaching order founded in 1206 by St Dominic to combat the Albigensians, and was appointed about 1235 as a travelling inquisitor. He adopted many stories from a collection formed by de Vitry, and their two collections circulated widely and contributed to others.

I have emphasized the fight against heresy, but of course the preachers ranged over the whole social scene, and their exempla enlivened their denunciations of public injustice as well as private sin. Preaching became more human; and the artful telling of stories contributed to popular drama, and before long to jest collections. Some of the de Vitry/de Bourbon stories lived on into later ages (see notes to Nos 55 and 90). One that recurs in many jestbooks from Poggio onwards is of the man whose wife falls into a river. He seeks her upstream: she had been so contrary in life that she was bound to have been so in death. (De Bourbon improved on the story by telling how she fell into the river. On a summer day, her husband invited some neighbours to a banquet in his riverside garden. The wife sat far from the table. Every time he urged her to sit nearer, she shifted her chair further back, until she went over the bank.) Misogynist jests were common; but there are other stories conveying a grimmer Christian message.

One example put before the faithful by de Vitry was of a man who passionately loved a girl, and was obsessed with her memory when she died. He cured himself by opening her grave and looking at the flesh he had once adored.

Lust, pride, envy, avarice—all the sins were dramatically exemplified and condemned. But too many of the preaching friars soon became notorious for the sins they denounced. Chaucer's Pardoner in the following century, with his fake relics, extorting money by preaching against avarice, living luxuriously and enjoying 'a joly wenche in every toun', was a great user of exempla:

> Thanne telle I hem ensamples many oon
> Of olde stories longe tyme agoon,
> For lewed peple loven tales olde;
> Swiche thynges kan they wel reporte and holde.

The friars themselves became the subjects of merry stories (which were a weapon in later waves of reform). And when *A Hundred Merry Tales* moralizes in the medieval manner—'By this tale ye may learn . . .'—it is adopting the preachers' method for comic effect or tongue-in-cheek satire.

With the Reformation, laughter in church goes out of fashion. If a clergyman collects jokes, they have no churchly message. Archbishop Sancroft (1617–93) jotted down more than a hundred, of which these are two:

> 'Why would you marry?' said a merchant to a sailor. 'While you are so long absent, your wife may—' 'Oh, sir', quoth he, 'that's done while you but walk to the Exchange.'

> 'How long have you been married, Dr Donne?' R. ''Tis the 7th year of her reign.' But he added not, 'Whom G. long preserve.'

They are the after-dinner stories of his day, useful no doubt for conversation at court.

III

Jesters and other entertainers have an uncertain place in society, and especially in the eyes of those whose role is to impose morality and order. Undirected merriment is disorderly. It makes brief moments of bliss on earth and turns men's thoughts from the hereafter. A Christian who pursued his belief to an extreme would smile only at the instant of death. To the holy mind, what is a greater illusion than laughter caused by a mimic, a singer, a teller of tales—men creating illusions for our delight? Yet churchmen themselves were seduced, early and often. The story of the Church's dealings with entertainers is well told in Sir Edmund Chambers's *The Medieval Stage*. He cites decrees from as early as A.D. 679 condemning singers, citharists, clowns, mimes, actors and especially *scurrae* (buffoons) and their jokes. The decrees were ineffectual. Again and again, in England as elsewhere, there were orders and invectives against wanton merriment and unholy japes not only among the common people, but countenanced and shared in by the clergy, and even in church. The impassioned sermons of Puritan divines in the sixteenth and seventeenth centuries were only the climax to a long series. And if with difficulty the church was somewhat purified, the people were being lured with new temptations:

> What multitude of books, full of all sin and abominations, have now filled the world! Nothing so childish, nothing so vain, nothing so wanton, nothing so idle, which is not both boldly printed and plausibly taken.... We have printed us many bawdy songs ... we have gotten our *Songs and Sonnets*, our *Palaces of Pleasure*, our unchaste fables and tragedies, and suchlike sorceries, more than any man may reckon.

The case is being stated here by a comparatively gentle Puritan who signs himself E.D., in *A briefe and necessary Instruction*, 1572. (*Songs and Sonnets* is Richard Tottel's famous miscellany; *The Palace of Pleasure*, by William Painter, 1566, contains stories from Italy that provided plots for more than forty Elizabethan plays, including *Romeo and Juliet*.) E.D. detests such books as 'the subtle sleights of Satan to occupy Christian wits in heathen fancies', and of course he deplores jestbooks—dismissing Howleglas and 'the fools of Gotham' (together with Robin Hood and Æsop) as 'witless devices'.

Not only Puritans, however, are disturbed by unlicensed foolery. It offends some civilized gentlemen, if only because it wastes

INTRODUCTION

time and money. In *Wits Miserie, and the Worlds Madnesse*, 1596, Thomas Lodge the poet and playwright has a description of a jester which is all the more telling for coming from this upholder of the theatre against Puritan attack. He is particularizing excesses to avoid. After drunkenness is 'immoderate and disordinate joy':

> This fellow in person is comely, in apparel courtly, but in behaviour a very ape, and no man. His study is to coin bitter jests, or to show antic motions, or to sing bawdy sonnets and ballads. Give him a little wine in his head, he is continually fleering and making of mouths. He laughs intemperately at every little occasion, and dances about the house, leaps over tables, outskips men's heads, trips up his companions' heels, burns sack with a candle, and hath all the feats of a Lord of Misrule in the country. Feed him in his humour, you shall have his heart. In mere kindness he will hug you in his arms, kiss you on the cheek, and rapping out a horrible oath, cry, 'God's soul, Tum, I love you, you know my poor heart, come to my chamber for a pipe of tobacco.' . . . Keep not this fellow company, for . . . your wardrobes shall be wasted, your credits cracked, your crowns consumed, and time, the most precious riches of the world, utterly lost.

'A very ape, and no man'—that is an aspect of actors as well as jesters that has troubled serious thinkers. The case is judiciously put by Thomas Fuller when in his *History of the Worthies of England*, 1662, he discusses (III, 47) that great clown from Condover, Shropshire, Richard Tarlton:

> Many condemn his (*vocation* I cannot term it, for it is a *coming* without a *calling*) employment as unwarrantable. Such maintain that it is better to be a fool of God's making, born so into the world, or a fool of man's making, jeered into it by general derision, than a fool of one's own making, by his voluntary affecting thereof. . . . Others allege . . . that jesters often heal what flatterers hurt, so that princes by them arrive at the notice of their errors, seeing jesters carry about with them an act of indemnity for whatsoever they do. . . . Our Tarlton was master of his faculty. When Queen Elizabeth

was *serious* (I dare not say *sullen*) . . . he could *undumpish* her at his pleasure. Her highest favourites would, in some cases, go to Tarlton before they would go to the queen.

The picture of the court jester telling home-truths is an enduring and attractive one, but it may be wondered how often monarchs permitted it; and how often they paid any heed. Tarlton, as a star of the theatre, was not a court parasite like other jesters, and it seems that he was outspoken sometimes with Elizabeth. Edmund Bohun says in *The Character of Queen Elizabeth*, 1693 (pages 352–3), that when Tarlton and others were brought to 'divert her with stories of the town . . . she would be much offended if there was any rudeness to any person, any reproach or licentious reflection used'. Bohun says that when Tarlton was presenting a play before Elizabeth, he dared to point at Sir Walter Raleigh and say, 'See, the knave commands the queen.' Although she frowned, he then reflected on 'the over-great power and riches of the Earl of Leicester', and according to Bohun there was such applause that the queen thought best to seem unconcerned, 'But yet she was so offended that she forbade Tarlton, and all her jesters, from coming near her table.'

She did not wish to be told her faults; and it is likely that the effective role of all jesters, even with less flattery-addicted monarchs, was to 'undumpish' them and sometimes to serve as go-between for courtiers. That is exactly the role that was played, we are told, by Will Sommers, Henry VIII's most famous fool (see notes to No. 177). Of another of Henry's fools, Lob, the point is made, in some verses with the flavour of John Heywood (MS. Rawl. C.258, Bodleian, printed in *Nugae Poeticae*, J. O. Halliwell, 1844), that he kept out of 'high matters':

> Thou wast neither Erasmus nor Luther.
>   Thou didst meddle no further than thy pot.
> Against high matters thou wast no disputer.
>   Among the innocents-elect was thy lot.
>   Glad may thou be thou hadst that knot [fool's cap?],
> For many fools by thee think themself none.
> Yet all be not dead, Lob, though thou be gone.

Fools by trade are not the only fools: that illuminates one satirical

INTRODUCTION

service that jesters could perform: they exposed the malice or idiocy of their betters, by being themselves. The poem goes on:

> Tyt Apguyllamys [Apwilliams], prepare his obsequy.
>   Nature constraineth you to do him good.
> The mad Lady Appleton, offer the mass-penny;
>   And ye as chief mourner in your own fool's hood.
>   Your wits were much like (though nothing of blood),
> Save in him was much goodness, and in you is none:
> Yet ye be a fool, and Lob is gone.

A century later, under James I, there were plenty of courtiers to compete for the fool's role, in a worldly-wise way. Sir Anthony Welldon says in *The Court and Character of King James*, 1650, that after supper the king—

> would come forth to see pastimes and fooleries, in which Sir Ed Zouche [Knight Marshal], Sir George Goring and Sir John Finet [Master of Ceremonies] were the chief and master fools; and surely this fooling got them more than any others' wisdom—far above them in dessert. Zouche's part it was to sing bawdy songs and tell bawdy tales; Finet to compose these songs; then were a set of fiddlers brought up on purpose for this fooling, and Goring was master of the game for fooleries—sometimes presenting David Droman, and Archie Armstrong the king's fool, on the back of the other fools [the courtiers] to tilt at one another till they fell together by the ears.

In a letter of 16 September 1620 John Chamberlain reports, 'Yet as hard as the world goes, Sir Edward Zouche, the Knight Marshal, hath Oking, with another lordship adjoining it (in all better than £500 a year), lately given him in fee-farm for masking and fooling.' Archie Armstrong, too, was well rewarded for his japes. These were not men to speak harsh truths to a king. (I cannot find, even, that they said anything very witty. James himself, says Welldon, 'had as many witty jests as any man living, at which he would not smile himself, but deliver them in a grave and serious manner.' His technique sounds good; but the quips that survive confirm the rule that royal wit is overrated.) Archie, it is true, got into trouble for impudence toward great persons, including the all-powerful Duke of Buckingham, but there is no sign that he worked to open the eyes of King James, who much needed undeceiving.

Perhaps Archie redeemed himself by the way he ended his career. In 1637, when Archbishop Laud's attempt to impose the Book of Common Prayer on Scotland began to cause unrest, Archie the Scot said to Laud, 'Whae's feule now?' This and other jibes so infuriated Laud that he tried to have Archie brought before the Star Chamber. The matter was settled by Charles I and his Council of State: in March 1637 they ordered that Archie 'shall have his coat pulled over his head, and be discharged of the king's service, and banished the court'. Soon the unwisdom of the men who banished him brought the country to civil war.

'He will not believe a fool,' says King Lear's Fool. When we see him telling Lear the sharp truth, it is too late; and the Fool has little to lose. Did he dare to speak out while Lear was in his pride and still had his kingdom?

The laughter that despots or lordly incompetents fear is the laughter of a public that will not be duped. Irreverent jokesters seldom achieve instant results, but they stimulate dangerous thoughts. It is perhaps in this way that creators of jest and repartee can have, if they wish, a lasting social effect: in sharpening the ordinary man's wits and making him less submissive.

The need continues. The content of most joking, however, is and always will be private—like most of the hours of men's lives. If jokes are considered for their purposes, it is here they go deepest. They can be medicine against neuroses, and perhaps against wives, or husbands. They convey intimate facts (that is one of the cultural roles of bawdry). They relieve us from the pressure of custom or conscience and give brief illusions of freedom. They can camouflage our thoughts, or expose hidden things.

When studying dreams, Freud found that they were full of jokes. He went on to write, in 1905, *Jokes and their Relation to the Unconscious*, a stimulating but not always merry work whose availability excuses me from offering a deep analysis myself. Freud's description of how a joke *occurs* rather than being made (page 167) is, however, worth quoting, 'We have an indefinable feeling . . . a sudden release of intellectual tension, and then all at once the joke is there—as a rule ready-clothed in words.' Jokemakers would probably give more credit to the conscious mind;

but the unconscious is at work. Release of tension is fundamental. Laughter is its symptom.

A few further words from Freud, in a letter in 1910 to Dr Friedrich Kraus, whose journal *Anthropophyteia* was publishing erotic and scatological stories from many lands: 'Many of the most admired jokes . . . owe their exhilarating and cheerful effect to the ingenious uncovering of what are as a rule repressed complexes. . . . The jokes, both erotic and of other sorts, which are in popular circulation provide an excellent auxiliary means of investigating the unconscious mind—in the same way as do dreams, myths and legends.'

To the seeker of laughter, that sounds utilitarian and clinical. However, the continuing study of the unconscious mind has not yet put us in danger of being saved from all our stimulating tensions and repressions. When there are no flaws in our inner or outer life, no bafflements, no fleshly incongruities, there will be no jokes; and those presented here will become puzzling relics of an untidy past. Meanwhile, they live, and can serve the pre-Freudian wisdom of that other doctor, Andrew Borde who wrote in an earlier unquiet age, 'Mirth is one of the chiefest things of physic'.

NOTE ON THE TEXT

The material in each of the five groups is placed in chronological order. Spelling and punctuation have been modernized throughout, but archaic words and phrases have been retained, and I have not tampered with pieces of loose syntax that might offend grammatical minds.

Occasionally a missing word is supplied. In a few stories, an ellipsis indicates that a word or two, or an unnecessary opening or closing passage, have been dropped.

Old words that might prevent instant comprehension are explained in square brackets. When a story raises other immediate questions, they are answered beneath it. But points of more general interest are dealt with in the notes at the end of the book—and more than sixty additional jokes will be found there, not counting simple variants.

The items are numbered for easy reference. Those with titles from the original sources are: Nos 1, 3–17, 26–9, 33–7, 65–75, 86–7, 92–104, 107–110, 124, 128–32, 138, 141, 149, 162–6, 177–81, 183–6, 219.

Sources are given, item by item, with the end-notes. When a story recurs in various books, the earliest discoverable example is used, except in rare cases in which it is markedly inferior, or when a later one has a special attraction.

The evolution of the language from the time of Richard III to the time of George III is here painlessly illustrated. I shall make only a few rapid points.

Caxton, who was born twenty-odd years after Chaucer died, says in the preface to his *Eneydos* in 1490, 'Certainly our language now used varieth far from that which was used and spoken when I was born.' When Caxton wrote, modern English was taking shape. Some men, he says in the same book, 'desired me to use old and homely terms in my translations', and others 'desired me to write the most curious terms that I could find. And thus between plain, rude and curious I stand abashed.' It was a time when men with literary pretensions were devising 'curious' ornate words from Latin and French. A contrast of styles may be seen in stories No. 1 and No. 2. The first is from a French book that was itself ornate in style, and there are many phrases ('full triste, thoughtful and melancholious') to please Caxton's seekers after curious terms. The second is told by Caxton himself, and we can overhear two Englishwomen conversing in 1484. Some phrases are utterly undated ('And what then?' said the widow).

In Henry VIII's time, *A Hundred Merry Tales* and Scoggin show a marked advance in narrative skill. There is confidence in the language. It is neither 'rude' nor 'curious'. Here we have the flavour of informal speech in the professional circles in which both John Rastell and Andrew Borde moved. In jestbooks at least, there is no hint of a language gulf between high and low. This continues to be true through the sixteenth and seventeenth centuries; and even in the eighteenth, when hack jestbook-compilers were sometimes seduced into Johnsonese, it is not hard to find the native English directness. And so we can enjoy the genuine British dialogue of No. 237—or of No. 240.

I

Husbands, Wives and Wenches

It is not surprising that stories of the loving battle of the sexes make up more than a quarter of this collection. All the jestbooks naturally make the most of the deceptions, strategies and incongruities of love, lust and marriage; moreover, in this realm of fundamentals most stories keep their point with the passing of time, and so survive for our pleasure.

Little here is obscene. The strongest things in Poggio, and in later Continental collections, were generally suppressed by their English adaptors. The English tone, in print at least, is cheerful rather than lascivious. Ideas of propriety were not a Victorian invention.

One thing is clear, in imported jokes and native English ones: girls and women are able to take care of themselves. Most of the time men are their victims. They know what they want. That upper-class erotic game, courtly love, has no place here.

I leave it to the girls of our age to say how radical their advantages are. No doubt there were more virgin brides in the old days; but girls tended to marry young, and wives had many freedoms, especially in England. The compulsive subject of cuckoldry must certainly have had some basis in fact. To our eyes, a picture of a medieval or Elizabethan woman in layers of ankle-length skirt suggests chastity and decorum; a miniskirt, liberation. But if the swing of fashion should put girls into full skirts with nothing worn underneath, like of girls of old, would guardians of morals be silent?

A word on a sterner subject. There is not one mother-in-law joke here. The reason is that I have not found one. They seem to begin in the Victorian age. Are they essentially a product of *petit-bourgeois* life? It may be that when more and more value was given to an appearance of domestic solidity, openly aggressive joking about the wife was softened, and the attack was diverted on to the person most closely associated with her. Perhaps anthropologists can offer a hypothesis. In societies with strong mother-in-law taboos, do men make mother-in-law jokes?

1 Of a young woman which accused her husband of culpe or blame

Poge Florentine saith that sometime there was a man named Nerus de Pacis, the which of his age was among the Florentines right sage and prudent, and right rich. This Nerus had a fair daughter, the which he married with a right fair young man and a rich and of good parentage or kindred; the which young man the next day after the feast of his wedding did lead her into his castle a little way without the city of Florence. And within few days after, this young man brought his wife again into Florence unto the house of her father Nerus, the which made then a feast, as it was customed to do at that time in some places, eight days after the wedding.

When this new-married or wedded woman was come again to her father's house, she made not over-good cheer, but ever she had her look downward to the earth, as full triste, thoughtful and melancholious. And when her mother perceived and saw her daughter so sorrowful and of mourning countenance, she called her within a wardrobe whereas [where] nobody was but they two, and asked of her the cause of her sorrow, saying, 'How fare ye, my daughter? What want you? Have you not all things coming to you after your desire and pleasance? Wherefore take ye so great thought and melancholy?'

And then the daughter, weeping full tenderly, said to the mother in this manner, 'Alas, my mother, ye have not married me to a man, for of such a thing that a man ought to have, he hath never a deal save only a little part of that thing for the which wedding is made.'

And then the mother, right wrath and sorrowful of this evil fortune, went toward her husband Nerus and told to him the evil adventure and hap of their daughter, whereof he was greatly wrath and sore troubled. And soon after, this fortune was also divulged, manifested and known among all the lineage of Nerus, whereof they were all sorrowful, and greatly abashed how this fair young man, to whom God had sent so many good virtues, and that had so many gifts of grace, as is beauty, richesse and good renommée . . . was indigent or fautif of that thing wherefore marriage is made. Nevertheless the tables were set and covered.

And when the time of dinner came, the young man came into the house of Nerus with his friends and parents. And incontinent [straightway] they set them all at the table, some with heavy and sorrowful heart, and the others with great joy and pleasure. And when the young man saw that all his friends made good cheer, and that all the parents [relations] of his wife were heavy and melancholius, he prayed and besought them that they would tell him the cause of their heaviness and sorrow; but none of them all answered. Nevertheless he prayed and besought them yet again; and then one of them, full of sorrow, and more liberal [outspoken] than all the other, said thus to him, 'Certainly, my fair son, thy wife hath told to us that thou art not man perfect.'

For the which words the man began to laugh, and said with a high voice, that all they that were there might understand what he said, 'My lords and my friends, make good cheer, for the cause of your sorrow shall soon be appeased.' And then he, being clothed with a short gown, untied his hosen [breeches] and woke his member with his hand, which was great and much sufficient, upon the table, so that all the fellowship might see it, wherefore the said fellowship was full glad and joyful. Whereof some of the men desired to have as much, and many of the women wished to their husbands such an instrument.

And then some of the friends and parents of Nerus' daughter went toward her, and said to her that she had great wrong for to complain her of her husband, for he had well wherewith she might be contented; and blamed her greatly of her folly. To whom the young daughter answered, 'My friends, why blame ye me? I complain me not without cause. For our ass, which is a brute beast, hath well a member as great as mine arm; and mine husband, which is a man, his member is unnethe [less than] half so great.'

Wherefore the simple and young damsel weened [thought] that the men should have it as great or greater than asses.

wardrobe   a room, not a cupboard.

indigent or fautif   lacking or faulty.

2 Of a fearless widow

There was in a certain town a widower wooed a widow for to have and bed her to his wife; and at last they were agreed and sured together.

And when a young woman, being servant with the widow, heard thereof, she came to her mistress and said to her, 'Alas, mistress, what have ye do?'

'Why?' said she.

'I have heard say,' said the maid, 'that ye be assured and shall wed—such a man.'

'And what then?' said the widow.

'Alas,' said the maid, 'I am sorry for you, because I have heard say he is a perilous man, for he lay so oft and knew so much his other wife that she died thereof. And I am sorry thereof, that if ye should fall in like case.'

To whom the widow answered and said, 'Forsooth, I *would* be dead! For there is but sorrow and care in this world.'

This was a courteous excuse of a widow.

3 Of the wife that made her husband to go sit in the arbour in the night while her prentice lay with her in her bed

A wife there was which had appointed her prentice to come to her bed in the night, which servant had long wooed her to have his pleasure; which according to the appointment came to her bedside in the night, her husband lying by her. And when she perceived him there, she caught him by the hand and held him fast, and incontinent wakened her husband, and said, 'Sir, it is so ye have a false and an untrue servant to you, which is William your prentice, and hath long wooed me to have his pleasure. And because I could not avoid his importunate request, I have appointed him this night to meet me in the garden in the arbour. And if ye will array yourself in mine array and go thither, ye shall see the proof thereof, and then ye may rebuke him as ye think best by your discretion.'

This husband, thus advertised [warned] by his wife, put upon him his wife's raiment and went to the arbour. And when he was gone thither, the prentice came into bed to his mistress, where for a season they were both content, and pleased each other by the space of an hour or two. But when she thought time convenient, she said to the prentice, 'Now go thy way into the arbour and meet him, and take a good waster [cudgel] in thy hand, and say thou didst it but to prove whether I would be a good woman or no, and reward him as thou thinkest best.'

This prentice, doing after his mistress' counsel, went to the arbour, where he found his master in his mistress' apparel, and said, 'Ah! Thou harlot, art thou comen hither? Now I see well, if I would be false to my master thou wouldst be a strong whore. But I had liefer [rather] thou wert hanged than I would do him so traitorous a deed. Therefore I shall give thee some punishment, as thou like an whore hast deserved,' and therewith lapped him well about the shoulders and back, and gave him a dozen or two good stripes.

The master, feeling himself somewhat to smart, said, 'Peace, William, mine own true good servant! For God's sake, hold thy hands! For I am thy master and not thy mistress.'

'Nay, whore,' quod he, 'thou liest. Thou art but an harlot, and I did but to prove thee,' and smote him again.

'Alas, man,' quod the master, 'I beseech thee, no more! For I am not she—for I am thy master. Feel, for I have a beard.'

And therewith he spared his hand, and felt his beard. 'Alas, master!' quod the prentice. 'I cry you mercy.'

And then the master went unto his wife, and she asked him how he had sped. And he answered, 'Iwis [for certain], wife, I have been shrewdly beaten. Howbeit, I have cause to be glad, for I thank God I have as true a wife and as true a servant as any man hath in England.'

By this tale ye may see that it is not wisdom for a man to be ruled always after his wife's counsel.

4 Of the woman that said her wooer came too late

Another woman there was that kneeled at the mass of requiem while the corpse of her husband lay on the bier in the church; to whom a young man came to speak with her in her ear, as though it had been for some matter concerning the funeral. Howbeit, he spoke of no such matter, but only wooed her that he might be her husband: to whom she answered and said thus, 'Sir, by my troth, I am sorry that ye come so late, for I am sped already—for I was made sure [engaged] yesterday to another man.'

> By this tale ye may perceive that women oft-times be wise and loath to lose any time.

5 Of the wedded men that came to heaven to claim their heritage

A certain wedded man there was, which when he was dead came to heaven-gates to Saint Peter, and said he came to claim his heritage which he had deserved. Saint Peter asked him what he was, and he said, 'A wedded man.' Anon Saint Peter opened the gate and bade him come in, and said he was worthy to have his heritage because he had had much trouble, and was worthy to have a crown of glory.

Anon after that there came another man that claimed heaven, and said to Saint Peter he had had two wives; to whom Saint Peter answered and said, 'Come in, for thou art worthy to have a double crown of glory, for thou hast had double trouble.'

At the last there came a third claiming heaven, and said to Saint Peter that he had had three wives and desired to come in. 'What!' quod Saint Peter, 'thou hast been once in trouble and thereof delivered, and then willingly wouldst be troubled again, and yet again thereof delivered; and for all that, couldst not beware the third time, but entered'st willingly in trouble again! Therefore go thy way to hell, for thou shalt never come in heaven, for thou art not worthy.'

> This tale is a warning to them that have been twice in peril to beware how they come therein the third time.

6 Of the Yeoman of Guard that said he would beat the carter

A Yeoman of the King's Guard dwelling in a village beside London had a very fair young wife, to whom a carter of the town, a tall fellow, resorted, and lay with her divers times when her husband was from home; and so openly known that all the town spake thereof. Wherefore there was a young man of the town, well acquainted with this Yeoman of Guard, that told him that such a carter had lain by his wife; to whom this Yeoman of Guard said, and sware by God's body, that if he met him it should cost him his life.

'Marry,' quod the young man, 'if ye go straight even now the high way, ye shall overtake him driving of a cart laden with hay toward London.'

Wherefore this Yeoman of Guard incontinent rode after this carter, and within short space overtook him and knew him well enough; and incontinent called the carter to him and said thus, 'Sirrah, I understand that thou dost lie every night with my wife when I am from home.'

This carter, being nothing afraid of the other, answered, 'Yea, marry! What then?'

'What then!' quod the Yeoman of Guard. 'By God's heart, hadst thou na' told me the truth I would have broken thy head.'

And so the Yeoman of Guard returned, and no hurt done nor stroke stricken nor proffered.

tall fellow brave, as well as strong.

7 Of the wife that bade her husband eat the candle first

The husband said to his wife thus-wise, 'By this candle, I dreamed this night that I was a cuckold.'

To whom she answered and said, 'Husband, by this bread, ye are none.'

Then said he, 'Wife, eat the bread.'

She answered and said to her husband, 'Then eat you the candle, for you sware first.'

By this a man may see that a woman's answer is never to seek.

8 Of the man that would have the pot stand thereas he would

A young man late married to a wife thought it was good policy to get the mastery of her in the beginning. He came to her, the pot seething [boiling] over the fire, [and] although the meat therein was not enough [not cooked], suddenly commanded her to take the pot from the fire; which answered and said that the meat was not ready to eat. And he said again, 'I will have it taken off for my pleasure.' This good woman, loath yet to offend him, set the pot beside the fire as he bade.

And anon after, he commanded her to set the pot behind the door, and she said thereto again, 'Ye be not wise therein.' But he precisely said it should be so as he bade. And she gently again did his commandment.

This man, yet not satisfied, commanded her to set the pot a-high upon the hen-roost. 'What!' quod the wife again. 'I trow ye be mad.' And he fiercely then commanded her to set it there or else, he said, she should repent. She, somewhat afeared to move his patience, took a ladder and set it to the roost, and went herself up the ladder, and took the pot in her hand, praying her husband then to hold the ladder fast for sliding—which so did.

And when the husband looked up and saw the pot stand there on height, he said thus, 'Lo, now standeth the pot there-as I would have it.'

This wife, hearing that, suddenly poured the hot pottage on his head, and said thus, 'And now ben [be] the pottage there-as I would have them!'

By this tale men may see it is no wisdom for a man to attempt a meek woman's patience too far, lest it turn to his own hurt and damage.

9 Of the husbandman that lodged the friar in his own bed

It fortuned so that a friar late in the evening desired lodgings of a poor man of the country; the which, for lack of other lodging, glad to harbour the friar, lodged him in his own bed. And after, he and his wife—the friar being asleep—came and lay in the same bed.

And in the morning after, the poor man rose and went to the market, leaving the friar in the bed with his wife. And as he went, he smiled and laughed to himself; wherefore his neighbours demanded of him why he so smiled. He answered and said, 'I laugh to think how shamefaced the friar shall be when he waketh, whom I left in bed with my wife.'

> By this tale a man may learn that he that overshooteth himself doth foolishly, yet he is more fool to show [reveal] it openly.

10 Of the husband that cried 'bleh' under the bed

In London there was a certain artificer, having a fair wife, to whom a lusty gallant made pursuit to accomplish his pleasure. This woman, denying, showed [revealed] the matter unto her husband, which, moved therewith, bade his wife to appoint him [the gallant] a time to come secretly to lie with her all night; and with great cracks [brags] and oaths swore that against his coming he would be ready harnessed [armed] and would put him in jeopardy of his life, except he would make him a great amends.

This night was then appointed, at which time this courtier came at his hour and entered into the chamber, set his two-hand sword down, and said these words, 'Stand thou there, thou sword, the death of three men.' This husband, lying under the bed in harness, hearing these words lay still for fear. The courtier anon got him to bed with the wife about his prepensed business. And within an hour or two, the husband, being weary of lying, began to remove him [move himself]. The courtier, that hearing, asked the wife what thing that was that removed under the bed; which, excusing the matter, said it was a little sheep that was wont daily to go about the house. And the husband, that hearing, anon cried 'bleh' as it had been a sheep. And so in conclusion when the courtier saw his time he rose and kissed the wife and took his leave and departed.

And as soon as he was gone the husband arose. And when the wife looked on him, somewhat abashed, she began to make a sad countenance and said, 'Alas, sir, why did ye not rise and play the man as ye said ye would?'

Which answered and said, 'Why, dame, didst thou not hear him say that his sword had been the death of three men? And I had been a fool then if I had put myself in jeopardy to have been the fourth.'

Then said the wife thus, 'But sir, spake not I wisely then when I said ye were a sheep?'

'Yes,' quod the husband. 'But then did not I more wisely, dame, when that I cried bleh?'

By this ye may see that he is not wise that will put his confidence too much upon these great crackers which ofttimes will do but little when it comes to the point.

11 Of the husband that said his wife and he agreed well

A man asked his neighbour, which was but late married to a widow, how he agreed with his wife, for he said that her first husband and she could never agree.

'By God,' quod the other, 'we agree marvellous well.'

'I pray ye, how so?'

'Marry,' quod the other, 'I shall tell ye. When I am merry, she is merry, and when I am sad, she is sad. For when I go out of my doors I am merry to go from her, and so is she. And when I come in again I am sad, and so is she.'

12 Of the burning of Old John

In a certain town there was a wife (somewhat aged) that had buried her husband, whose name was called John, whom she loved so tenderly in his life that after his death she caused an image of timber to be made, in visage and person as like to him as could be: which image all day long lay under her bed, and every night she caused her maid to wrap it in a sheet and lay it in her bed, and called it Old John.

This wife also had a prentice whose name was John, which John would fain have wedded his mistress—not for no great pleasure but only for her goods, because she was rich. Wherefore he imagined how he might obtain his purpose, and spake to the maid of the house and desired her to lay him in his mistress' bed for one night instead of the picture [statue], and promised her a reward for her labour. Which maid overnight wrapped the said young man in a sheet and laid him in his mistress' bed as she was wont to lay the picture.

This widow was wont every night before she slept, and divers times when she waked, to kiss the said picture of Old John; wherefore the said night she kissed the said young man, believing that she had kissed the picture. And he suddenly start [started] and took her in his arms and so well pleased her then that Old John from thenceforth was clean out of her mind, and [she] was content that this young John should lie with her still all the night, and that the picture of Old John should lie still under the bed for a thing of nought.

After this in the morning, this widow, intending to please this young John which had made her so good pastime all the night, bade her maid go dress some good meat for their breakfast to feast therewith her young John. This maid, when she had long sought for wood to dress the said meat, told her mistress that she could find no wood that was dry 'except only the picture of Old John that lieth under the bed'.

'Then,' quod the wife again, 'fetch him down and lay him on the fire, for I see well he will never do me good, nor he will never do better service though I keep him never so long.' So the maid by her commandment fetched the picture of Old John from under the bed and therewith made good fire and dressed the breakfast. And so Old John was cast out for nought and burnt, and from thenceforth young John occupied his place.

> By this tale ye may see it is not wisdom for a man to keep long or to cherish that thing that is able to do no pleasure nor service.

13 Of him that was called cuckold

A certain man which upon a time in company, between earnest and game, was called cuckold, went angrily home to his wife and said, 'Wife, I was this day in company called cuckold. Whether am I one or not?'

'Sir, truly,' said she, 'ye be none.'

'By my faith,' said he, 'thou shalt swear so upon this book,' and held to her a book [Bible].

She denied it long, but when she saw there was no remedy, she said, 'Well, sith I must needs swear, I promise you by my faith I will swear truly.'

'Yea, do so,' quod he.

So she took the book in her hand and said: 'By this book, sir, ye be a cuckold.'

'By the mass, whore,' said he, 'thou liest! Thou sayst it for none other cause but to anger me.'

> By this tale ye may perceive that it is not best at all times for a man to believe his wife, though she swear upon a book.

14 Of the jealous man

A man that was right jealous on his wife dreamed on a night as he lay abed with her and slept that the devil appeared unto him and said, 'Wouldst thou not be glad that I should put thee in surety of thy wife?'

'Yes,' said he.

'Hold,' said the devil. 'As long as thou hast this ring upon thy finger, no man shall make thee cuckold.'

The man was glad thereof: and when he awaked he found his finger in his wife's tail.

15 Of the young man of Bruges and his spouse

A young man of Bruges that was betrothed to a fair maiden came on a time when her mother was out of the way, and had to do with her. When her mother was come in, anon she perceived by her daughter's cheer what she had done; wherefore she was so sore displeased that she sued a divorce [breach of the betrothal] and would in no wise suffer that the young man should marry her daughter.

Not long after, the same young man was married to another maiden of the same parish. And as he and his wife sat talking on a time of the foresaid damsel to whom he was betrothed, he fell in a nice laughing.

'Whereat laugh ye?' quod his wife.

'It chanced on a time,' quod he, 'that she and I did such a thing together, and she told it to her mother.'

'Therein,' quod his wife, 'she played the fool. A servant of my father's played that game with me a hundred times, and yet I never told *my* mother.'

When he heard her say so, he left his nice laughing.

nice here this many-sided word suggests 'self-pleased'.

16 Of the widow that would not wed for bodily pleasure

There was a rich widow which desired a gossip of hers that she would get her a husband—'Not for the nice play,' quod she, 'but to the intent he may keep my goods together, which is a hard thing for me to do, being a lone woman.' Her gossip, which understood her conceit [true thoughts], promised her so to do.

About three or four days after, she came to her again and said, 'Gossip, I have found a husband for you that is a prudent, a ware and a worldly-wise man, but he lacketh his privy members— whereof ye force not [which does not matter to you].'

'Go to the devil with that husband,' quod the widow, 'for though that I desire not the nice play, yet I will that my husband shall have that wherewith we may be reconciled if we fall at variance.'

nice the word often had amatory implications. A British Museum MS. of about 1475 has a scrap of verse beginning, 'A nice wife and a back door.' About 1550 there was an interlude called *The Nice Wanton*.

17 Of him that feigned himself dead to prove what his wife would do

A young married man on a time, to prove, to hear and to see what his wife would do if he were dead, came into his house while his wife was forth washing of clothes, and laid him down in the floor as [as if] he had been dead. When his wife came in and saw him lie so, she thought he had been dead indeed; wherefore she stood even still and devised with herself whether was better to bewail his death forthwith or else to dine first: for she had eat no meat of all the day. All other things considered, she determined to dine first.

So she cut a collop of bacon and broiled it on the coals, and began to eat thereon apace. She was so hungry that she took no heed of drink. At last, the saltness of the meat made her to thirst so sore that she must needs drink. So, as she took the pot in her hand and was going down into her cellar to draw drink, suddenly came one of her neighbours for a coal of fire. Wherefore she stepped back quickly, and though she was right thirsty, yet she set the pot aside; and as [as if] her husband had then fallen down dead, she began to weep and with many lamentable words to bewail his death; which weeping and wailing and sudden death of her husband caused all the neighbours to come thither.

The man lay still in the floor, and so held his breath and closed his eyes that he seemed for certain to be dead. At last, when he thought he had made pastime enough—and hearing his wife say thus, 'Alas! dear husband, what shall I do now?'—he looked up and said, 'Full ill, my sweet wife, except ye go quickly and drink.' Wherewith they all from weeping turned to laughing, especially when they understood the matter and the cause of her thirst.

Whereby ye may see that not without a good skill the poet said, '*Ut flerent oculos erudiere suos*'.

Ut flerent, etc. Ovid, *Remedia Amoris*, l. 900—'They [women] taught their eyes to weep.'

18 Of the husband that lost his wager

There was a man in Gotham that laid a wager with his wife that she should not make him cuckold.

'No?' said she. 'But I can.'

'Spare not,' quoth he. 'Do what thou canst.'

On a time, she hid all the spigots and faucets in the house, and she went into her buttery and set a barrel abroach, and cried to her husband and said, 'I pray you, bring me hither a spigot and a faucet or else all the ale will run out.'

The good man sought up and down, and could find none. 'Come hither,' said she then, 'and hold your finger in the tap-hole.' She pulled out her finger and the good man put in his.

She then called [went] to her tailor, which did dwell at the next door, with whom she made a blind bargain. And within a while she came to her husband and did bring a spigot and a faucet with her, saying: 'Pull out thy finger out of the tap-hole, gentle cuckold: for you have lost your bargain.'

'I beshrew your heart for your labour,' said the good man.

'Make no such bargains then,' said she, 'with me.'

19 Of the twelfth father

When Henry the Eighth reigned, there was in London a gentlewoman, poor in goods but rich in beauty, and very wanton. She had twelve sons: the first was her husband's, the residue other men's.

Now she falling grievously sick, and waxing worse and worse, was suddenly in danger of death; wherefore upon a time, she, causing her husband to be called to her, said unto him, 'William' (so was he called), 'I must now mock thee no longer. Understand that of all these sons there is none thine but the eldest, because I was true to thee but the first year.' The husband was astonished, and all those children, which by chance sat there about the fire eating, were at a stay.

The mother followed her purpose, and began to reckon up in order their fathers. Which the youngest hearing (oh, mighty nature!), not above four years old, which had bread in one hand, and cheese in the other, laid down his meat [food], and holding up both his hands together, in trembling wise turned to her and said, 'Oh, my dear mam, give me, I pray you, a good father.'

The woman, coming to his father, named a famous and a rich man; wherefore the boy, being very merry and taking his meat again, said; 'I am in very good case, seeing that I have such a father.'

20 A chiding wife

A shrewd [shrewish] wife chid her husband out-of-doors, and he stepping forth into the street stumbled with his nose into the kennel [gutter]; and at rising up again, he said, 'Better here yet, than within-doors.'

21 A wife warned

A man had a shrewd wife, and he one day broke her head, the cure whereof cost him dear expense afterward; insomuch as his wife in regard thereof said on a time unto her gossips, 'Faith, my husband will not dare give me no more broken heads in haste, considering how dear he finds them in the cure.'

Her husband, hearing of such her braves, sent the next day for the surgeons and apothecaries, and in her presence paid them all their bills, and gave each of them twenty shillings over and above, saying, 'Hold this, sirs, against the next time.'

22 Of yielding women

One asked a gentlewoman why other females for the most part resist the male in generation, and only women most gently yield unto it. She answered, 'Because women are no beasts.'

23 A kind wife

A kind wife followed her husband to the gallows; and he requesting her not to trouble herself any further, she answered, 'Ah yes, dear husband, now that I am come thus far, faith, I'll see you hanged too, God willing, before I go.'

24 Home and weed!

A gardener being to be hanged, his wife came to give him his last kiss at the gallows—to whom he said, 'Fie on thee! Thus are we like to thrive well at the year's end! There cannot be a meeting in all the country, but still thou wilt be sure to make one. Home and weed, home and weed, with a very vengeance!'

country county.

25 How Tarlton was deceived by his wife in London

Tarlton being merrily disposed as his wife and he sat together, he said unto her: 'Kate, answer me to one question without a lie, and take this crown of gold'—which she took on condition that if she lost, to restore it back again. Quoth Tarlton, 'Am I a cuckold or no, Kate?' Whereat she answered not a word, but stood silent, notwithstanding he urged her many ways. Tarlton, seeing she would not speak, asked his gold again.

'Why,' quoth she, 'have I made any lie?'
'No,' says Tarlton.
'Why then, goodman fool, I have won the wager.'
Tarlton, mad with anger, made this rhyme:

> *As women in speech can revile a man,*
> *So can they in silence beguile a man.*

26 Of one that believed his wife better than others

A man whose wife was no better than she should be—nor so [good] neither—his friends counselled him to look better unto her. The man went home and sharply rebuked his wife, and told her what his friends said of her. She, knowing that perjury was no worse than adultery, with weeping and swearing denied the same, and told her husband that they devised those tales in envy, because they saw them live so quietly. With these words her husband was content and well pleased.

Yet another of his friends was at him again, and said that he did not well to let her have her liberty so much. To whom he answered, 'I pray you, tell me whether [which] knoweth my wife's faults best, she or you?'

They said, 'She.'

'And she that I believe better than you all saith you lie all like knaves.'

27 A tale of a merry Christmas carol sung by women

There was sometimes an old knight who, being disposed to make himself merry in a Christmas-time, sent for many of his tenants and poor neighbours with their wives to dinner; when having made meat to be set on the table, [he] would suffer no man to drink till he that was master over his wife should sing a carol to excuse all the company.

Great niceness there was who should be the musician, now the cuckoo time was so far off. Yet with much ado, looking one upon another, after a dry 'hem' or two, a dreaming companion drew out as much as he durst towards an illfashioned ditty.

When [he had] made an end, to the great comfort of the beholders, at last it came to the women's table, where likewise commandment was given that there should no drink be touched till she that was master over her husband had sung a Christmas carol: whereupon they fell all to such a singing that there was never heard such a caterwauling piece of music. Whereat the knight laughed so heartily that it did him half as much good as a corner of his Christmas pie.

28 The ninth gull, that wished for the wood

Among mad country wenches that when they sit a-milking will be talking of their sweethearts, it was my hap not long since, lying close under a bush, to hear a merry tale of a bird little wiser than a woodcock. . . . For as it fell out, a rich widow that was past a girl, and therefore knew what to do with a good thing when she had it, hearing divers reports of such persons as she was wished to make much of, among all she heard of one young man, a neighbour's son of hers, to be a sufficient man to do her much good service, either within the house or without, either for ploughing or threshing or sowing or such country work as best fitted her occupation. This young man she sent for, and as far as modesty might she made show of her affection; which the goose not perceiving, she carried him one day alone into her chamber where, she told him, she must have his help to remove a chest.

The fellow, understanding nothing more than was told him, went up with the widow, and all along from one chamber to another, the doors shutting after them; where she, often smiling at his either shamefacedness or foolishness, in the end carried him to a chamber where stood a chest that he could not remove; when, [he] saying he would fetch company to help him, she answered, 'No, now she was otherwise minded.' And so leading down again the good ass, she never sent more for him.

A friend of his, meeting of him coming forth, hoping of his good hap, knowing his being above with her alone, asked him how he had sped. Whose answer was, 'Oh, I wish I had had her in the wood, and then I would have told her my mind.'

Now what a notable gull was this, I leave to all goodhumoured wenches to consider.

ninth gull   This story and the next are from a series of twelve about gulls (bungling, simple or *gull*ible persons).

occupation   euphemism for lovemaking. The whole passage beginning 'a sufficient man' contains double meanings.

29   The tenth gull, that shook his gloves

This tale was no sooner ended but another wench began to quite [requite] her in this sort:

Nay, then I will tell thee of as good an ass as that was for his life. In our town not long ago, one of the chief of our parish, who was twice churchwarden and in election to be bailiff, a good fat gross churl, having a good house of his own, and well to take to [? more property coming to him], married a widow that dwelled three miles off—who having good cattle and corn and some household of her own, by the motion of good friends made a match together.

But this churl, being troubled with some sixteen diseases, lay himself in one bed, and his wife in another by him, who having a kind of more than good liking to a young man in the house, some kinsman of his, with sheep's eyes and smiles and such odd kind of wicked kindness she made him understand her mind. And being agreed one night to come into her chamber when [the husband] was asleep, she told him, for fear of the worst, that he should take a pair of her gloves, and flap them to and fro in his hand, which would make a noise like unto a great spaniel that used often to shake his ears: which lesson he forgot not.

Night was come, the candles out, they in bed, and he came

creeping like a dog. But the door creaking, the old man, half-awake or not fast asleep, asked who was there; when the fellow shaking of his gloves together made him think it was the dog—when saying, 'Oh, Troll,' he lay still, as though he slept. But the fellow, missing his way in the dark, running his head against his master's bedpost, upon a sudden the old man start up his head with 'How now? Who is there?'

The poor man, amazed, forgetting to flap his glove, answered, 'Forsooth, it is the dog.'

Whereat his mistress, laughing, bade, 'Hang him up!'

Whereat the fellow, as it were following in and seeking to drive him [the dog] forth, cried, 'Come out!'

But in the morning, as I have heard, the gull was put in a coop, where I heard no more of him.

'*Hang him up*' like a bird in a cage.

30 A loving scold

A poor labouring man was married and matched to a creature that so much used to scold waking that she had much ado to refrain it sleeping, so that the poor man was so batterfanged and belaboured with tongue-metal that he was weary of his life.

At last, four or five women that were his neighbours, pitying his case, came in his absence to his house to admonish and counsel his wife to a quiet behaviour towards her husband, telling her that she was a shame to all good women in her bad usage of so honest a painful [painstaking] man. The woman replied to her neighbours that she thought her husband did not love her, which was partly the cause that she was so froward towards him.

'Why,' said an old woman, 'I will show thee how thou shalt prove that he loves thee dearly. Do thou counterfeit thyself dead and lie under the table, and one of us will fetch thy husband, and he shall find us heavy and grieving for thee—by which means thou shalt perceive by his lamentation for thee how much he loves thee.'

This counsel was allowed and effected. When the poor man came home, he, hearing the matter (being much oppressed with grief), ran under the table bemoaning the happy loss of his most kind vexation; and making as though he would kiss her with a most loving embrace, to make all sure, he broke her neck.

The neighbours, pitying the man's extreme passion, in compassion told him that his wife was not dead, and that all this was done but to make trial of his love towards her. Whereupon they called her by her name, bidding her to rise and that she had fooled it enough with her husband. But for all their calling she lay still, which made one of the women to shake and jog her, at which the woman cried, 'Alas, she is dead indeed!'

'Why, this it is,' quoth her husband, 'to dissemble and counterfeit with God and the world.'

batterfanged this word of obscure origin neatly implies 'battered and slashed'.

31 The puzzled wife

A company of neighbours that dwelt all in one row in one side of a street—one of them said: 'Let us be merry, for it is reported that we are all cuckolds that dwell on our side of the street, except one.'

One of the women sat musing, to whom her husband said, 'Wife, what, all amort [pensive]? Why art thou so sad?'

'No,' quoth she, 'I am not sad, but I am studying which of our neighbours it is that is not a cuckold.'

32 A wife's warning

A man, going with his wife by a deep river side, began to talk of cuckolds, and withal he wished that every cuckold were cast into the river. To whom his wife replies, 'Husband, I pray you, learn to swim.'

33 Two old widows

Two old widows sitting over a cup of ale in a winter night entered into discourse of their dead husbands; and after the ripping up of their good and bad qualities, saith one of them to her maid, 'I prithee, wench, reach us another light, for my husband, God rest his soul, above all things loved to see good lights about the house, God grant him light everlasting!'

'And I pray you, neighbour,' saith the other, 'let the maid lay on some more coals or stir up the fire, for my husband in his lifetime ever loved to see a good fire, God grant him fire everlasting!'

34 Of a pretended rape

A wench accused a fellow for a rape. The judge asked her whether he offered her any violence, as to bind her hands or otherwise.

'Yes,' saith she, 'he bound my hands, and he would have bound my legs too, but he could not bring them together. I thank God I kept them far enough asunder.'

35 A silly young gentlewoman

A silly country gentlewoman, being begot with child by one that was much her inferior, to save her credit accused the man of rape; whereupon the matter was had in question before a neighbour justice of peace, who somewhat perceiving the matter, after he had heard her complaint how deeply she had been injured, as if pitying her case said, 'Alas, poor gentlewoman, I warrant this was not the first time the rogue ravished you.'

She, to aggravate his crime, replied, 'No, I'll be sworn he ravished me above twenty times,' which procured much laughter, and the fellow's freedom.

36 A wench's honesty

One was praising a wench's honesty, whom a stander-by knew to be a whore, wherefore he said to him, 'Is she honest? Pray, had she never a child?'

The first answered him, 'Indeed, she had a child, but it was a very little one.'

honesty chastity.

37 Of a country fellow and his wench

A country fellow and his wench, having been long in love together, made their appointed meeting in a park, and having choosed a convenient place for their privacy, he bade her lie down, which she refused unless he would throw her down.

The bashful fellow refused, and she appeared obstinate on the other side, insomuch that upon those terms they were ready to depart; which the wench perceiving, told him that if he would not cast her down, but to blow upon her and she would fall down: which was instantly done.

A woodman, standing behind a tree and observing all these proceedings, suddenly rushed out upon them and said to the fellow, 'Friend, by your favour, you have nothing to do here, for to *me* belong all the windfalls in this forest.'

windfalls selling windfalls for fuel was a forester's perquisite.

38 A wench's excuse

A wench came to Sir Henry Neville and made a pitiful complaint how such a man had ravished her. He granted a warrant and the fellow was brought, and upon examination, the wench having made her strongest allegations, the fellow confessed he had carnally known her, but not without her consent—'for if it please your worship,' says he, 'she took up her smock very willingly.'

'O Lord, sir,' says she, 'if I had not done so, he kept such a wimbling [wimble = gimlet], as he had bored a great hole in my smock presently!'

presently at once, right then.

39 A loose fit

A story that goes upon one Dr Burcott's wife, was not true by her, but by one Dr Matthias's wife. [He was] a German and famous physician that lived in Norwich, who (having been long absent, and suspecting foul play) said of his wife, 'By my trote [troth], when I went into Germany she was as fit for me as any woman in t' world. But when I come back, she is e'en so fit for me as my cap—' having then one of those same furred German caps on '—is for my t'umb—' putting the one upon the other.

40 Justice every day

A Suffolk gentleman in commission [as justice of the peace], that delighted much in examination of bawdy-body-businesses, had a pretty wench [who] came to complain that a young man of such a town had Done her Wrong. 'Then I am bound by oath,' says he, 'to Do thee Right,' and calls her (as his manner was) to auricular confession.

She opens her case [= body], he bestows a warrant on her. Next day she comes again, makes known the delinquent's contempt of his warrant, and craves justice. In he takes her again to the study, and does her justice to her mind. Next morning she appears again, reports a *fugem fecit*, the fellow's escape, and other fresh injuries, for which she begs justice.

She presently expected the closet; but the gentleman takes her aside, whispers her in the ear: 'Good wench, I prithee be gone. I am not now fit for thee. What, dost think I can do justice every day?'

41 The unsuspected hand

A tradesman's wife of the Exchange, one day when her husband was following some business in the City, desired him he would give her leave to go see a play, which she had not done in seven years. He bade her take his prentice along with her and go, but especially to have a care of her purse: which she warranted him she would.

Sitting in a box among some gallants and gallant wenches, and returning when the play was done—returned to her husband and told him she had lost her purse.

'Wife,' quoth he, 'did I not give you warning of it? How much money was there in it?'

Quoth she, 'Truly, four pieces, six shillings and a silver tooth-picker.'

Quoth her husband, 'Where did you put it?'

'Under my petticoat, between that and my smock.'

'What,' quoth he, 'did you feel nobody's hand there?'

'Yes,' quoth she, 'I felt one's hand there, but I did not think he had come for that!'

42 The tobacco-takers

A lady that could not endure tobacco herself, but her husband and both her sons (for she had two) took it roundly—one day she was at it—*why would they take it?*—to her sons. They told her, 'Oh, madam, 'tis good to preserve our chastity.'

With that—into the next room where her husband was. 'Say you so?' quoth she—hits him a good souse o'th' ear—'And what, then, does this old fellow take it for?'

43 Learning the truth

A woman told her husband he was a witch [wizard]. But he went to a cunning man to know the truth, who told him he was no witch, but he was a cuckold. So he comes home rejoicing to his wife; and told her that he said he was not a witch, but a cuckold. Says she, 'I am sure if thou art not a witch, he is one.'

cunning man soothsayer, as distinct from a witch or wizard possessed of infernal powers.

44 The experienced bride

A miller had wooed abundance of girls, and did lie with them, upon which he refused to marry them. But one girl he did solicit very much, but all would not do. Then he married her, and told her on the marriage-night, if she would have let him do as the rest did he would never have had her.

'By my troth, I thought so,' says she, 'for I was served so by half a dozen before.'

45 The silent maid

Says a lady to her maid, 'What, you are with child?'
  'Yes, a little, forsooth.'
  'And who got it?'
  'My master, forsooth.'
  'Where?'
  'In the truckle-bed, forsooth.'
  'Where was I then?'
  'Asleep in the high bed, forsooth.'
  'Why did you not call out then, you whore?'
  'Why,' says she, 'would you have done so?'

46 The lost fiddle

A fiddler was bragging what a chaste wife he had. Says a merchant, 'I'll lay my ship against thy fiddle, if I may have opportunity I get her good-will to lie with her.' The wager was laid and he had liberty to try her. But the fiddler in the meantime went to the window and sung this song:

> Hold out, sweetheart, hold out.
> Hold out but this two hours.
> If thou hold out there is no doubt
> But the ship and all is ours.

[Then she sang:]
> I'faith, sweet Robin, I cannot.
> He hath caught me about the middle.
> He hath me won, thou art undone.
> Sweet Robin, thou'st lost thy fiddle.

47 A willing servant

An impotent gentleman, having married a rich young gentlewoman whom he could not satisfy, gave a young lusty gallant fifty pounds a year to do the work. His waiting-man, seeing this gallant one day with his mistress, ran to acquaint his master; but he feigned as if he were in a sleep, and gave no answer: which made him cry the more urgently that his marriage bed was defiled.

When his master saw he would not be quiet, 'Peace, peace,' says he, 'I give him fifty pound a year for doing it.'

'Ah, sir,' replied the man, 'had I known that, I would have done it for half the money.'

48 The busy husband

A great scholar—or a mere one, as we say—that took care neither for wife, children nor anything but his book, was translating a Greek book into Latin, and at the same time one came and told him his wife was very sick. 'Well, I have but three or four sentences to do,' said he, 'and I will come.'

Presently came another and said she was dying. 'Well, I have but three lines,' said he, 'to do, and I come.'

Not long after came a third that said she was dead. 'Alas, I am sorry,' said he. 'She was a good woman.'

49 John and Will

There lived in a country village an idle companion who loved his pot better than his bed; and being till about one in the morning at an alehouse in company with a crew as good as himself, says he, 'I wish one good fellow or other would go lie with my wife in my stead this while.'

'Why, faith, John,' said one of the company, 'I will, if thou wilt have it so.'

'With all my heart,' says John.

'But how shall I get in?' says the other.

'Why,' replied he, 'you may find the key in the hole of the kitchen window.'

Away goes Will, takes the key, gets into the room without any words, lays down his clothes very orderly, and goes to bed to Grisel, giving her such entertainment as she was not used to; and having served up second course, puts on his clothes again and goes to his company. As he was coming down the stairs, he heard poor Grisel say, 'He came in like John, and went out like John. I pray God *be* John.'

50 Dead enough

A gentleman having sent his wife to be buried four or five hours after she was dead, one came and told him that she was scarce cold yet. 'No matter,' says he, 'do as you are bid. She is dead enough for me.'

51 Day of pleasure

Sudden transports of joy operate very powerfully on the spirits. One going to his wife's funeral said, 'Don't go so fast. What need we make a toil of a pleasure?'

52 Early to rise

A young lady who had been married but a short time, seeing her husband going to rise pretty early in the morning, said, 'What, my dear! Are you getting up already? Pray lie a little longer and rest yourself.'

'No, my dear,' replied the husband, 'I'll get up and rest myself.'

53 A smart message

An old fellow, having a great itch after his neighbour's young wife, employed her chambermaid in the business. At their next meeting, he inquired what answer the lady had sent him. 'Answer!' says the girl. 'Why, she has sent you this for a token'—giving him a smart slap on the chops.

The old fellow, rubbing his chops, cried, 'And you have lost none of it by the way, I thank you.'

54 An amorous fellow

An amorous young fellow making very warm addresses to a married woman, 'Pray, sir, be quiet,' said she. 'I have a husband that won't thank you for making him a cuckold.'

'No, madam,' replied he, 'but you will, I hope.'

55 A whore outwitted

A strammelling two-handed harlot, grenadier-height and limbed like a bacon-faced Dutchman, accused a little diminutive tailor once of a rape. The magistrate he was brought before ordered the fellow's purse to be taken from him and given to her, bidding her be sure to keep it; and so dismissed her.

As soon as she had turned her back, he bid the little nit-cracker follow her and take it from her again: upon which she quickly returned to make her complaint that, like an impudent rogue as he was, he would have robbed her of the purse.

'But I hope,' says the magistrate, 'you didn't let him.'

'Let him! No,' says she, 'I think not! 'Slife, I'd have tore his eyes out first.'

'Very well,' answered he, 'pray let me see if the money be all safe.' So, taking the purse, he returned it to the owner, and bid 'em give the whore forty lashes—with this instruction: 'If you had defended your honesty as well as you did your money, you had never been ravished, you whore, you.'

56 A strong constitution

Some years ago, when I was at Oxford, we had an amorous old fellow in our college that used often to make us merry when we could discover any of his intrigues; and happening one day to catch him in a very familiar posture with a very ugly cook-wench, we bantered him pretty much upon the oddness of his fancy.

'Why, look ye, gentlemen,' said he, 'though I am an old fellow, my constitution is good still, and I thank God I'm yet neither reduced to beauty or brandy.'

57 The embarrassing sign

Lady C———g and her two daughters having taken lodgings at a leather-breeches-maker's in Picadilly, the sign of the Cock and Leather Breeches, was always put to the blush when she was obliged to give anybody direction to her lodgings, the sign being so odd a one. Upon which my lady, a very good sort of woman, sending for her landlord, a jolly young fellow, told him she liked him and his lodgings very well but she must be obliged to quit them on account of his sign, for she was ashamed to tell anybody what it was.

'O! dear madam,' said the young fellow, 'I would do anything rather than lose so good lodgers. I can easily alter my sign.'

'So I think,' answered my lady, 'and I'll tell you how you may satisfy both me and my daughters. Only take down your Breeches and let your Cock stand.'

58 Taking the waters

Two ladies just returned from Bath were telling a gentleman how they liked the place and how it agreed with them. The first had been ill and found great benefit from the waters. 'But pray, what did you go for?' said he to the second.
　'Wantonness,' replied she.
　'And pray, madam,' said he, 'did it cure you?'

59 A knowing audience

When Mrs W―――n first acted Sir Harry Wildair at Drury Lane Playhouse, coming off the stage into the green-room, 'I believe,' said she, 'that one-half of the house take me really for a man.'
　To which said Mrs Clive, 'But the other half, madam, know to the contrary.'

W―――n Peg Woffington, actress (died 1760), famous for her lovers as well as her talent and beauty.

Wildair in George Farquhar's *The Constant Couple, or A Trip to the Jubilee*.

60 If this should come out

Two persons, male and female, having at once met with three irresistible temptations, time, place and consent, made use of the occasion, and were very wickedly busy, but the wench being more troubled about her credit than conscience, cries to him, 'If this should come out I am utterly undone.'
　To which he answered: 'If it do not, I am sure I shall be utterly undone.'

61 A disconsolate house

A man being asked by his neighbour how his sick wife did, made this answer, 'Indeed, neighbour, the case is pitiful. My wife fears she shall die, and I fear she will not die, which makes a most disconsolate house.'

62 The expensive wife

A gentleman one day reproached his wife with the prodigious sums of money she laid out on finery. 'When I had a girl,' said he, 'before I married, it seldom cost me above a guinea. But was I to keep an account, I am sure I never enjoy you that it costs me less than five.'

'That's no fault of mine, my dear,' replied the wife. 'I am always at your service. Come as often as you will. Why do not you contrive that it should not cost you above half a crown a time?'

63 Not ruined yet

It is now several years since one of the venerable inhabitants of King's Place told the Duke of Queensberry that she had just had consigned to her from Yorkshire a young and beautiful girl who would suit him to a T, as she was ignorant of life, unacquainted with the town, inexperienced, simple, captivating, etc., etc. The duke agreed to the terms, paid down the stipulated sum, fixed upon his hour, and was introduced to this paragon of innocence and simplicity—when, to his inexpressible surprise, he recognized an old acquaintance.

'Mercy on me!' said he. 'Why, I *ruined* you two months ago!'

'No, Your Grace,' replied she, 'you did not. I takes more *ruining* than you think for.'

King's Place it was in Westminster, and noted for brothels in the eighteenth century.

Queensberry the 4th Duke (1724–1810), 'Old Q', a notable racing man, gambler and wencher.

64 A lady's memory

A lady who had made several *faux pas* in life, being afterwards married very happily, a company of friends were talking over the circumstance, and mentioning that she had the frankness to tell her husband before marriage *all* that had happened. 'What candour! What honesty!' added they.

'Yes,' cried Foote, joining in the general praise, 'and what an *amazing memory, too!*'

Foote see additional notes.

2

Friars, Priests and Nuns

Jokes at the expense of the clergy, and especially of the friars, were common before and during the Reformation. For a time no doubt the friars often joined happily in the laughter. During Elizabeth's reign such jokes tend to fade away. It was wise to keep jestbooks fairly uncontroversial when, in all classes, all opinions could be found from Catholic to Puritan.

There are very few anti-Puritan jokes, even in the Commonwealth period when Cavaliers were freely lashing their enemy in pamphlet and song. Religion had become too serious for joking.

My hopes were raised when I found *The Tales and Jests of Mr. Hugh Peters*, published in 1660, for Peters, the Cromwellian chaplain, was an object of Cavalier execration and mockery. But this collection is made up almost entirely of old jokes. Peters' name is often dragged into them, with the result that he becomes quite likeable; and he does not suffer much from a story like this, almost the only topical one:

> Mr Peters, preaching immediately after the death of Oliver Cromwell, in his sermon brought in this expression: that he know Ol. Cromwell was in heaven as sure as he could then touch the head of his pulpit. And reaching up his hand, came short thereof by half a yard.

After the Restoration there is hardly a joke that exposes the established clergy even to light mockery. *Amusements Serious and Comical*, 1719, has one story with a little bite in it for those who wanted to take it that way. A woman is discussing wages and conditions with a maidservant she is hiring, and asks what her religion is. 'Alackaday, madam!' says the poor innocent girl. 'I ne'er troubled my head about that, for religion, I thought, was only for gentlefolks.'

The title is 'A servant-maid's simplicity.'

65 Of the Grey Friar that answered his penitent

A man there was that came to confess himself to a Grey Friar [Franciscan], and shrove him that he had lain with a young gentlewoman. The friar then asked him, 'In what place?' And he said it was in a goodly chamber all night long in a soft, warm bed.

The friar, hearing that, shrugged in his clothes and said, 'Now, by sweet Saint Francis, then wast thou very well at ease!'

66 Of the friar that said Our Lord fed five thousand people with three fishes

There was a certain White Friar [Carmelite] which was a very glutton and a great niggin [niggard], which had an ungracious boy that ever followed him and bare his cloak. And what for the friar's gluttony and for his churlishness, the boy where he went could scant get meat enough, for the friar would eat almost all himself.

But on a time the friar made a sermon in the country, wherein he touched very many miracles which Christ did afore His Passion; among which he specially rehearsed the miracle that Christ did in feeding five thousand people with five loaves of bread and with three little fishes.

And this friar's boy, which cared not greatly for his master, hearing him say so, and considering that his master was so great a churl and glutton, answered with a loud voice that all the church heard, and said, 'By my troth, master, then there were no friars there!'—which answer made all the people to fall on such a laughing that for shame the friar went out of the pulpit. And as for the friar's boy, he then departed out of the church, that the friar never saw him after.

> By this ye may see that it is honesty for a man that is at meat to depart with [share] such as he hath to them that be present.

67 Of the priest that said Our Lady was not so curious a woman

In the town of Botley dwelled a miller which had a good homely wench to his daughter whom the curate of the next town loved— and, as the fame [public report] went, had her at his pleasure.

But on a time this curate preached of these curious [fashion-mad] wives nowadays. And whether it were for the nonce [on purpose] or whether it came out at all adventures, he happened to say thus in his sermon, 'Ye wives, ye be so curious in all your works that ye wot not what ye mean. But ye should follow Our Lady. For Our Lady was nothing so curious as ye be, but she was a good homely wench like the miller's daughter of Botley.' At which saying, all the parishioners made great laughing, and specially they that knew that he loved that same wench.

> By this ye may see it is great folly for a man that is suspected with any person to praise or to name the same person openly lest it bring him in further slander.

68 Of the two nuns that were shriven of one priest

In the time of Lent there came two nuns to St John's in London, because of the great pardon there, to be confessed; of the which nuns, the one was a young lady and the other was old.

This young lady chose first her confessor, and confessed her that she had sinned in lechery. The confessor asked with whom it was. She said it was with a lusty gallant. He demanded where it was. She said, in a pleasant green arbour. He asked further, when it was. She said, in the merry month of May. Then said the confessor this wise, 'A fair young lady, with a lusty gallant, in a pleasant arbour, in the merry month of May: ye did but your kind! Now by my troth, God forgive you, and I do.' And so she departed, and incontinent the old nun met with her, asking her how she liked her confessor; which said he was the best ghostly father that ever she had, and the most easiest in penance-giving.

For comfort whereof, this other nun went to the same confessor, and shrove her likewise that she had sinned in lechery. And he demanded with whom; which said, with an old friar. He asked where. She said, in her old cloister. He asked, what season. She said, in Lent. Then the confessor said, 'An old whore, to lie with an old friar, in her old cloister, and in the holy time of Lent! By cock's body, if God forgive thee, yet will I never forgive thee!' Which words caused her to depart all sad and sore abashed.

> By this tale men may learn that a vicious act is more abominable in one person than in another, in one season than in another, and in one place than in another.

ye did but your kind   according to nature.

ghostly   spiritual.

69 Of the franklin's son that came to take orders

A certain scholar that was intending to be made priest, which had neither great wit nor learning, came to the bishop to take [holy] orders—whose foolishness the bishop perceiving, because he was a rich man's son, would not very strongly oppose him, but asked him this small question, 'Noah had three sons, Shem, Ham and Japhet. Now tell me,' quod the bishop, 'who was Japhet's father, and thou shalt have orders.'

Then said the scholar, 'By my troth, my lord, I pray you pardon me, for I never learned but little of the Bible.'

Then quod the bishop, 'Go home and come again and soyle [resolve] me this question, and thou shalt have orders.'

This scholar so departed and came home to his father, and showed [told] him the cause of the hindrance of his orders. His father, being angry at his foolishness, thought to teach him the solution of this question by a familiar example, and called his spaniels before him and said thus: 'Thou knowest well, Coll my dog hath these three whelps, Ryg, Tryg and Tryboll. Must not Coll my dog needs be sire to Tryboll?'

Then quod the scholar, 'By God, father, ye say truth! Let me alone now. Ye shall see me do well enough the next time.' Wherefore on the morrow he went to the bishop again and said he could soyle his question.

Then said the bishop, 'Noah had three sons, Shem, Ham and Japhet. Now tell me, who was Japhet's father?'

'Marry, sir,' quod the scholar, 'if it please your lordship, Coll, my father's dog.'

> By this tale a man may learn that it is but lost time to teach a fool anything, which hath no wit to perceive it.

oppose him   with questions.

70 Of the priest that would say two gospels for a groat

Sometime there dwelled a priest in Stratford upon Avon of small learning, which undevoutly sang mass, and oftentimes twice on one day. So it happened on a time after his second mass was done in Shottery, not a mile from Stratford, there met with him divers merchant-men which would have heard mass, and desired him to sing and he should have a groat; which answered them and said, 'Sirs, I will say mass no more this day. But I will say you two gospels for one groat, and that is dog-cheap a mass in any place in England.'

> By this tale a man may see that they that be rude and unlearned regard but little the merit and goodness of holy prayer.

twice on one day   to make more money.

gospels   excerpts from the Gospel.

71 Of the courtier that did cast the friar over the boat

A courtier and a friar happened to meet together in a ferry-boat, and in communication between them fell at words, angry and displeased each with other; and fought and struggled together so that at the last the courtier cast the friar over [out of] the boat. So was the friar drowned.

The ferryman, which had been a man of war the most part of his life before, seeing the friar was so drowned and gone, said thus to the courtier, 'I beshrew thy heart! Thou shouldst have tarried and fought with him a-land, for now thou hast caused me to lose a halfpenny for my fare.'

> By this tale a man may see that he that is accustomed in vicious and cruel company shall lose that noble virtue to have pity and compassion upon his neighbour.

72 Of the parson that stole the miller's eels

A certain miller there was which had divers ponds of eels, where was good store of eels; wherefore the parson of the town, which looked like a holy man, divers and many times stole many of them, insomuch that he had left few or none behind him. Wherefore this miller, seeing his eels stolen and witting [knowing] not by whom, came to the said parson and desired him to curse for them.

The parson said he would, and the next Sunday came into the pulpit with book, bell and candle, and perceiving there were none in the church that understood Latin, said thus, 'He that stole the miller's eels, *laudate dominum de coelis*, but he that stole the great eels, *gaudeat ipse in coelis*.' Therewith he put out the candle.

'Whoa, sir!' quod the miller. 'No more, for this sauce is sharp enough for him.'

> By this ye may see that some curates that look full holily be but dissemblers and hypocrites.

curse perform the ritual of anathematizing or excommunicating.

73 Of him that preached against them that rode on the Sunday

In a certain parish a friar preached, and in his sermon he rebuked them that rode on the Sunday, ever looking upon one man that was booted and spurred ready to ride. This man, perceiving that all the people noted him, suddenly half in anger answered the friar thus, 'Why preachest ye so much against them that ride on the Sunday? For Christ Himself did ride on Palm Sunday. As thou knowest well, it is written in Holy Scripture.'

To whom the friar suddenly answered and said thus, 'But I pray ye, what came thereof? Was he not hanged on the Friday after?' Which hearing, all the people in the church fell on laughing.

74 Of the curate that said Our Lord fed five hundred persons

A certain curate, preaching on a time to his parishioners, said that Our Lord with five loaves fed five hundred persons. The clerk, hearing him fail, said softly in his ear, 'Sir, ye err, the Gospel is five thousand.'

'Hold thy peace, fool,' said the curate. 'They will scantly believe that they were five hundred.'

75 Of him that had his goose stole

A man that had a goose stole from him went and complained to the curate, and desired him to do so much as help that he had his goose again. The curate said he would. So on Sunday the curate, as though he would curse, went up into the pulpit and bade everybody sit down. So when they were set he said, 'Why sit ye not down?'

'We be set already,' quod they.

'Nay,' quod the curate, 'he that did steal the goose sitteth not.'

'Yes, that I do!' quod he.

'Sayst thou that?' quod the curate. 'I charge thee, on pain of cursing, to bring the goose home again.'

curse see No. 72.

76 A penitent wife

A certain jealous husband followed his wife to confession; whom when the priest should lead behind the altar to be displied [disciplined by beating], the husband, perceiving it, and doubting the worst, cried unto him, saying, 'Hear ye, Master Parson, I pray you let me be displied for her.'

And kneeling down before the priest, 'I pray you,' quod the wife to the priest, 'strike him hard, for I am a great sinner.'

77 The penitent nun

The nuns of a certain monastery [nunnery] had this custom, that when any of them were delivered of child she should use recreations and bathings and other things necessary for a woman in that case, and the nuns would come a-gossiping unto her and bring her presents.

But because that the correction that belonged to the order should not be abrogated, at the month's end she must come naked into the chapter-house before them all, and receive three stripes at every one of her sisters' hands with a foxtail, which always hung up in the chapter-house for that purpose.

78 A good market

A thief, wandering in the woods, by chance met with a priest, and said unto him that he would fain be shriven, 'for,' said he, 'there passed today a priest by this way, and I took his horse from him, and therefore I pray you enjoin me penance.'

Then quod the priest, 'Give me five shillings to say mass for thine offence.'

And the thief told him out ten shillings into his hand, saying, 'Take here five shillings for the priest's horse which I took away this day, and because you make so good a market, I give you five more for the horse whereon you ride,' and so he took away his horse also.

make so good a market   deal so cheaply.

79 The hungry novices

One Friar Humbert, a master of the order [of Dominicans], carrying with him certain novices unto Lyons, came to a village where they could get no meat [food]. At length an old woman brought them a little bread unto the bridge whereon they sat; which when the novices had eaten, he asked her if she had any more, and she brought another piece, and the young men ate it immediately very greedily. The third time, he willed her to fetch more if she had any, which she did, and they ate it up all straightways.

Then said the master unto the novices, 'He will provide you bread, that increased the five loaves in the wilderness'—reciting unto them the whole story out of the Evangelist, and how there were twelve basketsful left, over and besides that which was eaten.

'Now, by Jesus!' quod the old woman, '*you* be no such, for you have left none at all!'

80 Brothers in Christ

A Scot was a-preaching how that all men are one another's neighbour and brother in Christ, 'even the Turk, the Jew, the Moor, the cannibal, the far Indian'—and then concluded, 'Yea, and the very Englishman is our neighbour too.'

81 Leave that to God

My Lord Brooke used to be much resorted to by those of the preciser sort, who had got a powerful hand over him; yet they would allow him Christian liberty for his recreations. But being at bowls one day in much company, and following his cast with much eagerness, he cried, 'Rub rub rub rub rub!'

His chaplain, a very strict man, runs presently to him, and in the hearing of divers, 'O good my lord, leave that to God, you must leave that to God,' says he.

Brooke Robert Greville, 2nd Lord Brooke (1608–43), Parliamentary general, killed at Lichfield.

82 The sleeping lord

A minister, in his sermon, spied a nobleman asleep, and another plain fellow over against him snorting very loud. He calls to his clerk; says he, 'Go wake that same snoring fellow. He'll wake my lord else.'

83 Never again

Andrew Downes was a great Grecian and a good scholar, but a very ordinary man in the pulpit; and preaching once at St Mary's was pitifully out, insomuch that he observed some to jeer him. Well, he rubbed through, and gave them a short benediction, but as he came down from the pulpit, 'By God,' says he, 'I'll ne'er come here again!'

Downes Regius Professor of Greek at Cambridge for thirty-nine years; a translator of the King James Bible; died 1628.

84 Ladies in breeches

The Bury [St Edmunds] ladies that used [took part in] hawking and hunting were once in a great vein of wearing breeches. And some of them being at dinner one day at Sir Thomas Lewknor's, there was one Mr Zephory, a very precise and a silenced minister, who frequented that house much; and discourse being offered of fashions, he fell upon this and declaimed much against it.

Rob Heigham, a jovial blade, being there, he undertook to vindicate the ladies and their fashion as decent and such as might cover their shame, 'For,' says he, 'if a horse throws them, or by any mischance they get a fall, had you not better see them in their breeches than naked?'

Says the over-zealous man, in detestation of breeches, 'Oh, no, by no means!'

'By my troth, parson,' says Rob Heigham, 'and I commend thee for't, for I am of thy mind too.'

precise and silenced Puritan; deprived of his living for refusing to conform to the Church of England.

85 A foolish question

A young maid came to a priest to be shrived, and she told him all her sins; but one among the rest was that she was with a young man in a hayloft. 'And what did you do there?' says the priest.

'Why, what an old fool are you,' says she, 'to ask what a young man and a maid should do together in a hayloft!'

86 Of a factious minister

A factious minister in the time of the Long Parliament . . . had this rhetoric in his pulpit prayer: 'Lord, thou hast been very good to us this last year. Lord, thou hast been good to us two years. Lord, thou hast been good to us three years. Yea, Lord, to say right thou hast been good to us these eighty years [since Bloody Mary's death]. But yet, Lord, thou art still wanting in one thing. Lord, thou wert with us at Edgehill, but Lord, why didst thou absent thyself from us when we were at Brentford?'

Edgehill . . . Brentford battles in 1642, won by Parliament and lost by Parliament.

87 Of a curate

A curate preaching to his parishioners of the Day of Judgment said, 'At that day,' said he, 'Christ will say to me, *Curate, what hast done with my sheep?*

'I shall answer,' said he, 'Beasts thou gavest them to me, and so I return them to thee.'

88 A contrary wind

The frequent prayers put up at present in the churches for rain remind us of the honest West Country parson who, when desired at a time like the present to pray for rain, answered, 'I'll willingly do it to oblige you: but it is to no purpose while the wind is in this quarter.'

3

From Marcolf to Scoggin

The four characters presented here (in a mere fifteen extracts from a large body of work) are all mockers, if not rebels, and it is no accident that the best known of them, Eulenspiegel, rose to extraordinary popularity in northern Europe at the time of the rebellion that we call the Reformation.

The conflict between the common man and authority—especially an authority that combines coercive power with high moral claims—is of course an ancient one. The origins of Marcolf, Solomon's earthy opponent, have been traced far back. Both Jews and Arabs told stories in which Solomon was not merely wise, but a powerful magician. Solomon puts the king of the demons, Ashmodai (Asmodeus) in his power by means of a magic ring, and plies him with questions, in which Solomon proves himself superior. But Ashmodai gets hold of the ring by a trick, assumes the shape of Solomon, sends the king into exile and for a time enjoys his wives and concubines, until he is unmasked and ousted. One element in this story may be the ancient New Year ritual in which a mock-king—a lowly person, often a criminal—ruled briefly (originally his days of glory ended in sacrificial death).

In the Dark Ages, Solomon was developed as a symbol of Christian power and wisdom. He was presented holding dialogues in which he dealt effectively with the sort of deep questions that would be asked by an awkward convert. His challenger thus became the spokesman of the suppressed forces of heathenism. (A recurrent problem: by denouncing subversive ideas, you spread them.) In Germany and France this challenger was very early given the name Marcolf or variations of it (Marculf, Morolf, Marolt in

Germany; Marcol, Marcoul, Marcun, Marcon in France). In England, but apparently not elsewhere, he was called Saturn.

Before dealing with Marcolf, something must be said of Saturn. Significantly, it is a name associated with New Year revelry, fertility, and pagan wisdom. The surviving Solomon-Saturn dialogues, in manuscripts of the tenth and eleventh centuries at Corpus Christi College, Cambridge, describe Saturn as a Chaldean —that is, a possessor of magical and occult lore—who has searched the Orient for the deepest truths. (And here there is a link with Marcolf, for one place Saturn visits is 'Marculfes eard', Marculf's land.) According to R. J. Menner (see bibliography), the two dialogues in the manuscripts, in Old English verse, probably date from the ninth or tenth centuries. Saturn is shown not as a peasant-like figure, but almost as Solomon's equal. He asks serious questions about the ways of Providence (I quote John M. Kemble's translation of 1848):

> But why falleth the snow,
> and hideth the earth,
> covereth the young shoots of herbs,
> weigheth down the fruits,
> twisteth and oppresseth them . . .?

And even more radical questions:

> But who then shall judge
> Christ the lord
> at doomsday when he
> judgeth all creatures?

It is an attitude of mind that implies agnosticism. Solomon speaks for the church, and he always wins, although sometimes his replies are arbitrary. To the question about doomsday, he says:

> Who then dare judge the lord
> who wrought us out of dust . . .?

Marcolf, says R. J. Menner, is first mentioned as debating with Solomon early in the eleventh century; but he finds the name Marchol as an alternative for Saturn as early as the seventh century. The name Marchol appears to have come from that of a Hebrew idol, Markolis, which was itself derived from another Roman god, Mercurius. Probably the earlier Marcolf-Solomon dialogues on the Continent were similar in tone to the Saturn-Solomon dialogues; but in the Marcolf manuscripts that survive from the Middle Ages, Solomon's challenger has become a grotesque peasant-like character whose role is to reply to Solomon's established wisdom with sardonic practical truths. He is a fool-figure who speaks underdog wisdom. Perhaps his grotesqueness was emphasized to make his subversive words seem of no consequence. As the centuries pass, his comic-earthy side tends to take over. In France, one version of the dialogue has Marcolf reply to everything with a blunt remark about whores:

> Solomon   *Chargez à jument*
> *Du plomb ou argent,*
> *Ne lui chaut lequel.*
>
> Marcon   *À putain ne chaut*
> *Qui sur son cul saut:*
> *Tout lui est un tel.*
>
> Solomon   *Qui langueur dura*
> *Tout joyeux sera*
> *Si vif en échappe.*
>
> Marcon   *Qui putain croira,*
> *Ne lui demeura*
> *Ni manteau ni chape.*

I quote from a copy in the British Museum, *Les dictz de Salomon: avecques les responces de Marcon / Fort joyeuses*, printed about 1500. (Probably the punning implications of *mar-con* helped to inspire the whore-lashing theme.) This French dialogue exists much earlier in manuscripts; one at Trinity College, Cambridge, is dated about 1430. A translation of the version I have quoted was printed about 1528 by Richard Pynson with the title *The sayinges or proverbes of king Salomon / with the answers of Marcolphus*. Here are the parallel verses:

> *Solomon*   Charge upon a beast
> Money or lead in a chest,
> Whether they nothing care. [which

> *Marcolf* A whore taketh no keep
> What man on her doth leap:
> All is to her one fare.
>
> *Solomon* Whosoever hath sickness
> Is very joyful, I guess,
> When he with life doth scape.
>
> *Marcolf* He that a whore believeth,
> Nothing with him abideth,
> Neither mantle nor cape.

A version in which Marcolf replied with general proverbial wisdom certainly existed in France, for Rabelais uses a snatch of it in *Gargantua*, I, ch. 33. Spadassin says, '*Qui ne se adventure n'a cheval ny mule, ce dist Salomon.*' Echephron replies, '*Qui trop se adventure perd cheval et mule, respondit Malcon.*'

It is time to turn to the English translation of Germany's Marcolf from which I am going to give extracts. It was printed in Antwerp about 1492. Marcolf is described like this when he arrives 'out of the east' to see Solomon:

> . . . of visage greatly misshapen and foul; nevertheless he was right talkative, eloquent and wise. His wife had he with him, which was more fearful and rude to behold. . . . This Marcolf was of short stature and thick. The head had he great; a broad forehead, red and full of wrinkles and frounces. His ears hairy and to the mids of the cheeks hanging. Great eyes, and running. His nether lip hanging, like a horse. A beard hard and foul like unto a goat. The hands short and blockish. His fingers great and thick. Round feet. And the nose thick and crooked. A face like an ass, and the hair of his head like the hair of a goat. His shoes on his feet were overmuch churlish and rude, and his clothes foul and dirty. . . .

'My wife,' he tells Solomon, 'is come of the blood and twelve kindreds of untidy wives.' They have an appropriate daughter: 'This Fudasa was short and thick. And thereto was she great with child, and thus was she thicker than she was of length.'

I can give only a fraction of the dialogue, which goes on until

Solomon gives up through weariness. He orders Marcolf to stay awake by him through the night. Marcolf dozes; and then we are given an explicit statement of his message:

Solomon Thou sleepest.
Marcolf I do not, but I think.
Solomon What thinkest thou?
Marcolf I think how that nature goeth afore learning.

Marcolf's mocking of the king, and his escape from hanging, are the climax of a long narrative that is thought to be a fifteenth-century supplement to the dialogue. It belongs to a tradition, again very old, of the scurrilous jesting trickster who cannot be put to death.

Subversive rogues flourished in Germany. Til Eulenspiegel had ancestors. In the thirteenth century, the exploits of Pfaff (Priest) Amis were recounted in German verse. He comes, it is said, from England ('*Er hat hus in Engellant*'), and in the end, repentant, he retires to a monastery there. His rogueries have a double message: he questions the established order by mocking and outwitting bishops and princes; and he is shown practising the mercenary tricks and indulging in the fleshly sins of the clergy. Pfaff Amis's story contributed in the next century to the verse-story of the Pfarrer von Kalenberg (the Parson of Kalenborow of No. 91), a similar ruthless cleric who happily dupes peasants and bishops alike.

A number of incidents from these two men's stories were taken over for Eulenspiegel—a wandering rogue like them, but a blasphemous secular rogue, owing not even a parasitic duty to the Church. The Eulenspiegel story seems to have been built up during the fifteenth century, and to have reached its grand total of ninety-five chapters about the time it came into print early in the sixteenth century. It was first told in the language of Lower Saxony, the region where Eulenspiegel performed most of his gross pranks. This was the region that produced Luther and tumultuously welcomed his revolt against the Church; and the remarkable popularity of Eulenspiegel in the first half of the sixteenth century coincided with the spread of Luther's ideas. It was a time when peasants at one extreme and humanist scholars at another impatiently revolted against an organization that demanded but did not deserve reverence. The mood of the time is tellingly expressed by Eulenspiegel's frequent acts of aggressive defecation. It is not irrelevant that the rebel-hero of the age, Luther, was an anally-oriented personality. In France, in Luther's lifetime, that more genial underminer, Rabelais, took the comic-satirical possibilities of defecation to heroic heights. In the year that *Gargantua* appeared, 1532, the first French edition of Eulenspiegel was printed; the rogue's great impact is attested by his gift to the French language of the words *espiègle*, waggish, and *espièglerie*, a roguish trick. That Eulenspiegel appealed to learned minds is shown by the fact that he was twice put into Latin verse, at Utrecht in 1538 and at Frankfurt in 1567.

The name Eulenspiegel (= owl-mirror, because by his ruses he shows solid citizens what owls they are) becomes Howleglas in England, which obscures the point a little. The printer William Copland's prologue (see page 152 for editions used) emphasizes Howleglas's merry side but contains a cryptic sentence:

> . . . This fable is not but only to renew the minds of men or women of all degrees from the use of sadness, to pass the time with laughter or mirth. And for because that simple knowing persons should beware if folks can see. Methink it is better to pass the time with such a merry jest and laugh thereat and do no sin, than for to weep and do sin.

That second sentence seems to allude to Howleglas's owl-mirror function.

As a frontispiece, Copland used a woodcut purporting to show Howleglas, but borrowed, in fact, from the Antwerp edition of *Solomon and Marcolf*. The drawing of Marcolf is not nearly as grotesque as the description of him, but it still gives an impression of peasant-like uncouthness. This is misleading, for on the Continent Eulenspiegel was depicted as a lithe, clean-cut fellow—like Pfaff Amis and the Pfarrer von Kalenberg before him—with the innocent-seeming face that a good trickster needs. He can be seen like this in an illustration of the wine-drawer story in an early edition of Howleglas printed in Antwerp.

The idea of Howleglas as a misshapen figure took hold in England. When Ben Jonson brings him on stage in his 1625 *Masque of the Fortunate Isles*, together with such assorted characters as John Skelton, Scoggin and Elinor Rumming the foul alehouse-keeper, he writes:

> An Howeleglass
> To come to pass
> On his father's ass:
> There never was
> By day nor night
> A finer sight,
> With feathers upright
> In his hornèd cap,
> And crooked shape
> Much like an ape,
> With owl on fist
> And glass at his wrist.

But by then Howleglas had served his deeper purposes and was being dismissed by the learned as an amusement only for the vulgar.

The history of the last rogue in this group, Scoggin, is given in the Introduction. Some of his debts to Eulenspiegel and other Continental forerunners are detailed in the Notes.

89 The dialogue of Solomon and Marcolf

Solomon A good wife and a fair is to her husband a pleasure.
Marcolf A potful of milk must be kept well from the cat.

Solomon Let us amend us in good, that [which] unwittingly we have misdone.
Marcolf As a man wipeth his arse he doth nothing else.

Solomon There are many that to their good-doers do evil for good.
Marcolf He that giveth bread to another man's hound shall have no thank.

Solomon He seeketh many occasions, that will [wants to] depart from his master.
Marcolf A woman that will not consent saith that she hath a scabbed arse.

Solomon He that stoppeth his ears from the crying of the poor people, our Lord God shall not hear him.
Marcolf He that weepeth afore a judge leeseth [wasteth] his tears.

Solomon For God's love, men are bounden to love others.
Marcolf If thou love him that loveth not thee, thou leeseth thy love.

Solomon He that is wine-drunken holdeth nothing that he saith.
Marcolf An open arse hath no lord.

Solomon As a man playeth upon an harp he cannot well indite.
Marcolf So when the hound shiteth, he barketh not.

Solomon If thou make friendship with a false and evilwilled man, it shall hinder thee more than profit.
Marcolf What the wolf doth, that pleaseth the wolfess.

Solomon Of abundance of the heart, the mouth speaketh.
Marcolf Out of a full womb [stomach] the arse trumpeth.

Solomon Were it so that God all the world under my power had set, it should suffice me.
Marcolf Men cannot give the cat so much but that she will her tail wag.

90 How Marcolf was banished and condemned to be hanged

[Marcolf has tricked Solomon into dispraising women, a thing that Solomon swore he would never do]

Then said the King Solomon, 'Go from hence out of my sight, and I charge thee that I see thee no more betwixt the eyes.' Forthwith was Marcolf cast out of the king's palace. . . .

It happened that the next night following fell a great snow. Marcolf took a little sieve or temse in his one hand, and a foot of a bear in the other hand, and he turned his shoes that stood forwards upon his feet, backward. And upon the morning early he began to go like a beast upon all four feet through the street, and when he was comen a little without the town, he found an old oven, and crept into it. [Solomon, with hunters and hounds, goes after the 'marvellous beast'.] . . .Marcolf lay all crooked, his visage from him-wards. He had put down his breech [trousers] into his hams, that he might see his arsehole and all his other foul gear. As the King Solomon, that seeing, demanded what lay there, Marcolf answered, 'I am here.'

Solomon 'Wherefore liest thou thus?'

Marcolf 'For ye have commanded me that ye should no more see me betwixt mine eyes. Now, and [if] ye would not see me betwixt mine eyes, ye may see me between my buttocks in the midst of mine arsehole.'

Then was the king sore moved [and] commanded his servants to take him and hang him upon a tree.

Marcolf, so taken, said to the king: 'My lord, will it please you to give me leave to choose the tree whereupon that I shall hang?'

Solomon said, 'Be it as thou hast desired, for it forceth not [dost not matter] on what tree that thou be hanged.'

Then the king's servants took and leddyn [led] Marcolf without the city and through the Vale of Jehoshaphat, and over the height of the Hill of Olivet from thence to Jericho, and could find no tree that Marcolf would choose to be hanged on. From thence went they over the Flume [river] Jordan, and all Araby through, and so forth all the great wilderness unto the Red Sea. And nevermore could Marcolf find a tree that he would choose to hang on. And thus he escaped out of the danger and hands of King Solomon, and turned again unto his house, and lived in peace and joy.

And so mote [may] we all do above with the Father of Heaven. Amen.

91 How the parson sold his wine

Our parson of Kalenborow had wine in his cellar which was marred; and because he would have [wanted] no loss by it, he practised a wile to be rid of it; and caused it to be published in many parishes thereabout that the parson of Kalenborow at a day assigned would fly over the river of Tonowa [Donau =

Danube] from the steeple of his church, and this he proclaimed in his own parish also.

And then he caused two wings of peacocks' feathers to be made; and also he caused his naughty [bad] wines to be brought under the church steeple whereas [where] he should stand for to fly over the river. And he gave the clerk charge of his wine, because he should sell it well and dear to the most profit.

And when the day was come that the parson should fly, many [a] one come thither to see the marvel, from far countries. And then the parson went upon the steeple arrayed like an angel ready for to fly, and there he flickered oftentimes with his wings, but he stood still. In the meanwhile that the people stood for to behold him, the sun shone hot and they had great thirst, for the priest did not fly. And he see [saw] that, and beckoned to them, saying, 'Ye good people, my time is not yet to fly, but tarry a while and ye shall see what I shall do.'

And then the people went and drunk apace of this wine that they see there for to sell, and they drunk so long that they could get no more wine for money, and cried out for drink and made great press. And within a little while after, the clerk come to the parson and said, 'Sir, your wine is all sold, and well paid for though there had been more.'

The parson, being very glad of this tidings, began to flicker with his wings again, and called with a loud voice unto the people, saying, 'Hark, hark, hark! Is there any among you all that ever see man have wings or fly?'

There stepped one forth and said, 'Nay, sir, nay.'

The parson answered again and said, 'Nor never shall, by my fay [faith]! Therefore go your ways home everyone, and say that ye have drunk up the parson of Kalenborow's evil wine, and paid for it well, and truly more than ever it cost him.'

Then were the villeins or peasants marvellously angry, and in their language cursed the parson perilously, some with 'a mischief!' and 'vengeance!' And some said, 'God give him a hundred drouse, for he hath made among us many a fool and totting [witless] ape.' But the parson cared not for all their curses, and this subtle deed was spread all the country about.

drouse apparently 'beatings'. Dialect dictionaries give an East Anglian word, 'droze', meaning 'to beat severely' (compare 'thrash').

92 How Howleglas deceived a wine-drawer in Lübeck

On a time came Howleglas to Lübeck, where is very strait justice. And while that Howleglas was there abiding, he heard tell of a wine-drawer that was in a lord's cellar, that was very proud and presumptuous and said that there was no man that could deceive him or pass him in wisdom; and there was none of all the lords that loved him. Then thought Howleglas in his mind how he might deceive him. . . .

> [He comes to the tavern with an empty pot and another full of water; conceals the full one; has the wine-drawer fill the other with wine; makes a fuss over the price, and refuses to pay; covertly substitutes the pot of water for the pot of wine. The wine-drawer angrily takes the pot of water down to his cellar and empties it into his barrel.]

. . . Then was the wine-drawer very angry . . . and said, 'Make ye me fill wine and ye have no money to pay for it! Ye ween [think] I be a fool!'

And then said Howleglas, 'Ye be beguiled of a fool,' and with that word went his way with the pots. And then the drawer, mistrusting Howleglas for the words that he said, took a sergeant and overtook him and searched him, and then they found that he had two pots under his mantle. Then took they Howleglas and peached [impeached] him for a thief and brought him to prison.

And then said some that he had deserved to be hanged. And some said that it was done for the nonce, to deceive the wine-drawer, and that was but well done, 'for he should have seen thereto before, for he saith daily that no man should beguile him'. But they that loved not Howleglas said that he was a thief and that he should be hanged. And then was Howleglas brought before the judges, and they gave sentence that he should be hanged. And on the morrow was he brought unto the gallows for to be hanged, for they that loved him not would fain have seen justice done on him, and there were gathered many of the town to see Howleglas suffer death.

But the lords of Lübeck were sorry for him; for some weened

that he could [knew] sorcery or witchcraft, that he therewith should be delivered. And as he was led toward the gallows he lay all still as though he had been all dead. And when he came under the gallows, then desired he to speak with the lords, and when the lords were come he fell upon his knees and prayed them that they would grant him a boon.

And the lords said that should be his life that he would ask.

And then said Howleglas, 'It shall not be my life, nor money,' nor it should not cost them one penny of cost.

And all the lords of Lübeck went to the other side of the gallows and took a counsel, and they repeated his words, and then agreed to grant him his petition, and came to him and bade him ask whatever he would, save those words that were above rehearsed.

And then thanked Howleglas the lords, and said, 'I pray you that every one of you will give me your hands thereon.' And then all together gave him their hands, so that all the lords had granted him both with word and hand. Then said Howleglas to the lords, 'Because I know that ye be so faithful of your words, I shall show [declare] to you my boon.' And then he said, 'This is my boon: that every lord of Lübeck do come to kiss my arse when that I am hanged upon the gallows by the space of three days long, with his mouth, in the morning fasting, and the boroughmaster first, and all the lords after in order.'

Then answered the lords to Howleglas and said that that was an unmannerly boon for to be asked.

And then said Howleglas to the lords of Lübeck, 'I know the council of Lübeck so sure of their promise, that they would hold that which they have promised both with hand and mouth.'

Then went the lords again to counsel, and then said the one to the other, 'This thing that he asks of us, it is unlawfully asked, for it were a great shame to us all that we, that be the greatest lords of the town, should come and kiss his arse. Better it were for us to give him his pardon and let him go his way, for it is but a small fault that he hath done. . . .'

lords these would be town councillors—powerful men in old Lübeck.

93 How Howleglas lay sick

... Then heard his mother say that he was sick. Then she came to him; and she had thought for to have had some money of him, for she was old and poor. And when she saw him she wept, and said, 'Where be ye so sick?'

And Howleglas said, 'Here, between the bed and the wall.'

Then said his mother, 'Speak to me one sweet word.'

Then said Howleglas to his mother, 'Honey—honey—is not that a sweet word?'

Then said his mother, 'Tell me something that may do me ease.'

Then said Howleglas to his mother, 'When that you fart, turn your arse with the wind, and then you shall feel no stink.'

Then said his mother, 'Give me some of your good [goods].'

Then said Howleglas to his mother, 'He that hath none shall give none. For my good is so secret that no man can find it. And if you can find any, take it.'

And then Howleglas waxed sicker and sicker, so that the folk asked him whether that he would be shriven, for they saw well that he should not recover. Then said an old sister [a Beguine] that was a good friend of his—she counselled him to be confessed and take repentance for his sins, and so to be the servant of God.

And Howleglas said, 'I will not confess me secretly, for all that I have done I have done it openly to many men in divers lands, and that is well known. For they that I have done good to, they will say good of me; and they that I have done harm to, they will say harm of me. But I am very sorry of two things that which I could never bring to pass in my life.'

Then said the sister, 'Be sorry of thy sins, and be glad that ye did not those two things, if that they were ill. And if they were good, be sorry because they were not done.'

Then said Howleglas, 'It is as men will take it. For I was sorry in my mind, when I saw a man pick his teeth with his knife, that I had not shitten on the end of it. The other is that I am sorry for, that I did not drive a wooden wedge in all women's arses that were above fifty year, for they be neither cleanly nor profitable. I desire it for no other cause but this: that is, that they should not shite on the ground, the which bringeth fruits.'

Then said the sister to Howleglas, 'God save all women of that age and all those that ben more! For I hear [understand] well, and [if] you were strong, and that you had your might as you have had before this time, you would ere you departed wedge mine arse with a wooden wedge, for I am a woman of sixty year and more.'

Then he answered to the sister, 'I am right sorry and heavy because it is not done.'

Then answered the sister, 'It were much better that the devil had thee!'

Then answered Howleglas, 'That is truth, for a woman is no sooner angry, but she is worse than the devil.'

And then the sister departed and let him lie.

94 How Howleglas deceived his ghostly father

And as Howleglas was thus sick . . . they brought to him a priest. And when the priest was come there, he thought in his mind, 'This hath been a great deceiver of the people and beguiler, wherewith he hath got much money.' And then came the priest unto him and said: 'Howleglas, remember yourself, for ye have done many sins, and now must you remember that you have a soul to keep, and how you have gotten much money by deceit and falsehood. And now bestow that money to the worship of God and poor priests, as I am; and that I counsel you for to do, and I shall order it well and remember you hereafter and do many masses for you.'

Then said Howleglas, 'Good father, if it please you to come at noon again, then shall I make ready some money for you.' Then was the priest glad, and then departed.

Then took Howleglas an earthen pot and filled it half-full of turds, and he strewed thereon a little money so that the dirt was covered. And when it was noon, the priest came and he said to Howleglas, 'Friend, shall I have that that you promised me?'

And Howleglas said, 'Yea.' Then he set the pot before him and said, 'Take now yourself, but be not too hasty, nor put not your hand too deep.'

Then said the priest, 'I shall do as you bid me.'

And Howleglas did open the pot and he bade the priest to gripe softly, for it was almost full. Then was the priest hasty and put his hand into the pot, and he griped a great handful. And when he felt it soft, he pulled out his hand, and it was all to-beshitten. Then the priest said, 'Ye may well be called a deceiver and beguiler, that have deceived his ghostly [spiritual] father, and when ye be at the point of death.'

Then said Howleglas to the priest, 'Good sir, did I not show unto you before that you should not gripe too deep? And if that ye were covetous, it was not my fault.'

Then said the priest, 'Ye pass in ungraciousness all others that ever I saw. In faith, it was great pity that thou scaped from hanging when thou shouldest have been hanged at Lübeck.' And then the priest departed from thence.

Then Howlegas called the priest again and he said to him, 'Master parson, come again and take your money with you!' But he went his way, and made it as [if] he heard it not.

95 How Jack made his master pay a penny for the herring bones

On a time, Scoggin did send Jack [a poor scholar, his servant] to Oxford to market to buy a pennyworth of fresh herring. Scoggin said: 'Bring four herrings for a penny, or else bring none.' Jack could not get four herrings, but three, for his penny; and when he came home, Scoggin said: 'How many herrings hast thou brought?'

And Jack said, 'Three herrings, for I could not get four for a penny.'

Scoggin said he would none of them.

'Sir,' said Jack, 'then will I, and here is your penny again.'

When dinner-time was come, then Jack did set bread and butter before his master, and roasted his herrings, and sat down at the lower end of the table and did eat the herrings.

Scoggin said, 'Let me have one of thy herrings, and thou shalt have another of me another time.'

Jack said, 'And if you will have one herring, it shall cost you a penny.'

'What!' said Scoggin. 'Thou wilt not take it, on thy conscience.'

Jack said: 'My conscience is such that you get not a morsel here, except I have my penny again.'

Thus contending together, Jack had made an end of his herrings. A Master of Art of Oxford, one of Scoggin's fellows, did come to see Scoggin; and when Scoggin had espied him [in the road] he said to Jack: 'Set up the bones of the herrings before me.'

'Sir,' said Jack, 'they shall cost you a penny.'

Then said Scoggin, 'What, whoreson, wilt thou shame me?'

'No, sir,' said Jack, 'give me my penny again, and you shall have up the bones, or else I will tell all.'

Scoggin then cast down a penny to Jack, and Jack brought up to Scoggin the herring bones; and by this time the Master of Art did come in to Scoggin, and Scoggin bade him welcome, saying, 'If you had come sooner, you should have had fresh herrings to dinner.'

96 How Scoggin sold powder to kill fleas

Scoggin divers times did lack money and could not tell what shift to make. At last he thought to play the physician, and did fill a box full of the powder of a rotten post, and on a Sunday he went to a parish church and told the wives that he had a powder to kill up all the fleas in the country, and every wife bought a pennyworth, and Scoggin went his way ere mass was done. The wives went home and cast the powder into their beds and in their chambers, and the fleas continued still.

On a time, Scoggin came to the same church on a Sunday, and when the wives had espied him, the one said to the other, 'This is he that deceived us with the powder to kill fleas.' 'See,' said the one to the other, 'this is the selfsame person.' When mass was done, the wives gathered about Scoggin and said, 'You be an honest man, to deceive us with the powder to kill fleas!'

'Why,' said Scoggin, 'are not your fleas all dead?'

'We have more now,' said they, 'than ever we had.'

'I marvel of that,' said Scoggin. 'I am sure you did not use the medicine as you should have done.'

They said, 'We did cast it in our beds and in our chambers.'

'Ay,' said he. 'There be a sort of fools that will buy a thing, and will not ask what they should do with it. I tell you all that you should have taken every flea by the neck, and then they would gape, and then you should have cast a little of the powder into every flea's mouth, and so you should have killed them all.'

Then said the wives, 'We have not only lost our money, but we are mocked for our labour.'

97 How Scoggin told those that mocked him that he had a wall-eye

Scoggin went up and down in the king's hall, and his hosen hung down, and his coat stood awry, and his hat stood *à bonjour*, so every man did mock Scoggin. Some said he was a proper man and did wear his raiment cleanly. Some said the whoreson fool could not put on his own raiment. Some said one thing and some said another.

At last Scoggin said, 'Masters, you have praised me well, but you did not espy one thing in me.'

'What is that, Tom?' said the men.

'Marry,' said Scoggin, 'I have a wall-eye.'

'What meanest thou by that?' said the men.

'Marry,' said Scoggin, 'I have spied a sort [gang] of knaves that do mock me, and are worse fools themselves.'

98 How Scoggin greased a fat sow on the arse

Scoggin had got a fat sow, and killed her under the court wall, beside the king's gate. He made a great fire, and got a great spit, and put the sow on the spit, and roasted her, and bought twenty pounds of butter, and still [without stopping] he poured the butter with a ladle on the sow's buttocks.

Divers men came to him and said, 'Why dost thou grease this fat sow on the arse?'

He said, 'I do as kings and lords and every man else doth: for he that hath enough shall have more, and he that hath nothing shall go without. And this sow needeth no basting nor greasing, for she is fat enough, yet shall she have more than enough.'

99 How Scoggin desired the king that he might say Ave Maria, gratia plena, Dominus tecum in his ear at certain times

On a certain time Scoggin went to the king's grace, and did desire that he might come to him divers times and sound in his ears, 'Ave Maria, gratia plena, Dominus tecum'. The king was content he should do so, except he were in great business.

'Nay,' said Scoggin, 'I will mark my time. I pray Your Grace that I may do thus this twelvemonth.'

'I am pleased,' said the king.

Many men were suitors to Scoggin to be good to them [put in a good word for them], and did give him many gifts, so that within the year Scoggin was a great rich man.

So when this year was out, Scoggin desired the king to break his fast with him. The king said, 'I shall come.' Scoggin had prepared a table for the king to break his fast, and made him a goodly cupboard of plate of gold and silver, and he had cast over all his beds and tables, and corners of his chamber, full of gold and silver.

When the king did come thither and see so much plate and gold and silver, he asked of Scoggin where he had it and how he did get all this treasure.

Scoggin said, 'By saying the Ave Maria in your ear—and seeing I have got so much by it, what do they get that be about Your Grace daily and be of your council, when that I with six words' speaking have gotten so much? He must needs swim that is held up by the chin.'

Ave Maria, etc.   opening words of the 'Hail Mary'.

100 How Scoggin desired of the queen to know whether riches would not tempt men, and especially women

On a time Scoggin was jesting with the queen, and said, 'Madam, riches—as gold, silver, precious stones, and dignity—do tempt men, and especially women, very sore, and cause women to fall to lechery and folly.'

The queen said a good woman would never be tempted with gold or silver or other riches.

'I pray you, madam,' said Scoggin, 'if there were a goodly lord or a knight that would give you forty thousand pound to dally with you, what would you say to it?'

The queen said, 'If any man living would give an hundred thousand pounds, I would not leese [lose] my honesty for it.'

Then said Scoggin, 'What if a man did give you a hundred thousand thousand pounds, what would you do?'

'I would,' said the queen, 'do no folly for so much.'

Then said Scoggin, 'What if a man did give you this house full of gold?'

The queen said, 'A woman would do much for that.'

'Lo!' said Scoggin. 'If a man had goods enough, he might have a sovereign lady.' For the which words, the queen took a high displeasure with Scoggin; wherefore it doth appear that it is not good jesting with lords or ladies, for if a man be plain, or do tell the truth, he shall be shent [ruined] for his labour.

101 How Scoggin in the French king's court came to a gentlewoman's door and whined like a dog

When Scoggin was thus commanded [into exile] by the king, he got him into France into the French king's court, and there he jested.

And first, there was a gentleman which made a gentlewoman [a] promise to come to her bed at nine o'clock at night; he did promise to come to her chamber-door and would scrape and scratch at the door like a dog, and would whine. Scoggin, hearing this bargain, before nine o'clock came to the door, and scraped with his nails, and did whine like a dog. Then the gentlewoman did rise and let him in.

Within a little while after, the gentleman did come and scrape and whine at the door like a dog. Scoggin arose and went to the door and said: 'Arre arre,' like another dog. And after that the French gentlewoman did love an Englishman.

Wherefore in such matters let a man make nobody of his counsel, lest he be deceived.

102 How Scoggin told the Frenchmen he would fly into England

On a time, Scoggin made the Frenchmen believe that he would fly into England, and did get him many goose-wings and tied them about his arms and legs, and went upon a high tower and spread his arms abroad as though he would fly, and came down again, and said that all his feathers were not fit about him, and that he would fly on the morrow.

On the morrow he got him up upon the tower, and there was much people gathered together to see him fly. Scoggin did shake his feathers, and said, 'All my feathers be not fit about me. Come tomorrow and I will fly.'

On the morrow Scoggin got upon the tower and did shake his feathers, saying, 'Go home, fools, go home. Trow you that I will break my neck for your pleasure? Nay, not so!'

There was a Frenchman had indignation at Scoggin, and he said, 'Tomorrow you shall see me fly to Paris.' And he got him wings, and went upon the tower, and spread his wings abroad, and would have flown, and fell down into the moat under the tower. Every man was diligent to get the man out of the water, and Scoggin did take him by the hand, and said, 'Sir, you be welcome from Paris. I think you have been in a great rain.'

> Here a man may see that one cannot have a shrewd turn in playing the fool, but he shall have a mock for his labour.

103 How the French king had Scoggin into his house of office [*privy*] and showed him the king of England's picture

On a time, when the French king went to his stool, he did take Scoggin with him. Then said the French king to Scoggin, 'Look behind thee, who is pictured on the wall.'

Scoggin looked, and said: 'It is a fair picture.'

The king said, 'Thou mayst see what I do make of a picture of thy king.'

Scoggin beheld the picture of the king of England, and said to the French king, 'Jesus Christ! Here is a wonderful thing! What would you do if you did see the king of England in the face as he is, when that for fear you do beshit yourself when that you look but upon a picture of him?'

Then the French king banished Scoggin out of France, and he came into England again.

104 How Scoggin came to the Court like a monstrous beast, and should have been hanged

Scoggin was weary of Cambridge, and could not tell how to do, because the king had commanded him to look him no more in the face.

At last he got him a bear's foot and an ox foot, and tied them under his feet. Then he took a horse foot in one of his hands, and his other hand served for another foot. And Scoggin lay about the Court, and on a certain night there fell a snow. Scoggin within half a mile of the king's palace went with his aforesaid three feet and his hand which served for the fourth foot, and when he had set a circuit, he went into an old house where there was an oven, and he crept into it, and set out [bared] his arse.

In the morning the trace of this monstrous beast was found, and well was he that might first come to the Court to tell the king what a monstrous beast this should be. . . . [The king and all go in chase.] There was a great yelping of hounds and blowing of horns, and at last the hounds did come to a bay. The king and the lords pricked forth their geldings and rode to the old house, and looked into the oven, and Scoggin did set out his bare arse.

'What knave is this?' said the king.

'I, sir,' said Scoggin, 'whom you charged not to look you in the face, wherefore I must needs turn mine arse to you.'

'Well, knave,' said the king, 'thou shalt be hanged for this prank doing.'

Scoggin leapt out of the oven, and pulled up his breech, and said, 'I desire Your Grace, if I shall be hanged, let me choose the tree I shall be hanged on.'

'I am content,' said the king.

Four men were appointed to hang Scoggin.

Scoggin had provided a bottle of wine, and sucket [candied fruit], and marmalade, and green ginger; and said to them that should hang him, 'Masters . . . in the Forest of Windsor be goodly trees, and thither will I go.'

Scoggin went before them, and ever looked upon many oaks and trees, and ever was eating of his sucket, and marmalade, and green ginger; and drank still on his bottle, saying, 'God knoweth, the pangs of death are dry.'

When night was come, the men, being all day without meat and drink, fainted [became faint], and said, 'Good Scoggin, the night draweth on and we have eaten no meat today, and where we shall lie tonight we cannot tell. Choose one tree or other to be hanged on.'

'O masters,' said Scoggin, 'make no haste for my hanging, for it would grieve the best of you all to be hanged.' Scoggin wandered about here and there until it was a good while within night. Then said Scoggin, 'Here is a fair tree. Let us go lie under it all night.'

The men said, 'We are so faint that we cannot tell what to do.'

'Well,' said Scoggin, 'you seem to be honest men. Go to our king, and have me commended to him, and tell him that I will never choose a tree to be hanged on. And so fare you well. He is a mad man that may save his own life, and will kill himself.'

4

Quips, Retorts, Tricks and Blunders

This section unites a medley of things in which the fun arises less from plausible situations than from a play on words and ideas. Acts of outwitting have their echo in follies. (Folly, like sex, is an undying topic.)

I resisted most puns. It was not hard. Shakespeare's are sometimes an embarrassment, but they scintillate beside most of the puns that proliferated in the seventeenth century. Here is an average item from *Conceits, Clinches, Flashes and Whimzies*, 1639: ' "A smith," said one, "is the most pragmatical fellow under the sun, for he hath always many irons in the fire." ' And another: 'One asked why B stood before C. "Because," said another, "a man must B before he can C." '

I prefer the story in the same book about a gentleman who went hawking on a farmer's land. The farmer was angry; the gentleman spat in his face. 'What is your reason for that?' said the farmer. 'I cry you mercy,' said the gentleman. 'I gave you warning, for I hawked before I spat.'

And here is a gem from *Pinkethman's Jests*, 1721: 'A gentleman, having some friends about him, says to one of 'em he could find in his heart to leave him the gout for a legacy. "Faith," says another, "I should be loath to have such a leg-as-he." '

This section contains a number of bulls. They became popular early in the seventeenth century. In 1630, John Taylor describes his *Wit and Mirth* as 'fashioned into Clinches, Bulls, Quirkes, Yerkes, Quips, and Jerkes', and a good number of his jokes are bulls. The origin of the term is obscure, but I see a clue in my No. 143 and in the French original given in the note to it. I offer the theory that when this joke came into English, perhaps before

1620, the bull-speaker said he saw someone riding 'a-horseback on a cow', and the Gaulard original was improved upon with the reply, 'That's a bull'—which then became a catch-phrase applied to all such unwittingly ludicrous turns of phrase.

Irishmen began to be the general butt of bull stories in the eighteenth century. But an Irish servant figures in one in the 1633 *Banquet of Jests*. His master tells him to bring a pint of claret and a pint of sack. He pours both into one pot, and says, 'I prethee, master, drink off thy claret first, for i'faith the sack is all in the bottom.'

105 Demands joyous

How many calves' tails behoveth to reach from the earth to the sky?
—No more but one, and [if] it be long enough.

What beast is it that hath her tail between her eyes?
—It is a cat when she licketh her arse.

Which is the most cleanliest leaf among all other leaves?
—It is holly leaves, for nobody will not wipe his arse with them.

How may a man know or perceive a cow in a flock of sheep?
—By sight.

Wherefore set they upon church steeples more a cock than a hen?
—If men should set there a hen, she would lay eggs and they would fall upon men's heads.

What is it that freezeth never?
—That is hot water.

What thing is that, that is most likest unto a horse?
—That is a mare.

Which is the cleanliest occupation that is?
—That is a dauber, for he may neither shite nor eat till he hath washed his hands.

What thing is it, the less it is, the more it is dread?
—A bridge.

Which was first, the hen or the egg?
—The hen, when God made her.

Why doth an ox or a cow lie?
—Because she cannot sit.

What people be they that love not in no wise to be prayed for?
—They be beggars and poor people, when men say 'God help them' when they ask alms.

What time in the year beareth a goose most feathers?
—When the gander is upon her back.

dauber   who mixed or applied the daub of wattle-and-daub houses.

106 Penning the cuckoo

On a time, the men of Gotham would have penned in the cuckoo, whereby she should sing all the year in the midst of the town. They made a hedge round in compass, and they had got a cuckoo, and had put her into it, and said, 'Sing here all the year and thou shalt lack neither meat nor drink.' The cuckoo, as soon as she perceived herself encompassed within the hedge, flew away. 'A vengeance on her!' said they. 'We made not our hedge high enough.'

107 Of the courtier that bade the boy hold his horse

A courtier on a time that alighted off his horse at an inn gate said to a boy that stood thereby, 'Ho, sir boy, hold my horse!'

The boy, as [as if] he had been afeared, answered, 'O master, this is a fierce horse. Is *one* able to hold him?'

'Yes,' quod the courtier, 'one may hold him well enough.'

'Well,' quod the boy, 'if one be able enough, then I pray you hold him your own self.'

108 Of him that would give a song for his dinner

There came a fellow on a time into a tavern and called for meat. So when he had well dined, the taverner came to reckon and to have his money; to whom the fellow said he had no money—'But I will,' quod he, 'content you with songs.'

'Nay,' quod the taverner, 'I need no songs, I must have money.'

'Why,' quod the fellow, 'if I sing a song to your pleasure, will ye not then be content?'

'Yes,' quod the taverner.

So he began, and sung three or four ballads, and asked if he were pleased.

'No,' said the taverner.

Then he opened his purse and began to sing thus:

> When you have dined make no delay
> But pay your host and go your way.

'Doth this song please you?' quod he.

'Yes, marry,' said the taverner, 'this pleaseth me well.'

'Then, as covenant was,' quod the fellow, 'ye be paid for your victuals.' And so he departed and went his way.

This tale sheweth that a man may be too hasty in making of a bargain and covenanting, and therefore a man ought to take good heed what he saith; for one word may bind a man to great inconvenience if the matter be weighty.

109 Of the scoffer that made a man a soothsayer

There was a merry scoffing fellow on a time, the which took on him to teach a man to be a soothsayer. When they were agreed what he should have for his labour, the scoffer said to the man, 'Hold: eat this round pellet, and I warrant thou shalt be a soothsayer.'

The man took and put it in his mouth and began to champ thereon, but it savoured so ill that he spit it out forthwith and said, 'Fie! This pellet that thou givest me to eat savoureth all of a turd.'

'Thou sayest truth,' quod the scoffer. 'Now thou art a soothsayer, and therefore pay me my money.'

soothsayer   literally 'truth-sayer'.

110 Of the doctor that went with the fowler to catch birds

There was a doctor on a time which desired a fowler that went to catch birds with an owl, that he might go with him. The birder was content, and dressed [camouflaged] him with boughs, and set him by his owl, and bade him say nothing. When he saw the birds alight apace, he said, 'There be many birds alighted! Draw thy nets,' wherewith the birds flew away. The birder was very angry and blamed him greatly for his speaking. Then he promised to hold his peace.

When the birder was in again, and many birds were alighted, master doctor said in Latin, '*Aves permultae sunt*,' wherewith the birds flew away. The birder came out right angry and sore displeased, and said that by his babbling he had twice lost his prey.

'Why, thinkest thou, fool,' quod the doctor, 'that the birds do understand Latin?'

111 Augustus outjested

There came unto Rome a certain young gentleman very like unto Augustus, whom when the emperor had seen, he demanded of him if his mother had sometime been at Rome or not.

'No,' quod the gentleman, 'but my father hath been often.'

112 The horseless cart

John-a-Nokes was driving his cart toward Croydon, and by the way fell asleep therein. Meantime a good fellow came by and stole away his two horses and went fair away with them.

In the end he, awaking and missing them, said, 'Either I am John-a-Nokes, or I am not John-a-Nokes. If I be John-a-Nokes, then have I lost two horses, and if I be not John-a-Nokes, then have I found a cart.'

113 A manmade squirrel

A cockney, seeing a squirrel in a shop, greatly admired it, and said, 'Jesu God, what pretty things are made for money!'

cockney originally a countryman's derisive term for a townsman—the converse of bumpkin.

114 No more now

A drunkard passing over a bridge, his eyes so glared that he thought they were two bridges; and stepping upon the wrong bridge, down he tumbled into the brook; where drinking his belly full of water, he continued saying, 'No more now, hostess, no more now.'

115 Hold the ship

A passenger at sea, feeling his stomach rise, said to the master of the ship, 'I pray, hold still the ship a while till I vomit.'

116 Man of few words

Two travellers met together at an inn, and a fat capon was served up to their board. At dinner-time one asked the other whether he had a father living or no. He answered 'No', and withal told him a long discourse how, and where, and how long since his father died.

Meantime the other ate up the best of all the capon, which the tale-teller at last perceiving, half-angry said unto him, 'Now that you have heard the discourse of my father's death, I pray you tell me, have you also e'er a father living?'

He answered, 'No.'

'Now I pray you then tell me,' quoth the other, 'how he died.'

He, very earnestly at his victuals, briefly answered, 'Suddenly, very suddenly.'

117 First and last

One said to his host, 'This fruit that you serve first into this board, in my country useth to be served in last.'

The host answered, 'Yea, and here too for this once.' For it was all his fare at that time.

118 Too many Spaniards

A Spaniard travelling on the way alighted at a poor inn, and they asked him his name. He answered, 'Don Pedro Gonzales Gayetan de Guevara.' Whereunto they replied, 'Sir, we have not meat enough for so many.'

119 No marvel

A gallant was brought before a merry recorder of London for getting a maid with child, and the recorder said, 'It is a marvel, Master N., that you, being a gentleman of good quality, would venture to get maids with child.'

The gentleman answered, 'Nay, rather were it a marvel if a maid had gotten me with child.'

120 The colewort-liar

A traveller affirming that he saw a colewort so monstrous huge that five hundred men on horseback might stand in her shade, another answered, 'And I for my part did once see a cauldron so wide that three hundred men wrought therein, every one distant twenty yards from other.'

Then the colewort-liar asked him to what use that cauldron was made.

He answered, 'To seethe [boil] your colewort in.'

colewort   a kind of cabbage.

121 No fool he

A serving-man was jesting with his master's fool, and made him believe he would cut off his head. The fool ran straight to his master and told him of it: who answered, 'He shall not cut off thy head. If he do, I'll hang him the next day after.'

'Nay, I pray,' replied the fool, 'rather hang him a day before.'

122 Hangman's advantage

A felon at the gallows said unto the hangman, 'Villain, better yet be hanged than be a hangman, like thee.'

'True,' answered the hangman, 'were it not for hanging.'

123 If the shoe fits

Somebody having stolen away a stump-footed fellow's shoes, he said, 'Now I pray God, whoever hath them, well may they fit him.'

124 The answer of a gentleman's man to his master

A worshipful gentleman of London . . . on a time invited divers of his friends to supper to his house. And being at supper, the second course coming in, the first [waiter] was one of the gentleman's own men bringing a capon. And [he] by chance stumbling at the portal door, the capon flew out of the platter and ran along the boards [floor] to the upper end of the table where the master of the house sat; who, making a jest of it, said, 'By my faith, it is well. The capon is come first. My man will come anon too, I hope.'

By and by [straight away] came his man; and takes up the capon and lays it in the platter and sets it on the board.

'I thank you, sir,' quoth his master. 'I could have done so myself.'

'Aye,' quoth his man. ''Tis a small matter, sir, for one to do a thing when he sees it done before his face.'

125 Two good legs

A gentleman, seeing a gentlewoman garter her stockings in the street, said, 'Gentlewoman, you have a good leg.'
'Sir,' said she, 'I have two.'
'Then,' said he, 'they be twins.'
'Not so,' said she, 'for there was a man borne between.'

126 Value for money

One met his friend in the street and told him he was very sorry to see him look so ill; asking him what he ailed. He replied that he was now well amended, but he had been lately sick of the pox.

'What pox, the smallpox?' said his friend.

'Nay,' quoth the other, 'my mind was not so base, for I had the biggest pox that I could get for my money.'

127 Bargain in oysters

An apprentice in the market did ask the price of a hundred oysters. His friend persuaded him not to buy them, for they were too small. 'Too small!' replied the apprentice. 'There is not much loss in that, for I shall have the more to the hundred.'

128 A man on the gallows

One passing by and seeing a poor fellow, in a very cold morning, upon the gallows in his shirt, and after a short confession ready to be turned off the ladder, 'Alas, poor man!' saith he, 'I much pity him. He will stand so long yonder in the cold, I am afraid he will go near to catch his death.'

129 A drunken man's mistake

A waterman, being very drunk, sat down in frosty weather on the shore near the Tower Wharf at a low water, in a moonshine night, and fell fast asleep, and slept so long until the tide came in and flowed by degrees even up to his mouth, the moon shining in his face. Whereupon, suddenly awakening, he said, 'No more drink, I thank you heartily. But a few more clothes if you please, and then put out the candle.'

130 Of a tiler

A tiler and his man were together at work upon a house when, the rafters breaking, his man fell down through the roof. The tiler, looking after him, said, 'I like a fellow that will go through his work.'

131 A foolish resolve

Two scholars having been abroad tippling, etc., about eight or nine resolved at last to go home and study like horses; wherefore they agreed to lock each other into their studies.

132 A witty inscription

Witty was that conceit of him who bestowed this inscription on the door of a jakes [privy]: Here are farts to be let.

133 I'll die first

Two gentlemen fought a duel. One overthrew the other and disarmed him. 'Now beg your life and take it,' says he, 'for you lie at my mercy.'
   'I'll die first!' says the other.
   'Nay, faith,' says he, 'if it be not worth your asking, it's not worth my taking.' And so he let him go.

134 Room at the inn

A merry fellow came late to his inn, very wet and cold; and the kitchen fire so thronged as there was no access to it. He calls presently to the ostler to give his horse a peck of oysters.
   'You mean oats, sir,' says he.
   'No, sirrah,' says he, 'I say a peck of oysters.'
   The ostler obeys his command. Out run the people from the fireside into the stable to see the sea-horse eat oysters. In the meantime he gets the warmest seat, and they return like fools, as they went. And the ostler brings him word, his horse did not like such provender, for he would eat no oysters.
   'No?' says he. 'I prithee bring them to me then and I'll eat 'um myself.'

135 A fair offer

One being condemned to throw himself from a precipice, ran often to the brink of it, stopped, and retreated. Some appointed for supervisors of the execution began to intrepate [embolden] and hearten him, for they had other business in hand and must not stand there and see the law mocked.

'Why, pray,' says he, 'how often have I run?'

'Five times,' said they.

'Before God,' says he, 'I'll give any man here six to do it, for a hundred pounds.'

136 I'LL try thee

A sturdy vagrant on the highway begged good-saucily on Sir Dru Drury. 'Ay, sirrah,' says he. 'Such as you make all your kin fare the worse. For this is your fashion: deny ye but once, though happily not in earnest, a man's back is no sooner turned but ye curse him to the pit of hell.'

'Ah, sir,' says he, 'your worship is mistaken in me. I am none of those.'

'I'faith,' says Sir Dru. 'I'll try thee for this once,' and away he rides.

137 That was a bull

A controversy being at Bury [St Edmunds] Assizes about wintering cattle—before Baron Trevor, then judge upon the bench—and the demand being extreme high, 'Why, friend,' says he, 'this is most unreasonable. I wonder thou art not ashamed! For I myself have known a beast wintered one whole summer for a noble' [6s. 8d.].

'That was a bull, my lord, I believe,' says the fellow—at which ridiculous expression of the judge and sly retorted jeer of the countryman, the whole court fell into a most profuse laughter.

138 A witty answer of a lady

One following a gentlewoman that was very handsome-bodied—as he passed by her, viewed her face, and not finding those features to answer his expectation, said, 'Lady, if I had liked you as well before as behind, I would have kissed you.'

  'Kiss where you like, sir,' quoth she.

139 More riddles

What is the likest to a cat in a hole?
—A cat out of a hole.

How should one stop three holes with one thing?
—By putting one man's nose in another man's——.

What is the best recipe to make a fat lady lean?
—To keep her eyes open, and her mouth shut.

What is the difference between a lord and a meaner man?
—A word.

Why are there so many cuckolds?
—Because so many marry.

What was the greatest cause of the Indians' undoing?
—Their gold.

How do young men and women love one another?
—Like anything.

What is the difference between a rich usurer and a rich man that is no usurer?
—Six per cent.

Why is it so impossible to ravish some lasses?
—Because they are willing.

140 Proverbs with commentaries

Love, though he be blind, can smell
—This is the reason that a man that runs passionately after a woman is said to have his nose in her tail, and is called a smell-smock.

'Tis a trouble to ride, and death to go on foot
—What a devilish lazy fellow was he that invented this proverb!

Fast bind, fast find
—This proverb caused the invention of the Italian padlocks [chastity belts].

Grass grows not in hot ovens
—He that made this proverb was bound, sure, to speak truth for a wager.

A gentle shepherd makes the wolf shite wool
—'Tis a very fine way to be eased of the trouble of sheepshearing.

Hungry dogs love dirty puddings
—There's many a man hath lost his nose by verifying this proverb.

lost his nose: with the pox.

141 On a tapster and gentleman

A tapster bringing a can of beer to a gentleman that had froth about the top of it, the tapster unmannerly blew it off with his mouth, whereupon the gentleman struck him a box on the ear. The tapster very angrily asking if he struck him for blowing the froth off his beer—'Yes,' said the gentleman, 'I did but give you blow for blow.'

142 Half measures

An Englishman and a Scotchman were both in the hold of a ship together in the last engagement at sea, and as they were in the heat of the fight, says the Englishman to him, 'Come, let's go up and partake with our brethren in the fight, and not stand here like drones and do nothing.'

'Be God,' says he, 'wi' aw my heart.'

And as the Englishman led the way, when he was halfway up a great bullet [cannonball] came in and cut him just in two in the middle.

'Uds bread!' says the Scotchman. 'What the de'il! Dost gang up to fight and leave thy arse behind thee?'

143 No bull

A gentleman and his man riding, his man saw one riding on a cow. 'Look, master,' says he. 'Yonder is a fellow rides a-horseback on a cow.'

'That's a bull,' says he.

'No, sir,' says he, 'I know 'tis a cow by his teats.'

144 The new way

A witty young fellow was tried for his life, since the King's Restoration; and being condemned, they told him he must be hanged. He argued pro and con in his defence. At last he desired the judge that if he must be hanged, he might be hanged after the new way, as Oliver was, three or four years after he was dead.

new way In January 1661, on Charles II's orders, the bodies of Cromwell and other regicides were exhumed and hung up on the gallows at Tyburn. (It was a little over two years after Cromwell's death, not three or four.)

145 All the prisons

A nobleman of this kingdom that was often put into the Tower by the Rump and Oliver for his loyalty to the King, was followed by a cripple (which was a Cavalier also), who begged earnestly of him, 'for my lord,' says he, 'you know that you and I have been in all the prisons in London.'

'Out, you lying rogue!' says he. 'I never was in any prison but the Tower.'

'Yes,' says he, 'and I have been in all the rest.'

146 Off with his leg

A country fellow pressed in the late wars, having been at a fight and being asked what exploits he had done there, he said that he had cut off one of the enemy's legs. And being told that it had been more manly if he had cut off his head, 'Oh,' said he, 'you must know that his head was off before.'

147 The imported house

A gentleman, none of the wisest, seeing a house very stately built, told the porter it was much of the Italian mode, and asked whether it were made in England. The porter, seeing his simplicity, said, 'No, sir, it was made in Venice, and brought hither by two merchants.'

148 Have a care

A carpenter passing by with a deal board on his shoulder hit a gentleman on the head with the end of it, whereupon he, perceiving his fault, cried, 'Have a care, sir!'

'Why,' quoth he, 'do you intend to hit me again?'

149 Notable bulls

One asked a fellow if he would go into the water with him. 'No,' says he, 'I'll never go into the water till I have learnt to swim.'

One saying that the fenny-countries were very unhealthy—'I am of your mind,' said another, 'for I lived there once, and I believe if I had lived there till this time, I had died seven years ago.'

150 The bull-speaker

Mr Amner passing through the street, two boys looked out of a tavern window and said, 'There goes Mr Amner, the bull-speaker.'

He, hearing them, looked up, saying, 'You rascals, I know you well enough, and if I had you here I'd kick you downstairs.'

151 Escape route

Mr Amner being with some gentlemen in a tavern near Charing Cross, their chief discourse was about what William Lilly [the astrologer, 1602–81] had prophesied, that the next Monday the world would be at an end, calling it Black Monday. It being then the Saturday before, many fears and doubts did arise among them.

'Well well,' said Mr Amner, 'if I were sure it would be so, I would go over into Holland.'

152 Poor Patty

One Irishman, meeting another, asked what was become of their old acquaintance Patrick Murphy. 'Arrah now, dear honey,' answered the other, 'poor Patty was condemned to be hanged. But he saved his life by dying in prison.'

153 Wary Teague

A Munster man being on board a man-of-war was desired by his messmate to go down to the steward-room for a can of small beer.

Teague, perceiving that preparations were then making for sailing immediately, refused to go, saying, 'Arrah, by my shoul, and so while I am after going into the cellar to fetch drink for you, the ship will be after sailing and leave me behind.'

Teague   nickname for Irishmen.

154 Taking his measure

A humorous fellow, a carpenter, being subpoena'd as a witness on a trial for an assault, one of the counsel, who was very much given to browbeat the evidence, asked him what distance he was from the parties when he saw the defendant strike the plaintiff.

The carpenter answered, 'Just four feet five inches and a half.'

'Prithee, fellow,' said the counsel, 'how is it possible you can be so very exact as to the distance?'

'Why, to tell you the truth,' says the carpenter, 'I thought perhaps that some fool or other might ask me, and so I measured it.'

155 A lying dog

In the heat of an engagement a sailor took his wounded comrade on his shoulders—and [as he was] carrying him down to the surgeon, the fellow in his way lost his head. 'Why,' says the surgeon, 'do you bring me a man without a head?'

'Odso!' says the sailor, 'he told me he had only lost his leg, but he was always a lying dog.'

156 A great slaughter

A certain swaggering Irish officer, being in company with Mr Charles B——der, bragged egregiously of the number he had slain by his own hand abroad, insomuch that by his own account he had demolished at least five hundred.

'Sir,' says Charles, 'I have killed in my time—let me see—five at Madrid—ten at Lisbon—twenty at Paris—thirty at Vienna—and double the number at the Hague. But at length coming over from Calais to Dover, I had scarcely disembarked before a desperate son of a bitch of a fellow killed me.'

'Killed you!' says the officer. 'Damn you, what do you mean by that?'

'Sir,' replied Charles, 'I did not dispute your veracity, and why should you question mine?'

B——der Brander, according to *Wits Museum*, 1780. Apparently a forgotten wit of the 1760's.

157 The yellow peas

A certain punster being at dinner at a tavern where there was a dish of green peas which the cook had boiled very yellow, 'Here, fellow,' said he, calling to one of the waiters, 'take these peas to your cook and desire her to carry them to Hammersmith.'

One of the company asking what she should do with them there, 'Why, you blockhead,' added he, 'is not that the way to Turn'em Green?'

158 Guinea toothpicks

The Marquis of Carmarthen, being at Mitchener's Coffee-room at Margate, was much solicited by a poor man to buy some toothpicks. 'Well,' says the marquis, 'what is the price of your toothpicks?'

'A guinea apiece,' replied the man.

'A guinea apiece!' said the marquis. 'Why, toothpicks must be very scarce at Margate, surely, by your asking such an exorbitant price.'

'No,' replied the man, 'toothpicks are not scarce here, but marquises are.'

159 Sixpence extra

The late Stephen, Lord Holland, who was *the fattest man of his height in England*, and his brother Charles, coming out of the Thatched House Tavern one night together, a chair was called for Lord Holland; who, altering his mind, agreed to go home in his brother's carriage, which was in waiting. The chairmen, however, being disappointed of their fare, he gave them a shilling.

'Long life to your honour,' says Paddy. 'Sixpence more for your poor chairmen.'

'What!' says he. 'Have I not given you your full fare?'

'Oh, yes, your lordship, but consider how you frightened us.'

160 A good joke

A Fellow of a certain college, seeing Tom Brown in a tattered garb, said, 'Tom! Your gown's grown too short for you.'

'Ah!' replied Tom. 'That's true, but it will be long enough before I get another.'

This repartee so diverted the Fellow that he continued laughing till he met with a brother of the same college, who asked him what he laughed at. 'Why,' says he, 'at an excellent joke. I just now told Tom Brown his gown was grown too short for him, and he said it would be a long time before he should have another.'

'Well, and pray where is the joke in that?'

'I don't know,' replied he, 'but I am sure it was a good joke when I heard it.'

5
Men and Manners

The eighty-four stories in this concluding section might have been put into further categories such as 'crime and disaster' and 'master and man', but that would have caused too much fragmentation.

Although stories in which lowly men assert themselves against gentlemen and courtiers occur in the sixteenth century, and occasionally in the mid-seventeenth century (Nos. 182, 208, 209), they are rare thereafter. The era of British middle-class humour in which the lower orders were at best the object of complacent laughter began long before the establishment of Punch. A few hints of radicalism are heard, however, at the end of the eighteenth century. It was a time when even future laureates had revolutionary thoughts.

It is worth quoting the *New Joe Miller* of 1800 on a question that has still to be settled:

> A gentleman expatiated on the justice and propriety of an hereditary nobility. 'Is it not right,' said he, 'in order to hand down to posterity the virtues of those men who have been eminent for their services to the country, that their posterity should enjoy the honours conferred on them as a reward for such services?' 'By the same rule,' said a lady, 'if a man is hanged for his misdeeds, all his posterity should be hanged too.'

161 Of a proud Frenchman

He [Poggio] telleth also that there was a carrack of Genoa hired into France for to make war against Englishmen; of the which carrack the patron [master] bare in his shield painted an ox head: which a nobleman of France beheld and saw, and said he would avenge him[self] on him that bare those arms. Whereupon arose an altercation so much that the Frenchman provoked the Genoese to battle and fight therefor.

The Genoese accepted the provocation, and came at the day assigned into the field without any array or habiliments of war. And that other Frenchman came in much noble apparel into the field that was ordained.

And then the patron of the carrack said, 'Wherefore is it that we two should this day fight and make battle?'

'For I say,' said that other, 'that thine arms be mine, and belonged to me to-fore that thou hadst them.'

Then the Genoese said, 'It is no need to make any battle therefor, for the arms that I bear is not the head of an ox, but it is the head of a cow.'

Which thing so spoken, the noble Frenchman was abashed, and so departed half mocked.

162 Of the gentleman that taught his cook the medicine for the toothache

In Essex there dwelled a merry gentleman, which had a cook called Thomas that was greatly diseased with the toothache and complained to his master thereof—which said he had a book of medicines, and said he would look up his book to see whether he could find any medicine there for it; and so sent one of his daughters to his study for his book, and incontinent looked upon it a long season, and then said thus to his cook:

'Thomas,' quod he, 'here is a medicine for thy toothache, and it is a charm, but it will do you no good except ye kneel on your knee and ask it for saint-charity.'

This man, glad to be released of his pain, kneeled and said, 'Master, for saint-charity let me have that medicine.'

Then quod this gentleman, 'Kneel on your knees and say after me.' Which kneeled down and said after him as he bade him.

This gentleman began and said thus: 'The sun on the Sunday.'

'The sun on the Sunday,' quod Thomas.

'The moon on the Monday—'
'The moon on the Monday.'
'The Trinity on the Tuesday—'
'The Trinity on the Tuesday.'
'The wit on the Wednesday—'
'The wit on the Wednesday.'
'The holy, holy Thursday—'
'The holy, holy Thursday.'
'And all that fast on Friday—'
'And all that fast on Friday.'
'Shite in thy mouth on Saturday—'
This Thomas cook, hearing his master thus mocking him, in an anger start up and said, 'By God's body, mocking churl, I will never do thee service more!' and went forth to his chamber to get his gear together, to the intent to go thence by and by [there and then]. But what for [what with] the anger that he took with his master for the mock that he gave him, and what for the labour that he took to gather his gear so shortly together, the pain of the toothache went from him incontinent, that his master came to him and made him tarry still, and told him that his charm was the cause of the ease of the pain of his toothache.

By this tale ye may see that anger oft-times putteth away bodily pain.

163 Of the courtier and the carter

There came a courtier by a carter, the which in derision praised the carter's back, legs and other members of his body marvellously; whose jesting the carter perceived, and said he had another property than the courtier espied in him. And when the courtier had demanded what it should be, he looked aside over his shoulder upon the courtier and said thus, 'Lo, sir, this is my property. I have a wall-eye in my head, for I never look over my shoulder this wise but I lightly [surely] espy a knave.'

By this tale a man may see that he that useth to deride and mock other folks is sometimes himself more derided and mocked.

164 Of Saint Peter, that cried 'Caws pob'

I find written among old jests how God made Saint Peter porter of heaven, and that God of His goodness, soon after His Passion, suffered many men to come to the kingdom of heaven with small deserving; at which time there was in heaven a great company of Welshmen which with their cracking [bragging] and babbling troubled all the others. Wherefore God said to Saint Peter that He was weary of them and that He would fain have them out of heaven. To whom Saint Peter said, 'Good Lord, I warrant you, that shall be done.'

Wherefore Saint Peter went out of heaven-gates and cried with a loud voice, '*Caws pob!*'—that is as much as to say 'roasted cheese'—which thing the Welshmen hearing, ran out of heaven a great pace. And when Saint Peter saw them all out, he suddenly went into heaven and locked the door, and so sparred all the Welshmen out.

> By this ye may see that it is no wisdom for a man to love or to set his mind too much upon any delicate or worldly pleasure whereby he shall lose the celestial and eternal joy.

165 Of the two men that drank a pint of white wine together

Two homely [simple, unpolished] men of the country came into a tavern to drink a pint of wine. So they sat still, and wist [knew] not what wine to call for. At last, hearing every man to call for 'white wine as clear as water of the rock', they bade the drawer bring them a pint of the same.

The drawer, seeing and perceiving by their words that they were but blunt fellows, brought them a pint of clear water. The one of them filled the cup, and drank to his fellow, and said, 'Hold, neighbour, by mass, chad [I had] as lief drink water, save for the name of wine.'

166 Of him that said he was the devil's man

In the civil seditious time of Edward the Fourth and Henry the Sixth, one chanced to meet with a company that quickly asked him, 'Whose man art thou?'

'King Edward's,' quoth he.

'Art thou so?' quoth they, and all to-beat him, for they were of Henry's side.

Wherefore to the next company that met him and demanded whose man he was, he answered, 'King Henry's.'

'Art thou so?' quoth they, and likewise all to-beat him, for they were on Edward's part.

The fellow, thus sore beaten, went forth [on], and met with another rout, who asked him, 'Whose man art thou?'

He being at his wits' end what to say, answered, 'The devil's man.'

'Then go—the devil go with thee,' said they.

'Amen!' quoth he. 'For it is the best master that I served this day.'

By this tale ye may perceive how grievous and perilous all civil seditions be; so doubtful may it stand that a man cannot tell on which side to hold, for he that now is stronger, another time is weaker, as Fortune list to turn her wheel.

civil seditious time   the Wars of the Roses.

167 A high hat

A gentleman sitting at a play, a merchant by chance sat afore him whose hat was so high and broad that it hindered his view of the play, whereupon he said unto him, 'My good friend, I beseech you, do off your hat a while, for I assure you it will greatly benefit my eyesight.'

168 Bearing the shame

A Spanish gentleman had a many Moors to his slaves, and in the winter-time he kept them cold and bare. A churchman, rebuking such his uncharity and hard heart, and saying that it was a shame unto him, he answered, 'Pass they over the cold, and I'll pass over the shame well enough.'

169 A Spaniard's brag

At the siege of Barcelona, a Portugal horseman entered pell-mell in the enemy's throng into the town gate, and wrote with a chalk within the gate: *Hitherto adventured Vasco Fernandes*. The next day, a Spaniard, hearing him boast thereof, was no less adventurous, and bravely hazarded himself the next skirmish in at the same gate, and wrote with a coal beyond his, *Hitherto Vasco Fernandes did not adventure*.

170 I have no brains

A Gallego [Galician] of Spain went to the wars, and was shot with an arrow into the head. The surgeon searching the wound said that he could not possibly live, for that the arrow had pierced his brain.

The Gallego answered, 'That cannot be, for I have no brain at all. Had I had brains, I trow I had never come to the wars.'

171 Tiling for tomorrow

A tiler and his son were a-tiling of a house, and the father did his work so loosely that his son found fault therewith. Whereunto he answered, 'Do it well today, and beg tomorrow.'

172 Change of diet

Certain servingmen complained to their niggardly master how that his steward allowed them but only salads and cheese to their suppers a-nights.

Whereupon the gentleman called his steward before him, and in a great chafe said unto him, 'Is it true, N., that you give my men salads and cheese to their suppers? I charge you do no more so, but give them their salads one night, and their cheese another, and so in order.'

173 Confess and be hanged

A Biscayan was sore tormented to confess his committed felony, and he would not do it to die. At last when they had tormented him almost to death, they took him off the torture and bespake him fair, saying, 'Well, we see your invincible heart. You are truly a man every inch of you. But, faith, tell us now, even as you are a gentleman, did you it not?'

Then the Biscayan answered, 'Aye, marry, sirs! As I am a gentleman: that's another matter. Why said ye not so at the first? Go to, I did it. Confess and be hanged.' And so he was.

Biscayan   a Basque (a butt of Castilian jokes).

174 Did you ever see the like?

A country maid coming to market, her mare stumbled in the market-place and down she fell over and over, showing all that ever God sent her; and then at rising up again, she turned her round about unto the people and said, 'Gog's life, sirs, did you ever see the like before?'

175 I'll break your arrow

A countryman standing at a mark [target], an arrow lighted on his nose and spitted it through. At last, the archer coming to the mark to take up his arrow, the swain met him with it in his hand, and asked him whether it were his arrow.

'Yea,' he answered, 'where had ye it?'

'Marry, see here,' replied the swain, pointing to his nose. 'You have made me a proper nose, so you have. Indeed if you serve me so any more, I'll break your arrow.'

176 Goodnight

A serving-man having but one eye came into a fence-school and played with another at fence, and it was his chance to have the other eye strucken out too. He then seeing himself all in dark laid down the foils and said unto the company, 'My masters, God give you all goodnight.'

177 How this merry fool Will Sommers, to make the king merry, asked him three questions

Howsoever these three things came in memory, and are for mirth inserted into stage plays, I know not; but that Will Sommers asked them of the king, it is certain: there are some will affirm it now living in Greenwich.

The king [Henry VIII] upon a time being extreme melancholy and full of passion, all that Will Sommers could do would not make him merry. 'Ah,' says he, 'this cloud must have a good shower to cleanse it,' and with that goes behind the arras. 'Harry,' says he, 'I'll go behind the arras, and study three questions, and come again. See therefore you lay aside this melancholy muse and study to answer me.'

'Aye,' quoth the king. 'They will be wise ones, no doubt.'

At last, out comes William with his wit, as the fool of the play doth, with an antic look to please the beholders. 'Harry,' says he, 'what is that, the lesser it is, the more it is to be feared?'

The king mused at it; but to grace the jest the better, he answered, he knew not. Will made answer, it was a little bridge over a deep river: at which he smiled.

'What is the next, William?' says the king.

'Marry, this is next: What is the cleanliest trade in the world?'

'Marry,' says the king, 'I think a comfit-maker, for he deals with nothing but pure ware, and is attired clean in white linen when he sells it.'

'No, Harry,' says Will, 'you are wide.'

'What say you then?' quod the king.

'Marry,' says Will, 'I say a dirt-dauber' [who applied the daub of wattle-and-daub houses].

'Out on it!' says the king. 'That is the foulest, for he is dirty up to the elbows.'

'Aye,' says Will, 'but then he washes them clean again, and eats his meat cleanly enough.' [*But see No.* 105.]

'I promise thee, Will,' says the king, 'thou hast a pretty, foolish wit.'

'Aye, Harry,' says he, 'it will serve to make a wiser man than you a fool, methinks.'

At this the king laughed; and demands the third question.

'Now tell me,' says Will, 'if you can, what it is, that being born without life, head, lip or eye, yet doth run roaring through the world till it dies?'

'This is a wonder,' quod the king, 'and no question. I know it not.'

'Why,' quod Will, 'it is a fart.'

At this the king laughed heartily and was exceeding merry; and bids Will ask any reasonable thing, and he would grant it.

'Thanks, Harry,' says he. 'Now, against I want, I know where to find—for yet I need nothing, but one day I shall. For every man sees his latter end, but knows not his beginning.' The king understood his meaning, and so pleasantly departed for that season. And Will laid him down amongst the spaniels to sleep.

178 A jest of a felon at Oxford

The assizes being at Oxford, among the rest there was a felon that had the benefit of the clergy, to have his book—but he could read never a word, which a scholar perceiving, stood behind and prompted him with his verse that he was to read. And coming to the latter end, he held his thumb upon the book, that the scholar could not see, wherefore he bade him softly, 'Take away thy thumb.'

He thinking that the same was so in the book, said aloud, 'Take away thy thumb,' which the judge perceiving, bade, 'Take him away.'

And so he was condemned: and being upon the ladder ready to die, and the rope about his neck, he said, 'Have at yon daisy that grows yonder,' and so leapt off the gallows.

to have his book A first offender, if sentenced to hang, could get off if able to read a verse of Latin (usually the first verse of the 51st Psalm, 'Miserere mei . . .').

179 How a madman in Gloucestershire answered a gentleman

In Gloucestershire dwelt one that cured frantic men in this manner: when their fit was on them, he would put them in a gutter of water—some to the knees, some to the middle, and some to the neck, as the disease was on them. So one that was well amended, standing at the gate by chance, a gentleman came riding by with his hawks and his hounds. The fellow called to him and said, 'Gentleman, whither go you?'

'On hunting,' quoth the gentleman.

'What do you with all those kites and dogs?'

'They be hawks and hounds,' quoth the gentleman.

'Wherefore keep you them?' quoth the other.

'Why,' quoth he, 'for my pleasure.'

'What do they cost you a year to keep them?'

'Forty pounds,' quoth the gentleman.

'And what do they profit you?' quoth he.
'Some ten pounds,' quoth the gentleman.
'Get thee quickly hence,' quoth the fellow, 'for if my master find thee here he will put thee into the gutter up to the throat.'

180 A gentleman and a barber

A barber coming finically about a gentleman was (as the most of them are) terribly full of talk. At length he found the leisure to ask how he would be trimmed. 'Marry, my friend,' replied the gentleman, 'if thou canst possibly, do it in silence.'

181 Gentlemen at an ordinary

Certain gentlemen being in game at an ordinary [eating-house], everyone complained of a filthy rank smell that was amongst them, which grew still hotter and hotter in their noses. At length saith one of them jestingly, 'I pray you, gentlemen, which of you amongst us here useth to wear socks?'

A country gentleman, one of the company, presently answered, 'Not I, I protest. I never knew what belongs to them.'

useth to wear wears.

182 Pay like a gentleman

A collier [coalman], coming into a tobacco shop, sat him down and observed two gentlemen who called either [both] of them for a fresh pipe; who when they had drunk [smoked] them off, being well acquainted with the man of the house, bade him farewell and they would pay him the next time they came that way—who told them they were welcome, and so let them go.

The collier then he calls for his pipe; and having whiffed it off, was walking away without paying. But the man, calling him back, asked him for money. 'For money?' saith he. 'Why, what dost thou take me to be?'

'Marry,' saith the man, 'by thy habit I take thee to be a collier.'

'A collier?' replied he. 'I tell thee, friend, I have called for tobacco like a gentleman, I have drunk it like a gentleman, and I will pay thee like a gentleman. Farewell—it shall be the next time that I come this way.'

183 A braggart

A terrible braggart boasted how it was his chance to meet with two of his arch-enemies at once. 'The one,' saith he, 'I tossed so high in the air, that had he had at his back a baker's basket full of bread, though he had eaten all the way, he would have been starved in the fall ere he would have reached the ground.' And the other he struck so deep into the earth that he left him no more to be seen above ground but his head and one of his arms—and these to no other end than to put off his hat to him as he had occasion to pass that way.

184 Of one that delivered a message to a lady

A gentleman-usher being on a serious message unto a great lady, and having a long tale to deliver her, in the midst of his speech, not able to contain it, he let a great fart which was heard all over the chamber, at which the lady's gentlewomen and chambermaids began to tee-hee and laugh. And one of them, in holding in her breath because she would not laugh too loud, chanced to do the like; which he observing, abruptly broke off his discourse, and turning to them, said: 'Aye, marry, young gentlewomen, you do well! I know it is for your ease. I beseech you, let it go in order round. When it shall come again to my turn I will make proof what I can do.'

185 Of a cheesemonger

A Puritan coming to his neighbour, a cheesemonger, to buy a gossips' or groaning cheese because his wife was ready to lie down, the master of the shop offered him a taste of that which he seemed best to like: who, as he put it to his mouth, so he put his hat to his eyes and began a long grace—which the cheesemonger seeing, 'Nay,' saith he, 'since you mean instead of a taste to make a meal out of my cheese, I assure you you shall buy none here, for I cannot afford it after that weight and measure.'

186 Two ancient companions

Two old soldiers and companions that had served in the Low Countries twenty-odd years together, in the last German war took pay under the King of Sweden. And whilst His Majesty lay with his army before Frankfurt, it chanced as they two with some others were tippling, just as one of them was heaving up a great bombard of beer to fill his cup—it chanced, I say, that a bullet from the besieged wall struck the jack out of his hand, and with it half his head off. The other, his ancient familiar and acquaintance, seeing it, 'Zounds!' saith he, swearing like a madman, 'the drink's all spilt!'

jack usually a large leather drinking-cup; here, the container from which he was pouring.

187 A bush and no wine

Sir William Cornwallis, meeting Sir Henry Wotton one time, asked him where he had been. He answered, 'Faith, Will, at a bawdy-house, where I met with the strangest thing that ever man saw—a wench that was all hair and nothing else.'

To whom Sir Will replied:

'A bush and no wine?
Down with the sign!'

bush and no wine   a play on the bush, extended on a pole, used as a sign by taverns.

188   Good for an old woman

Sir Henry Sidney drank one time to an old woman (that was exceeding deaf and sat at the lower end of the table) in a glass of sack, but with the annexion of this phrase, 'That I be your bedfellow this night.'

She, seeing the sack (her eyes being better than her ears), replied, 'I thank your good worship, with all my heart, sir. You know what's good for an old woman.'

189   A generous servant

The Lord Richardson, as he went to Westminster Hall, spied his man Williams at a tavern window in the Strand; and when the court was risen there was no Williams to be found. So when he came home, he told him, 'Sirrah, I must be mine own man for all you, for you are revelling at a tavern when you should attend me. I saw you well enough, sirrah, at the window today.'

'In faith, my lord,' says Williams, 'I am sorry at my heart I did not see you, for if I had, I would have given you a quart of sack.'

Richardson   Lord Chief Justice; died 1634.

Westminster Hall   where the law courts sat.

190   Zounds!

A braggadocio relating a skirmish betwixt himself and another in a tavern, says he, 'As he reached for his rapier I put out the candle and ran under the table, because I was unarmed. Then, groping up and down the room, "Zounds!" said he. And "Zounds!" thought I.'

191 I have one quality

A fantastic gallant coming to an ordinary [eating-house] where they were all strangers to him, thinking to put a brave upon the company, as soon as they were set, told them, 'Gentlemen, I have one quality which I must needs give you notice of, for the peace and quiet of the company: that if any man takes away my bread by my trencher, I must strike him.'

Presently upon that, his next neighbour (Sir Francis Vane), putting off his hat, 'Gentlemen,' says he, 'I pray take notice also of another quality that I have: that if any man strikes me, I ever strike him again'—and with that, takes away his bread. At which my gallant was as mute as a fish.

192 A doomed oyster

Sir Robert Bell, eating of oysters, and meeting with one that was much tainted, began to smell to it. 'Are you stinking?' says he. 'By God, you shall not 'scape so, for I'll make you stink worse before you and I part.' And so he ate it.

193 Bless her heart

Sir Martin Stuteville's father riding abroad one day, with him [Martin] attending on him, he rode by the nurse's house that overlaid his eldest son, at which time the nurse stood at the door. 'Look you there, Martin,' said his father. 'There stands she that made you an elder brother.'

'Is that she, sir?' says he. 'Marry, God's blessing on her heart for it!'—and presently gallops up to her and gives her a couple of shillings.

194 Paper after shot

A physician's man being to give Sir Henry Berkley a clyster [enema], had prepared a great piece of brown paper, wrung round like a plug. And as soon as he had pulled out the pipe, in he began to crowd the paper with as much expedition as might be (for the day before he had given one to a gentleman that was not very retentive, but shot it back on his face), for fear the liquor should fly out. But Sir H., feeling that pudder in his backside, began to look over his shoulder, and asked him what 'a devil he meant to do.

'Oh, nothing, sir,' says he, 'but put in paper after my shot.'

paper in muzzleloading guns, a wad of paper had to be rammed in to stop the ball from falling out.

195 Hear my prayer

An atheistical fellow in a storm began to use this rhetoric to God for his life, 'Lord, I beseech thee, hear my prayer now, for thou knowest I trouble thee but seldom.'

196 Sprinkling the table

Climme Hoe being at a supper-feast where his mistress was at the table—what with the spirit of claret and her presence he swelled so fast and with so much provocation to make water, as he knew not what shift in the world to make, for he was wedged in on the bench side with much company on each hand.

At last he resolved, having a winter boot on with a huge large top, to force his instrument downward and discharge all into that. Very silent and intent he was about it, but to avoid suspicion, still played with his eyes above-board. Yet his cousin, Serjeant Atthow's wife, sitting at his elbow (a woman quick-sighted in any knavery, and of infinite boldness), observed him, and in the midst of his career, catching him suddenly by the arm, snatched it to her with these words, 'What, art melancholy, coz?'

With that his water-bottle sprang up and all besprinkled the table and the opposite company, to the excessive laughter of all, and unexpressible comfort of his mistress.

197 Wiggett in peril

Wiggett, the famous facetious fool, being at Hunstanton in Sir Nicholas Strange's time, where Sir John Heydon and divers others came to be merry—as they were one night at a sack posset before they went to bed, Wiggett thrust in his spoon amongst them. Sir J. Heydon watched him the next time he came, and daubed up his eyes with a spoonful of posset. The fool still offered to eat, and Sir J. as often threatened. But Wiggett, turning his back with a seeming fear to shun him, got that advantage to piss in his spoon; and bringing on't closely to the basin, offered to dip for more.

With that, Sir John lets fly posset again at the fool, and he piss at Sir John; and serves him thus twice or thrice before he perceives anything. But at last, smelling out his knavery, 'Ud's zounds!' says Sir J. Heydon, 'this villain hath thrown piss on my face,' and presently whips out his rapier, and after the fool.

But he, spying him come in that fury, and finding no evasion, turns out his buttocks just as he was ready to tilt at him. 'Hold, hold, hold, I prithee, Jack,' says he. 'Run't into the old hole for fear of hurting the skin.' Which knavish retort of the fool stopped him in the career of his rage, and struck him into such a laughter that he could scarce hold his sword in his hand; otherwise Wiggett in every man's judgement was in great danger, for Sir J. Heydon was a man of choler, and would bear as little himself as any man, though his pregnant wit would lay on load upon others.

sack posset   milk and sack, hot, with spices and sugar.

turns out his buttocks   pulls down his breeches.

198 Wiggett ingratiates himself

At the same time, about 12 o'clock that night, after they had been frolic and eaten their sack posset, 'Gentlemen,' says Wiggett (and the rather to ingratiate himself again), 'if you will be whist and silent but a little, I'll show you as good sport as ever you saw in your lives.' They promised him they would be as silent as the night itself.

The fool presently goes to a postern door that led out of that chamber into a room where the mother of the maids lay and all her retinue (for Sir Nich. Strange, being a widower at that time, left the domestic government of his house principally to an old virgin), and steals in very softly into the wenches' chamber, where they all slept very supinely at that time. And he to his work at the beds' feet, drawing down the clothes softly and leisurely—for as soon as he perceived but a limb to stir, he was quiet for a while, and then to't again—till by degrees, at last he uncovered them all.

Then out he goes to the company, and taking a candle in his hand, 'Now, gentlemen,' says he, 'do but follow me easily, and you may see the naked truth of the business.' So when they came there, he presented them with that object, the wenches snorting in their several postures, and some with their bare bellies, and told Sir N. Strange that he might now perceive how he was cheated in his dairy, 'For before God,' says he, 'these ranni-gutted sows eat so much unstrained cream that you may see the very hairs grow through their bellies.'

199 A fair exchange

A gentleman at a play sat by a fellow that he strongly suspected for a cutpurse, and for the probation of him took occasion to draw out his purse, and put it up so carelessly as it dangled down (but his eye watched it strictly with a glance), and he bent his discourse another way; which his suspected neighbour observing, upon his first fair opportunity exercised his craft, and having got his booty began to remove away; which the gentleman noting, instantly draws his knife and whips off one of his ears—and vowed he would have something for his money.

The cutpurse began to swear and stamp and threaten. 'Nay, go to, sirrah,' says the other. 'Be quiet. I'll offer you fair. Give me my purse again—here's your ear—take it and be gone.'

200 Have it for five

A gentleman overtakes in the evening a plain country fellow, and asks him how far it was to such a town.
'Ten miles, sir,' says he.
'It is not possible,' says the gentleman.
'It is no less,' says the fellow.
'I tell thee 'twas never counted above five.'
''Tis ten indeed, sir,' says the fellow. And thus they were arguing *pro et con* a long time. At last, says the countryman to him, 'I'll tell you what I'll do, sir, because you seem to be an honest gentleman, and your horse is almost tired. I will not stand with you; you shall have it for five; but as I live, whosoever comes next shall ride ten.'

201 Advice at the gallows

One of the bailiffs of Colchester had a man was to be hanged, and just as the fellow was ready to be turned off, his master came puffing into the crowd—'By your leave, by your leave, my masters.'
The people made way; the executioner paused, and his man; and all looked for a pardon at least. But he had nothing to say but, 'Oh, John, John, put the knot behind thine ear. Thou't find much ease on't.'

202 Drunken music

The organist at Ely began a wrong anthem, and the bellows-blower was drunk. Up comes a boy from the choir and cries, 'False, false! Y'are out, y'are out!'

'It may be so,' says the bellows-man, 'when I blow one thing, and he plays another.'

203 A naughty nickname

Serjeant Atthow's wife, a woman of great boldness and audacity, the first time that ever she saw Sir John Pooly, at a great meeting, before all, proffered him to teach him an excellent way how to kiss a woman without ruffling her ruff. He desiring to know how, she told him he must set her on her head and kiss her arse.

'I thank you, good Mrs Arsehole' (for Mrs Atthow), said Sir John; which nickname stuck so by her—as he calling her by no other, and telling many stories of her by that name—at the Earl of Warwick's, the countess ignorantly saluted her by that name, coming one day to visit her.

204 One push more

At the siege of Sluis, a quarter-shot struck away the very belly of a soldier in the defending of a breach, being come to push of pike; and his guts fell dangling upon the ground. Colonel Baskervill rushing in to make good that place, and seeing him in what case he was, bade him step by [aside], for he was but a dead man. The soldier replied to Baskervill, who trod unawares on his guts, 'Nay, tread but off my shirt, and I'll warrant you I'll give them one push more.'

205 No nose for me

Tom Brewer, my musical servant, through his proneness to good-fellowship having attained to a very rich and rubicund nose, being reproved by a friend for his too frequent use of strong drinks and sack as very pernicious to that distemper and inflammation in his nose, 'Nay, faith,' says he, 'if it will not endure sack, it's no nose for me.'

206 A waggish wench

A man walking the street let a great fart, upon which he jestingly said, 'Crack me that nut.' It being heard of a waggish wench that was in a chamber over his head, she being well provided at that time with a perfumed chamber-pot, throws it out of the window upon his head, saying, 'There's the kernel of your nut, sir.'

207 Fruitful Wales

There fell a great dispute betwixt Jockey, a Scotchman, and Jenkin, a Welshman, and the subject of it was the fruitfulness of their countries, and thus Jockey began, 'There was not a braver, fruitfuller country in the world than Leith in Scotland.'

The Welshman answered him again, 'Py Cot, that was false, for there was no place so full of all sorts of fruit as was in Wales.'

Jockey replied again that he knew a piece of ground in Scotland where the grass grew up so suddenly [rapidly] that if you threw a staff in it overnight, in that time the pasture would so overgrow it that you could not see it again the next morning.

But Jenkin, hearing this with a great scorn, made him this answer, 'py Saint Taff,' that the throwing so small a thing as a staff was nothing, 'for,' quoth Jenkin, 'we have tivers pieces of cround in our country, that if you turn your horse into them, you shall not see him next morning.'

not see him because he has been stolen.

208 The way to Salisbury

A mad young gallant . . . having rid, as he feared, out of his way, overtook a blunt country fellow and asked him which was the way to Salisbury. The countryman, intending not only to set him right, but withal to know whether or no he had committed any error in his way thither, asked him, as the manner is, whence he came; **to** which the surly gallant answered, 'Why, what is that to you—from whence I came?'

'You say true, master,' quoth the bumpkin. 'It is nothing to me from whence you come nor whither you go.' So he walked away with his hands coupled behind him, and left the gentle fool to study out his way to Salisbury.

209 Hard at the bottom

Another gentleman as mad as the former, riding over a hill and being doubtful [fearing] that the descent was boggish, called rudely to a fellow (as cross as himself) who was making of a hedge, 'You, sirrah rogue!'

'Aye, master,' quoth the hedger.

'Do you live here?' quoth the gallant.

'Yes, and please your worship,' quoth the ditcher.

Quoth the gentleman, 'Is it hard at the bottom?'

'Aye, sir,' replied the country fellow, 'very hard at the bottom.'

The gentleman, being thus assured, set spurs to his horse and rid down the hill pell-mell, but before he had rid out of call from the country fellow his horse was up to the belly in a slough, where he stuck fast and durst not alight—but in great fury called to the ditcher: 'You base lying rogue you, did not you tell me that it was hard at the bottom?'

'True, master,' replied the countryman, 'so it is, but you are not at the bottom yet.'

210 The glory of the West

There was a gentleman whose only study and practice was manhood, as football-playing, wrestling, pitching the ball, throwing of weights, riding and fencing, in which active practices he was so perfect that he overmatched all men that came over him, insomuch that he was the glory of the West of England, and he was conqueror of all men that came to him, and grew troubled that he could not find any man fit to match him. But it happened that one day after hunting, at a drinking-match in an alehouse, by chance he met a North-Countryman who was highly extolling a great gamester like himself in the North who performed all exercises that were manly, and that was an overcomer of all that durst engage him.

The Western gentleman desired his name and habitation, which was soon told him; but when he heard, he was impatient of further delay, and therefore in order for a journey to him he provided himself of all conveniences and rid into the North, where with little inquiry he found the gentleman's house, and knocking at the gate, he was informed by a servant that his master was in his park a mile off. The traveller returned thanks, and with his horse in his hand (guided by the servant's direction) he went to him, where he found him mending of a pale.

Now take notice that this North Country gentleman was a very stout man but of very few words, and the Western gentleman of as many: who thus began to accost him, 'Sir, I have intelligence that you are the stoutest man in all the North, and I am as highly reputed in the West, which hath provoked me to find you out, that we may try both our strength and our skill so far that fortune and fame may crown one of us the only glorious man in England.'

The North-Countryman was still at his work, but heard distinctly all that he said—but returned no answer. Only when the other had ended speaking and expected a reply, the North-Countryman comes fairly to him, puts his hand under his twist, and pitches him over the park pales.

The West-Countryman, seeing him do that so easily, began to think there was no contending with him, and therefore very civilly with his hat in his hand gave him a return in these words, 'I thank you, sir, heartily. Pray throw over my horse too.'

pale boundary fence.
twist crotch.

211 A vomit without physic

A gentlewoman would needs have a vomit, but would take no physic. 'Well, then I'll tell you what you must do,' saith Dr B.

'Put the little finger of one hand into your mouth and t'other in your breech for half an hour, and see if that won't do.'

But 'twouldn't do. 'No?' quoth he. 'Then change fingers.'

212 A cure by a humour

A gentlewoman fallen into a melancholy, Dr B. sent for, consulted with, undertakes her cure. Commands all to depart the room, bars the door, tells the gentlewoman now she must lie down upon the bed, close upon her face. She lies down as he appoints. When he sees a convenient opportunity, he takes and flings up all and hits her a good clap. With that she starts up in a most passionate heat. 'Well, Mistress—you're well, and do but keep your own counsel and I'll keep mine.'

213 Of a barber

One asking a barber, that never before had been at Court, what he saw there, 'Oh,' said he, 'the king was excellently well trimmed.'

214 No forenoons

An Oxford scholar having been ten days at Cambridge together, it seems they kept him drinking so all night that he never could rise before dinner [at noon]; and being asked how he liked Cambridge, said, 'I like the place well enough, but that there are no forenoons in't.'

215 A carpenter!

A valiant captain that had lost his leg formerly in the wars was nevertheless for his great prudence and courage made captain of a ship; and being in the midst of an engagement, a cannon bullet took off his wooden supporter so that he fell down. The seamen—forasmuch few knew he had a wooden leg—called out for the surgeon. 'The surgeon, a pox on you all!' said he. 'A carpenter, a carpenter!'

216 A passionate gamester

A gentleman playing a game at tables [backgammon] in a chamber in Fleet Street, four storeys high, had so ordered his game that no chance of the dice could lose it but one. Yet it so happened that that chance came, whereupon he grew so passionate that, bringing down the tables into the street, he made a stop; and asking the next gentleman that came if he understood the game, the gentleman said he did. 'Then pray, sir,' said he, 'what do you think could lose me the game?'

Then pausing a little—'I think there's nothing but—' such a chance.

'Why then,' said the passionate gamester, 'God damn me if I have not thrown it!'

217 A poor scholar

A poor boy, knowing what esteem learning had in the world, begged under colour of being a poor scholar. A gentleman passing by took pity on him, and asked him in Latin what his friends were, whether they were alive, and the like—but still he cries in the same tongue: 'Pray, sir, pity a poor scholar.'

'Why, you rascal,' quoth the gentleman, 'do you say you are a scholar, and you understand not one word of Latin?'

''Tis true,' said the boy, 'I understand no Latin, and scarce can read English, and that is the reason I desire you to give something to a very poor scholar.'

218 A butcher's bargain

A country woman that was a bold gossip came to a butcher's in Oxford, and when she saw a shoulder of mutton hang up, she asked him what she should give him for it. He told her two shillings and a half.

'Two farts and a half!' says she.

'Why,' says he, 'give me two farts and a half and thou shalt have it.'

'Sayst thou so, boy?' says she. 'Why then, have at it.'

Then she lifted up her pretty right leg and let a good one. 'Well,' says he, 'there's one.'

Then, sweet soul, she lifted up her left leg, and let another as good. Then lifting up her two legs one after another, she let a lusty one. 'Well,' says he, 'there's three. But where's the half one?'

'Why,' says she, 'take which half you will of the last, for that was a rousing one.'

219 Some probable stories told by several persons in a room together

... Another that had been a soldier, and newly come back from the great and long siege of Ostend—one asked him, 'What news there?'

He swore there was a great want of bread; but one day when some was brought in, he saw a lusty soldier that was one of their regiment take up a loaf, 'and having a very large and sharp knife, he sliced quite through the loaf, and himself (being eager at it) and two more soldiers behind him. And by that means we got their shares, and so fared the better'—and to the confirmation of it, added some lusty oaths.

'Nay,' said they, 'we'll believe this, 'cause 'tis a well-bred story.'

Ostend presumably the siege by the Spaniards, 1601–4, was in mind.

220 Another probable story

Then another told a story that a miller had a horse for many years together whose name was Roan, and being tired with working all day, poor jade, slept soundly at night; which a thievish fellow espying, flayed off his skin whilst he slept and went away with it. But old Roan, when he awaked—though 'twas a bitter cold night—yet, poor thing, he came home to the mill-door and neighed very loud, which the honest miller hearing, awaked his wife and asked her 'whether that was not the neighing of our old Roan?'

'Truly, husband,' says she, 'it is. Let's rise and see what's the matter with him.' And when they came out, they wondered to see him in such a pickle. 'Well, husband,' says she, 'since 'tis as 'tis, I'd have you kill five or six of our sheep (and tomorrow being market-day, we can sell their flesh there) and take all the skins and clap 'em hot upon poor Roan.' Which he presently did with his dear wife's help, and clapped them hot upon the horse's flayed back; which with the cold night were presently frozed on, and the horse as well or rather better in health than ever he was in his life, and I am sure you'll say warmer.

And this horse, says he, he kept for many years after, and every year it brought him thirty tod of wool. And I hope you will believe it, but if you don't believe it, I pray take notice that I am not bound to find you stories and belief too.

Then they all concluded it was true-lie so.

thirty tod   840 lb.

221 And another

Another story was that he being in a low [downstairs] room with some gentlemen, a-drinking of bottle ale, he saw the man of the house open a bottle, and the cork flew up with such a violence that it struck his hat off his head, and after that went through the ceiling of that room and another room above that, which was two pair of stairs high, and killed a man and his wife as they lay in bed, and from there flew up into the garret, and they could not get it out with a hammer and mallet.

Sir (says another), to make good your story, which I saw with my own eyes—being with some others in an upper room, one was then opening a bottle of ale, and the cork then flew up with such violence through the top of the house that it broke the ceiling and the tiles also, and killed a kite as he was flying just then over the house. And the hole was so big which the cork had made, that down fell the kite through that hole, and they, opening the kite to see where she was wounded, found two great chickens in her belly, which they sold to pay for their drink; and after that would never drink in any other room in that house.

But I don't know that it ever happened so again; for these things, though there be truth in 'em, don't happen every day so.

222 How to catch a hare

A country fellow told his wife that he started a hare in his ground, 'and I ran,' says he, 'after to catch her, and the devil was in her, I think, for she outran me, though I was ten times bigger than her—for she was no bigger than the calf of my leg.'

'Well, husband,' says she, 'if ever you catch him there again, mark which side his head lies, and hold your hat just against it, and then make a great noise, and I'll warrant you she runs into your hat.'

'Say you so?' says he. 'Then I am sure I shall *ha't*. Oh,' says he, 'these women are pestilent wits!'

223 I know it

At a certain battle, while the party defeated were fleeing, one of them had got an arrow in his breech, but fear of life made him run, not regarding it. One of his followers . . . cries out, 'Ho you! Look behind you, with a pox to you—there is an arrow sticking in your arse.'

'Don't you trouble yourself about that,' said he, 'for I know it as well as you do.'

224 Where I starve

One meeting an old acquaintance whom the world had frowned on a little, asked him where he lived. 'Where I live, I don't know,' says he, 'but I starve down towards Wapping and that way.'

225 Hot custard

One making a furious assault upon a hot custard burnt his mouth till the tears ran down. His friend asked him why he wept.

'Only,' says he, ''tis just come into my mind that my father died this day twelvemonth.'

'Phoo!' says the other. 'Is that all?' So whipping his spoon in, he quickly sympathized with his companion; who, seeing his eyes brimful, with a malicious sneer asked him why he wept.

'A pox on you,' says he. 'Because you were not hanged the same day your father died.'

226 God bless Tadloe!

Dr Tadloe, who was a very fat man, happening to go thump, thump with his great legs through a street in Oxford where some paviours had been at work, in the midst of July, the fellows immediately laid down their blocks. 'Ah, God bless you, master!' cries one of them, 'it was very kind of you to come this way. It saves us a great deal of trouble this hot weather.'

blocks rammers.

227 No room at the top

A gentleman coming to an inn in Smithfield, and seeing the ostler expert and tractable about the horses, asked how long he had lived there, and what countryman [of what county] he was.

'I'se Yorkshire,' said the fellow, 'an' ha' lived sixteen years here.'

'I wonder,' replied the gentleman, 'that in so long a time, so clever a fellow as you seem to be have not come to be master of the inn yourself.'

'Aye,' said the ostler, 'but maister's Yorkshire too.'

228 Deaf old Cross

Although the infirmities of nature are not proper subjects to be made a jest of, yet when people take a great deal of pains to conceal what everybody sees, there is nothing more ridiculous. Of this sort was old Cross the player, who, being very deaf, did not care that anybody should know it.

Honest Joe Miller, going with a friend one day along Fleet Street, and seeing old Cross on the other side the way, told his acquaintance he should see some sport. So beckoning to Cross with his finger, and stretching open his mouth as wide as ever he could as if he halloo'd to him, though he said nothing—the old fellow comes puffing from t'other side the way. 'What a pox,' said he, 'do you make such a noise for? Do you think one can't hear?'

229 Watch and watch about

Some 'dear joys' [Irishmen], waiting to get commissions to serve in the kingdom of Ireland, had little or no money to procure lodgings. Some of the richest hired a room with two beds, and they found means for sixteen to lie therein: four of them going to bed, and other four relieving each other every four hours—and crying, 'Be Chreest, joy, dish vill mauke ush all sholdiers!'

230 A deserving case

As the facetious Harry Woodward, comedian, was one day walking with a friend under Covent Garden piazza, a poor miserable-looking wretch asked his charity. Seeing the beggar's shocking countenance, Harry put his hand in his pocket and relieved him, saying at the same time, 'This fellow is certainly either a great object of charity, or a very good actor.'

Woodward   comic actor, died 1777.

231 A loud hint

Quin having an old gentleman for a constant guest, whom he did not choose to affront, that was very nauseous at table by frequently belching over the victuals—hearing of a man that could break wind backwards at will, engaged him to come one day as an old acquaintance and sit opposite to his constant guest.

The windy gentleman soon began his old practice. The first salute was returned by the adept in the opposite way; a repetition procured a double, and a third time a triple discharge. The old gentleman appeared greatly surprised at the stranger's ill manners; and upon a fifth peal, rose up in great consternation and asked him if he was not ashamed to affront all the company in that manner.

'Oh, never mind him,' said Quin. 'Sit down and eat your dinner. It is a foible he has. What he does, goes under the table. Now,' said he, 'if he were to *belch*, it would go over the table and the victuals too.'

Quin   comic actor (1693–1766); see notes.

232 Quin inconvenienced

Quin went one morning to a friend of his who had built a new house at Bath, before it was quite finished; when, being affected in a certain natural way, after having inquired of the servant if his master was at home, and being answered in the negative—'Well,' said he, 'however, show me your little-house.'

'Yes, sir,' replied the servant, keeping the street door in his hand, 'the house is *small*, but it is very compact.'

'I mean,' continued Quin, 'your necessary-house.'

'Yes, sir,' replied the servant, 'I believe my master will find it very *necessary* when he comes down, and much better than lodgings.'

'Your conveniency, I mean,' said Quin.

'Very convenient, I can assure you,' still continued the servant.

Quin, no longer able to contain himself, cried with some emphasis, 'G-d d—n you, you rascal, show me your sh-t-house, or, by G-d, I shall befoul my breeches!'

'Oh, Lord, sir,' said the servant, '*that* is not built yet.'

233 The cost of living

Quin being asked why he did not marry, take a house, and set up an equipage, said he always carried a wife, a dinner and a coach in his pocket, in the shape of half a guinea, half a crown and a shilling.

234 Up with the tide

Mr [John] Wilkes, seeing an Irish gentleman superbly dressed just after he had taken the benefit of the Insolvent Act [become a bankrupt], said, 'Throw an Irishman into the Thames naked at low water, and he will come up with the tide at Westminster Bridge with a laced coat and a sword on.'

Wilkes   the politician (1727–97).

235 My best razor!

The late Mr D———t, the player—a man of great humanity, as will appear by the story—having had an intrigue with his landlady's maid, she took an opportunity to go into his chamber one afternoon and cut her throat with one of his razors; of which an account being brought to him behind the scenes during the time of the play the same night, D———t, with great concern and emotion, cried out, 'Zoons! I hope it was not with my best razor!'

236 Hard at work

Quin [the actor] used to apply the following story to the then ministry [government]:
  A master of a brig calls, 'Who is there?'
  A boy answers, 'Will, sir.'
  'What are you doing?'
  'Nothing, sir.'
  'Is Tom there?'
  'Yes,' says Tom.
  'What are you doing, Tom?'
  'Helping Will, sir.'

237 Genuine British

A gentleman (an enemy to *anarchists*) lately ordered a glass of brandy in a coffee-house, adding, 'Take care there is none of your damned French stuff in it.'
  The waiter replied, 'Genuine British, sir, I assure you.'

anarchists French revolutionaries.

238 A polite hint

In the parlour of a public house in Fleet Street there is written over the chimney-piece the following notice: 'Gentlemen learning to spell are requested to use yesterday's paper.'

239 Poor dog

The favourite lapdog of a lady having bitten a piece out of a male visitor's leg, she exclaimed, 'Poor little dear creature! I hope it will not make him sick.'

240 Paid in advance

The same learned judge's [Lord Kames's] *wit* would occasionally get the better of his *parsimony*. One day, after coming out of the court at Edinburgh, he went to make water at a place where the sentinel on duty assumes a power of levying a fine for such transgressions.

'My lord,' said the soldier, 'you are fined.'
'For what?'
'For pissing at this place.'
'How much?'
'Threepence, my lord.'
'There is sixpence for you, then, sir; and remember you owe me a piss.'

Kames   see additional notes.

241 A nice corner

Mr Elwes's nephew, Colonel Timms, being on a visit to him at his seat at Marcham [Berkshire], in the night a quantity of rain fell, which, penetrating the roof of the old crazy mansion, soon wet the colonel through the bedclothes. He got up and moved the bed, but he had not lain long before he found the same inconvenience. Again he got up; and again the rain came down. At length, after pushing the bed quite round the room, he got into a corner where the ceiling was better, and slept there till morning. When he met his uncle at breakfast, he told him what had happened.

'Aye, aye!' said the old man. 'I don't mind it myself; but to those who do, that's a nice corner in the rain!'

Elwes   see additional notes.

242 White man's justice

A negro in Jamaica was tried for theft and ordered to be flogged. He begged to be heard; which being granted, he asked, 'If white man buy stolen goods, why he no be flogged too?'

'Well,' said the judge, 'so he would.'

'Dere den,' replied Mungo, 'is my massa. He buy 'tolen goods. He knew me 'tolen, and yet he buy me!'

243 War and peace

A Quaker being lately taken before a justice of peace in a country town on account of some religious scruple, the magistrate, in a voice much above its usual key, cried, 'Well, I understand thou art a Quaker!'

'I am,' replied the Friend, 'and what hast thou to say against that?'

The justice, with his wonted sagacity, and forgetting the extensive meaning of the word ALL, observed, 'I have only to say that if *all* men were Quakers, Bonaparte might come and slaughter us as soon as he pleased.'

'Nay,' answered the man of peace, 'thou'rt mistaken, friend, for if *all* men were Quakers, then would Bonaparte be one also, and if he were, I'm sure he would kill no man.'

244 What's become of Wilkes?

A quondam politician, returning a few years since from the Indies, where he had seldom seen a newspaper, asked Harvey Coombe, 'What is become of *Wilkes and Liberty* now?'

'They are both dead,' was the reply.

Wilkes and Liberty   slogan of John Wilkes and his followers in their fight for political reform. Revolution and the rise of Napoleon in France permitted a drastic suppression of reform in England. *Coombe (or Combe)*   Lord Mayor of London, 1800; a Whig.

SOURCES

The main sources are outlined here, under short titles. The source of each jest is given in the Notes beginning on page 156. (The location of a book or manuscript is stated only when it is not in the British Museum.)

BANQUET 1630   *A Banquet of Jeasts, or Change of Cheare, Being a collection of Moderne Jests, Witty Jeeres, Pleasant Taunts, Merry Tales. Never Before Imprinted*, 1630 (Bodleian; among Robert Burton's books).

When a later edition of this book was reprinted in 1889 by an anonymous editor, he attributed it to Archie Armstrong, the jester of James I and Charles I. The reprint is still listed under Armstrong's name in the British Museum library and elsewhere; but the attribution is certainly wrong. The 1889 editor could not have seen the 1633 'Second Part' containing the verses addressed to Archie which I quote in my Introduction, and he evidently was not worried by the fact that the edition he printed includes an anecdote (a thin one) *about* Archie. The jester was no author. The 1633 verses say, with some reason, 'If he can read . . .'.

A different jestbook published in 1660 did claim to be derived from Archie. This was *A Choice Banquet of Witty Jests. . . . Being an Addition to Archee's Jests, taken out of his Closet, but never publisht by him in his life time*. The compiler said many of the jests (in fact largely taken from earlier collections) 'were found in Archee's Cabinet after his death, and communicated by a kinsman to my disposal'. This was a lie, for Archie was then living in retirement in Cumberland, and survived until 1672.

SOURCES

BANQUET 1633   A Banquet, etc. The Second Part, newly published, 1633.

BANQUET 1639   A Banquet, etc. The fifth Impression, with many additions, 1639.

BANQUET 1640   A Banquet, etc. The sixth Impression, 1640 (Cambridge University Library).

CAMBRIDGE J.   Cambridge Jests, or Witty Alarums for Melancholy Spirits. By a Lover of Ha, Ha, He, 1674.

CAXTON   William Caxton's edition of Æsop's Fables, 1484 (see Introduction).

COFFEE J.   Coffee-House Jests. By the Author of the Oxford Jests, 1677. (The book reached a fifth edition, 'refined and enlarged', in 1688.)

COMPLETE J.   The Complete London Jester, or, Wit's Companion. Containing all the Fun and all the Humour, all the Learning and all the Judgment, which has lately flowed from the Two Universities, from the Two Theatres, from White's Chocolate-house, from the Bedford Coffee-house; or, from the Spouting Clubs, and Choice Spirits' Clubs in London and Westminster. Second edition, 1765.

GOTHAM   The Merry Tales of the Mad-Men of Gottam, gathered together by A.B. of Physicke Doctor (that is, Andrew Borde), 1630 (Bodleian; among Burton's books). Nineteenth-century bibliographers speak of editions printed in the 1560s.

GRATIAE   Gratiae Ludentes. Jests from the Universitie. By H.L., Oxon, 1638.

HOWLEGLAS I   First English version of the Howleglas (Eulenspiegel) stories, printed in Antwerp about 1519. Only five stories survive in the British Museum's unique copy (shelfmark C. 34. f. 41).

HOWLEGLAS II and III   Editions of Howleglas printed by William Copland 'in Tames strete at the Vintre on the thre Craned wharfe'—where Copland was established about 1560–62. (B.M. shelfmarks C.21.c.53 and C.21.c.57.) There are sure to have been earlier London editions; the wording, where comparison can be made, is very little changed from Howleglas I. The book begins, 'Here beginneth a merye Jest of a man that was called Howle-glas, and of many mervaylous thynges and Jestes that he dyd in his lyfe, in Eastland and in many other places.'

HOWLEGLAS IV   Edition printed by Copland in Lothbury, where he worked during 1562–8 (Bodleian). It fills in some gaps in the other copies.

JOLLY J.   *The Jolly Jester; or The Wit's Complete Library, by Marmaduke Momus, Esq., H.I.B.Q., President of the Imperial Society of Grinners*, 1794.

L'ESTRANGE   MS. Harl. 6395 (see introduction).

LONDON J.   *London Jests: or, A Collection of the Choicest Joques & Repartees, out of the Most Celebrated Authors Ancient and Modern, With an Addition of above One Hundred Never before Printed*, 1688.

MERRY 1526   A.C.*Mery Talys* (A Hundred Merry Tales), printed by John Rastell, 1526. The only complete copy known to survive is in the Niedersächsische Staats- und Universitätsbibliothek, Göttingen, Lower Saxony. It turned up at Lüneburg in 1767. The British Museum has an undated copy, also printed by Rastell, which was rescued from the binding of a book early in the nineteenth century and has gaps on nearly every page. Scholars have differed over which copy is the earlier. Four stories in the 1526 edition (second, seventh, ninety-first, ninety-eighth) are not in the British Museum copy. Three stories in the B.M. copy (ninety-seventh, ninety-eighth, ninety-ninth) are not in the other. (The B.M. copy was made up one short of the hundred.) It seems probable that if one were throwing out a few stories and inserting others, the rejects would have random positions, and the additions would be made at the end. That would make the 1526 edition earlier. Furthermore, I find the three stories at the end of the B.M. copy more attractive on balance than the four that it lacks. One of the three is of the hot custard (see No. 225 and notes). Another is of a man who, before going abroad, painted a lamb on his young wife's belly 'and prayed her it might remain there till he came home again'. Both of these turn up in later jestbooks; but the four unique to the 1526 copy do not. (For Rastell, see introduction.)

MERRY 1535   *Tales, and quicke answeres, very mery, and pleasant to rede.* Printed by Thomas Berthelet about 1535. Contains 114 stories, nearly all from Poggio (Huntington Library, San Marino, California).

MERRY 1567   *Mery tales, wittie questions and quicke answeres.* Printed by Henry Wykes, 1567, with twenty-six additional stories from various sources (Harvard University).

MILLER 1739   *Joe Miller's Jests*, first edition, 1739 (see introduction).

MILLER 1740   Fourth edition, 1740.

MILLER 1742   Fifth edition, 1742.

MILLER 1745   Eighth edition, 1745.

MILLER 1780   Undated, about 1780.

MIRTH   *Mirth in Abundance. Set Forth and made manifest in many Jests, upon severall occasions, full of Wit and Truth. Contrived to relieve the Melancholy, and rejoyce the Merry, to expell sorrow, and advance Jollity. All of them New and Noble, free from Rayling, Baudery, Blasphemy, or Incivility*, 1659.

OXFORD J.   *Oxford Jests*, fifth edition, 1684. A third edition, 1671, is in the Huntington Library. The compiler, Captain William Hicks, produced *Coffee-House Jests* (which uses some Oxford J. stories), as well as collections of merry verse such as *Oxford Drollery*, 1671.

PASQUIL   *Pasquils Jests, Mixed with Mother Bunches Merriments*, 1604. Many of the fifty-two stories are rewritten from Merry 1535/67. Mother Bunch was an alewife in Elizabethan farce. Later editions described her. I quote one of 1650: '. . . Now for Mother Bunch, the only dainty, well-favoured, well-proportioned, sweet-complexioned and most delightful hostess of England . . . she spent most of her time in telling of tales, and when she laughed, she was heard from Aldgate to the monuments at Westminster, and all Southwark stood in amazement. . . . She was an excellent companion, and sociable. She was very pleasant and witty, and would tell a tale, let a fart, drink her draught, scratch her arse, pay her groat, as well as any chemist of ale whatsoever. From this noble Mother Bunch proceeded all our great greasy tapsters and fat swelling alewives, whose faces are blown as big as the froth of their bottle-ale, and their complexion imitating the outside of a cook's greasy dripping-pan; and you could hardly go round about her in a summer afternoon. . . .'

PILKINGTON   *Mrs. Pilkington's Jests: Or the Cabinet of Wit and Humour*, 1759. Mrs Pilkington, a woman with a reputation for wit, had a 'pamphlet-shop' in St James's Street.

PINKETHMAN   *Pinkethman's Jests: or, Wit Refined*. Second edition, 1721.

POLLY   *Polly Peachum's Jests*, 1728 (for Pinkethman and Polly, see introduction, with Joe Miller).

SCHOOLMASTER   *The Schoolemaster or Teacher of Table Philosophie*, 1583 (first published 1576). Translation by Thomas Twine of the fifteenth-century *Mensa Philosophica*, which is derived in part from the *Saturnalia* of the fifth-century Latin writer Macrobius. The stories are from the last section of the book, 'which compriseth merry honest jests, delectable devices and pleasant purposes, to be used for delight and recreation at the board among company'. *Mensa Philosophica* contributed to early jestbooks in Germany and England (see Nos. 75, 92). Another translation appeared in 1609 with the title *The Philosophers Banquet*.

SCOGGIN   *The First and best Part of Scoggins Jests, gathered by Andrew Boord, Doctor of Physicke*, 1626. (See Appendix.)

TAYLOR   *Wit and Mirth. Chargeably Collected out of Taverns, Ordinaries, Innes, Bowling-Greenes and Allyes, Ale-houses, Tobacco-shops, Highwayes, and Water-passages. Made up, and fashioned into Clinches, Bulls, Quirkes, Yerkes, Quips, and Jerkes. Apothegmatically bundled up and garbled at the request of old John Garretts Ghost. By John Taylor, the Water-Poet*, 1630. (John Garrett was a jester.)

WITS   *Wits, Fittes and Fancies*, 1595 (Bodleian). The running title also has 'Wits, Fits' and 'Wittes, Fittes'. (See introduction.)

WITS 1614   *Wits, Fits, and Fancies. Newly Corrected and augmented, with many late, true, and wittie accidents*, 1614. The additions amount to very little.

WITS MUSEUM   *Wits Museum, or the New London Jester*. About 1780.

NOTES

1. Husbands, Wives and Wenches

1 OF A YOUNG WOMAN Caxton

This is Poggio xliii, *De adolescentula quae virum de parto priapo accusavit*. (Poggio numbers cited follow the Paris Latin-English edition of 1879.)

2 OF A FEARLESS WIDOW Caxton

Not from Poggio; apparently Caxton's own. It is followed by the last tale in the book, a moral one 'which a worshipful priest and a parson told me late'.

3 OF THE WIFE . . . IN HER BED Merry 1526

This trick is found in the *Decameron* (seventh tale, seventh day), but may have come to England by another route. It is in several other Italian collections, and there are French *fabliau* versions. On the Elizabethan stage the story became a jig (a farce performed by singers), of which a manuscript survives at the Bodleian (Rawl. poet. 185; printed by C. R. Baskervill). The jig ends:

Husband	O John, thou art my servant true!
	And my love—and my love—
	I'll change for no new.
John	A servant's duty pricked me on.
Husband	Now Jesus bless thee, gentle John!
	Oh, joy out of measure
	To have such a treasure
	Of such a servant—and love, and love. . . .

In the seventeenth century, La Fontaine used the story for his '*Cocu battu et content*'.

4 OF THE WOMAN THAT SAID HER WOOER CAME TOO LATE Merry 1526

In Bebel (II, 69). The preceding story in Merry 1526 is of a woman who weeps bitterly as she follows her fourth husband's coffin to the graveyard. To those who try to console her, she explains why she weeps: when her previous husbands died, she was 'sure always of another husband before that the corse came out of my house', but this time she is not. The moral: 'By this tale ye may see that the old proverb is true, that it is as great pity to see a woman weep as a goose to go barefoot.'

Merry 1535 has a young widow who goes on weeping inconsolably even when her father promises he will quickly find a new husband for her. At last, at table after the funeral, 'between sobbing and weeping she rowned [whispered] her father in the ear and said, "Father, where is the same young man that ye said should be mine husband?"'

The Aratoon collection of Hodja stories has a woman weeping at the bedside of her seventh husband, who is very ill. Who will take care of her when he dies? 'Your eighth husband,' says Hodja.

In China there are similar jokes, but about brides. In George Kao's collection, a bride weeps bitterly as she is being carried to the wedding in a sedan-chair. The carriers offer to take her home again. She says, 'The crying's stopped now.' Another girl, crying desperately on her wedding morning, hears the servants say they cannot find the sedan-chair poles anywhere in the house. The girl, still sobbing, says, 'Mother, tell them the poles are behind the door.'

5 OF THE WEDDED MEN Merry 1526

Wits has a parallel item: 'A politician wonted to say, "Whoso deceives me once, God forgive him; if twice, God forgive him, and God forgive me; but if thrice, still God forgive him, but ne'er forgive me."' Macrobius (II, v) quotes a maxim of Publilius Syrus: *Improbe Neptunum accusat qui iterum naufragium facit* (If you shipwreck a second time, it is not wise to blame Neptune).

6 OF THE YEOMAN OF GUARD Merry 1526

Wits tells the same story of a Croydon collier and 'a lubberly gallant'. The collier 'stood to his tacklings at the whip's end, and behaved himself so valiantly therewith that the cuckold's pottage was soon cooled'.

7 OF THE WIFE THAT BADE HER HUSBAND Merry 1526

This was put into verse later on. In MS. Sloane 1489 (about 1620) it reads:

> 'Cis, by this candle, in my dream methought
> One told me of thy body thou wert nought.'
> 'Good husband, he that told you lied,' she said,
> And swearing, laid her hand upon the bread.
> 'Then eat the bread,' quoth he, 'that I may deem
> Fancy was false which true to me did seem.'
> 'Nay, dear,' quoth she. 'The matter right to handle,
> Sith you sware first, you first must eat the candle.'

The lines were printed in *Wits Interpreter*, a miscellany of 1655.

NOTES

8 OF THE MAN THAT WOULD HAVE THE POT STAND Merry 1526

9 OF THE HUSBANDMAN Merry 1526

Wits has this: A cuckold-innocent being informed that such a one was abed with his wife, he answered, 'Knowing him as I do to be a right honest man, I dare adventure my wife abed with him.'

10 OF THE HUSBAND THAT CRIED 'BLEH' Merry 1526

11 OF THE HUSBAND THAT SAID HIS WIFE AND HE AGREED Merry 1526

Sir Thomas More, who married a widow, may have provided this one. William Camden tells of the Mores in his *Remains* (1605 edition, page 223):

> One day when she came from shrift [confession], she said merrily unto him, 'Be merry, Sir Thomas, for this day was I well shriven, I thank God, and purpose now therefore to leave off all my old shrewdness [shrewishness].' 'Yea,' quoth he, 'and to begin afresh.'

12 OF THE BURNING OF OLD JOHN Merry 1526

I have seen no sign of this story in southern Europe, but there is an Icelandic version (MS Add. 11153, f.225).

It recurs in jestbooks well into the eighteenth century. A version in *England's Jests*, 1693, is worth quoting in part:

> ... and casting her hand over her dear statue (as she thought), she felt a more agreeable warmth than usual; nay, fancied 'twas alive and had motion. She was not frighted at it (which is not a little wonderful), but by degrees crept closer and closer to her side-mate, till at length they were locked in mutual embraces; by which she with pleasure found that it was not her wooden bedfellow.
>
> In the morning her maid called at the chamber-door as she used to do, 'Madam, what will you please to have for dinner today?'
>
> She replied, 'Roast the goose, and the two pheasants that were brought in yesterday. Boil a leg of mutton and cauliflowers, and get a good dish of tarts and custards, and a dish of good dried fruit.'
>
> 'Madam,' says the maid, 'I think we have hardly billets enough for a quick fire.'
>
> 'You may burn Old Simon,' says she, 'burn Old Simon.'

13 OF HIM THAT WAS CALLED CUCKOLD Merry 1535

A similar reversal is in Gibb's *History of the Forty Vezirs*. A queen hastily hides her lover in a chest. The king suspiciously demands to be told what is in the chest. She says, 'It is my lover.' He is furious. She says, 'Would I say he is in the chest? I did it to test you to see if you trusted me.' He asks to be forgiven.

14 OF THE JEALOUS MAN Merry 1535

Poggio cxxxiii: the finger was *in uxoris cunno*. Poggio tells it of Francesco Filelfo (died 1481), a Florentine scholar with whom he carried on a scurrilously insulting war of words. Rabelais adopts the story and has Friar John recommend this charm against cuckoldry to Pantagruel (Book III, chap. 28). La Fontaine puts the story into verse—'L'Anneau d'Hans Carvel'—and so does Matthew Prior.

15 OF THE YOUNG MAN OF BRUGES Merry 1535

Poggio clvii. His young man is a Florentine. The English version drops out a piece of Italian naughtiness. After the girl has been told the marriage is off, the man comes back and finds the girl, alone, in tears. She says she wants to obey her mother. He tells the girl that the power to dissolve the engagement lies in herself—'*Antea,*' ait, '*inferiores partes egisti; nunc superior evadas oportet, ut per contrarium actum dissolutio matrimonii fiat.*' *Consensit illa, et matrimonium dissolvit.* (Before she played an inferior role with him; now she will perform in the contrary manner. . . .)

The story goes on. At the young man's wedding to someone else, the girl is present; their eyes meet; and with the memory of what happened they cannot help smiling—*praeteritorum memoria, invicem subridere coepissent.* The bride notices; that is how the old affair comes up. (And see No. 44.)

16 OF THE WIDOW Merry 1535

Poggio ccix. In Pasquil, this becomes 'Of the rich widow of Abingdon.' Sir Roger L'Estrange includes the story among twenty-two of Poggio at the end of his *Fables of Aesop*, 1692. The change of tone after five generations is amusing. The widow says, 'For the coarse, common business of matrimony—as I am an honest woman, the very thought on't turns my stomach.' The story ends: 'For turning your stomach—my life for yours, madam, he's not in a condition to give you any qualms that way.' 'Away, ye fool you!' says she, 'I hate the infirmity, though I love the virtue.'

L'Estrange censors the point about matrimonial reconciliation—what Poggio calls the Peacemaker (*Pacialis*). L'Estrange's moral is: Women are all of a make, and in some things, most of them in a mind. One woman feels another woman's pulse in her own veins; and there is *no halting before cripples.*

It will be thought typically French that *La Gibecière de Mome*, a jestbook published in Paris in 1644, makes the most of the widow's excuse by adding: '*Après qu'elle en eût trouvé un à sa fantaisie, jugez si elle ne le querella pas souvent.*'

17 OF HIM THAT FEIGNED HIMSELF DEAD Merry 1535

Poggio cxvi; he says the husband was 'a gardener I knew in Montevarchio'. Pasquil's version begins, 'In Kingston dwelt one Rawlins, newly married . . .'. (See No. 30.)

NOTES

18 OF THE HUSBAND THAT LOST HIS WAGER Gotham

19 OF THE TWELFTH FATHER *The Garden of Pleasure* . . . Done out of Italian into English by James Sanforde, Gent., 1573

The book is a translation of the *Detti et Fatti Piacevoli et Gravi* of Lodovico Guicciardini (1523–89).

20 A CHIDING WIFE Wits

21 A WIFE WARNED Wits

22 OF YIELDING WOMEN Wits

From Macrobius (II, v); the woman says '*Bestiae enim sunt.*' The same book gives a witticism of Augustus's daughter Julia. When her friends, knowing how wantonly she lived, marvelled that all her sons looked like her husband Agrippa, she said, '*Numquam enim nisi navi plena tollo vectorem*' (I take no passengers aboard unless the hold is full).

23 A KIND WIFE Wits

A similar kind wife is in the twentieth story of Timoneda's *El Sobremesa*. A man and wife had lived like cat and dog (*como perro y gato*). Sentenced to be hanged, the husband asks to be allowed a last word with the wife. She arrives as he is being led to the gallows. He stops to talk. She says, '*Andando y hablando; no perdamos tiempo*' (Walk and talk; let's not waste time).

There are more kind wives in Taylor. One who has come to see her husband hanged with some other men makes a special request to the sheriff. 'It is not his life that I ask'—but she has a long journey home and her mare is old and stiff—'therefore I would entreat you to let my husband be hanged first.' Another wife follows her husband when he goes to a river to drown himself. She says, 'cast not yourself into this shallow place here, for it will grieve my heart to see how long you will be a-dying.'

24 HOME AND WEED Wits

25 HOW TARLTON WAS DECEIVED *Tarltons Jests: Drawn into these three parts: His Court-witty Jests. His sound City Jests. His Country pretty Jests. Full of delight, Wit, and honest Mirth*, 1638

Richard Tarlton, comedian, died in 1588. A book of jests in his name was first published in the 1590s, for a 'second part' was entered n the Stationers' Register on 4 August 1600 (the same day as *England's Helicon*, the poetry miscellany). Most of the stories in *Tarltons Jests* are borrowed; and those that do seem to originate with him depend more on his merry memory than on intrinsic wit. He was a clown who could make almost anything sound funny. Here is one of his less faded quips:

> A gentlewoman, merrily disposed, being crossed by Tarlton and half-angry, said, 'Sirrah, a little thing would make me requite you with a cuff.' 'With a cuff, lady?' says Tarlton. 'So would you spell my sorrow forware; but spell my sorrow backward, then cuff me and spare not.'

There are some verses about Tarlton's wife in the jestbook. They run slightly better in MS. Sloane 1489:

> 'Now woe worth thee, Tarlton, that e'er thou wert born!
> Thy wife doth play the harlot, and thou must wear the horn.'
> 'Now what care I for that, sir? For I am ne'er the worse:
> She keeps me like a gentleman with money in my purse.'

26 OF ONE THAT BELIEVED HIS WIFE Pasquil

Rewritten, like most of the Pasquil stories, from Merry 1535 (or some later edition of that book). I give the Pasquil version partly because it shows that 'no better than she should be' was current in 1604.

Merry 1535 has a moral: 'This was well and wisely done; for one ought not to give light credence to those things wherein resteth perpetual grief of mind.'

27 A TALE OF A MERRY CHRISTMAS CAROL Pasquil

The Pasquil author, or printer, seems to have been a careless fellow. In the phrase about the cuckoo time, 'though' would make better sense than 'now'. (A cuckold was called 'a summer's bird'. Wives had more opportunity in fine weather.) 'A dreaming companion' should probably be 'daring'. At the end, 'half' ought to be 'twice'.

28 THE NINTH GULL Pasquil

29 THE TENTH GULL Pasquil

This story takes many forms. In *Banquet* 1640, a lover, surprised by the husband's unexpected return, runs to hide in the pigsty. The pigs, awakened, 'began to grunt and make a great noise'; the husband 'began to wonder' and went and asked who was there.

> The fellow answered nothing, but grunted like one of the hogs. But the other more earnestly clamoured, 'Who is there? And what art thou?' At last the fellow, forgetting himself through fear, answered, 'I am one of thy hogs.'

In China, the lover is hastily thrust into a rice sack. The husband is suspicious and asks the wife 'What is in that sack?' The wife is tongue-tied with fear; the lover calls out, 'Only rice!'

An old American vaudeville joke has an inept chicken thief rousing up the whole henhouse. The farmer shouts, 'Who's there?' The thief: 'Ain't nobody here but us chickens.'

30 A LOVING SCOLD Taylor

31 THE PUZZLED WIFE Taylor

An enduring joke. In *The Covent Garden Magazine*, vol. 2, 1773, it appears in verse:

> A husband, a little suspicious one day,
> Addressed himself thus to his wife:
> 'Every man in this court is a cuckold, they say,
> Except one.' 'Who is that, my dear life?'

32 A WIFE'S WARNING Taylor

In Tabourot's *Bigarrures*; the wife says, '*Savez-vous bien nager, mon ami?*' MS Sloane 1489 has, at a date a little earlier than Taylor:

> One wished all cuckolds in the seas.
> Then answered him
> His fair young wife, 'Sir, for your ease,
> Learn first to swim.'

33 TWO OLD WIDOWS Banquet 1630

Also in Wits, but this version is neater.

34 OF A PRETENDED RAPE Banquet 1633

Wenches' ready excuses make a great many jokes; see Nos. 35, 38, 45. In Merry 1567 (from Johannes Pauli's jestbook *Schimpf und Ernst*, 1519) is a story of a nun found to be with child. She said she was forced.

> Then said the abbess, 'Thou mightest have been held excused if thou haddest cried.' The nun said, 'So would I have done, had it not been in our dortour [dormitory], where to cry is contrary to our religion.'

> In *Les Récréations françoises*, 1681, a girl accusing a youth of rape tells the court he trapped her against a wall. The judge, sceptical, points out that she is two feet taller than the youth. She says, '*Mais je me baissais un peu.*'

35 A SILLY YOUNG GENTLEWOMAN Gratiae

36 A WENCH'S HONESTY Gratiae

Dictionaries of quotations attribute this joke to Captain Frederick Marryat (*Midshipman Easy*, 1836, chapter 3: 'If you please, ma'am, it was a very little one.') Bar-Hebraeus has the germ of the joke in the thirteenth century. A noodle's neighbour says, 'I see your wife is with child.' He replies, 'Slightly—not very much.' And see the maid's reply in No. 45.

37 OF A COUNTRY FELLOW Banquet 1639

38 A WENCH'S EXCUSE L'Estrange
Sir Henry Neville: perhaps of Billingbear, Berkshire, who died 1629.

39 A LOOSE FIT L'Estrange

40 JUSTICE EVERY DAY L'Estrange
The capitalization of Done her Wrong is L'Estrange's. Clearly it was already a current phrase.

41 AN UNSUSPECTED HAND Henry Peacham, *The Art of Living in London* 1642
In *La Gibecière de Mome*, 1644, there is a wife who showed herself to be even less resistant to strangers. A husband arrives home one night after a three-month absence, eager to embrace his wife—

> Sa femme lui ayant ouvert la porte, il n'eut la patience d'entrer plus avant, mais il l'accommode dans l'allée sans autre figure de procès. Ayant fait, et sa femme le regardant au visage, connaissant que c'était son mari, lui va dire en riant, 'Ma foi, si j'eusse pensé que c'eût été vous, je vous assure que vous eussiez attendu jusqu'à ce soir.' (. . . when she saw it was her husband, she told him with a laugh, 'By heaven, if I had thought it was you, I assure you that you'd have waited till tonight.')

42 THE TOBACCO-TAKERS MS Sloane 1925
Opponents of tobacco said it affected one's virility. For a poem on the subject, see No. 229 in my *Love and Drollery*.

43 LEARNING THE TRUTH Oxford J.
MS. Sloane 384, of about the same date, has a variant. A man and his wife are passing by some gipsies:

> 'You black devil,' said he to one of them. 'Can you tell me my fortune?' 'Yes, that I can,' said she. 'It is not long since your wife made you a cuckold.' His wife, hearing her to say so, 'I think,' said she, speaking drawlingly, 'that these same gipsies do know everything.'

44 THE EXPERIENCED BRIDE Oxford J.
Earlier version in *Wits*; the bride says, 'Faith, I thought as much—but such a one taught me more wit than so, seven years ago.'

Taylor tells of a lusty miller who makes a bargain with each girl he enjoys that she shall give him a cake on his wedding day—'and those aforesaid free-hearted wenches sent each one their cakes, to the number of ninety-nine.' His bride wonders; he explains; she says, 'If I had been so wise in bargaining as you have been in your time, the young men of my acquaintance would have sent me a hundred cheeses to eat with your cakes.'

Timoneda's *Buen Aviso* (II, 13) has a husband who, in a merry mood after making love to his wife, pays her. She exclaims, 'What a lot my father's servants owe me!'

In *Apollo's Feast*, 1703, a bride has a just retort. A 'well-experienced fellow' thinks his bride is a maid—

> But finding so much facility in the first charge, he began to be in great passion against his bride, and cried out, 'You damned whore, you are no maid!' To whom she as confidently replied, 'A pox on you for a whoremaster rogue! Who made you so skilful?'

45 THE SILENT MAID Oxford J.

46 THE LOST FIDDLE Oxford J.

47 A WILLING SERVANT Cambridge J.

48 THE BUSY HUSBAND Cambridge J.

Perhaps it was this scholar who said, when his wife shouted that the house was on fire, 'You know I never trouble myself with household matters.'

49 JOHN AND WILL London J.

50 DEAD ENOUGH *Delight and Pastime: or, Pleasant Diversion for Both Sexes . . . free from Obscene and Prophane Expressions, too frequent in other works of this Kind.* By G. M. 1697

51 DAY OF PLEASURE Pinkethman

Miller 1742 contains an epitaph these husbands might have written:

> Here lies my poor wife without bed or blanket,
> But dead as a doornail, God be thankèd.

52 EARLY TO RISE Pinkethman

53 A SMART MESSAGE Pinkethman

54 AN AMOROUS FELLOW Pinkethman

NOTES

55 A WHORE OUTWITTED Pinkethman

This is from the East (it is in Gladwin's *Persian Moonshee*) by way of de Vitry and de Bourbon. Cervantes used it in *Don Quixote*.

56 A STRONG CONSTITUTION Polly

This story provides a good example of how the Joe Miller compiler worked when he troubled, as he occasionally did, to camouflage his thefts. Miller 1739 reads: 'Poor Joe Miller happening one day to be caught by some of his friends in a familiar posture with a cook-wench almost as ugly as Kate Cl—ve [see below, No. 59], was very much rallied by them for the oddness of his fancy....' It ends, in case the point were missed, 'beauty or brandy to whet my appetite'.

57 THE EMBARRASSING SIGN Miller 1739

One of the few really naughty Miller jokes. It was soon dropped.

58 TAKING THE WATERS Miller 1745

59 A KNOWING AUDIENCE Miller 1745

Kate or Kitty Clive (1711–85), who played Lucy in *The Beggar's Opera*, was noted for her blunt speech and unblemished character. The story, probably genuine, must date from 1742, when Peg Woffington had a great success in a Drury Lane revival of *The Constant Couple*. Later jestbooks give the riposte to the actor James Quin.

60 IF THIS SHOULD COME OUT Miller 1745

The awkward phenomenon touched on here, known medically as vaginismus, is almost as rare in jokes as in life; but in the franker fourteenth century, when La Tour Landry wrote a book of moral tales 'for my daughters to learn to read, and understand how they ought to govern themself and to keep from evil', he included two stories about lecherous priests who were victims of vaginismus— and in church. The book had a long popularity in France and England.

61 A DISCONSOLATE HOUSE Complete J.

62 THE EXPENSIVE WIFE Wits Museum

An almost literal translation of Poggio cxxviii, with the insertion of the sentence 'When I had a girl . . . above a guinea.' I have not seen it in earlier English collections. It is in *Le Courrier Facétieux*, Lyons, 1668 (licensed 1647); the husband complains, '*qu'il ne lui faisait fois qu'il ne lui coûtât plus d'un écu,*' and the wife retorts, '*Faites-le si souvent qu'il ne vous revienne pas à un liard.*' An *écu* was three French pounds; a *liard* a quarter of a sou.

63 NOT RUINED YET *The Town and Country Joker*, about 1800 (Douce Collection, Bodleian).

64 A LADY'S MEMORY *Memoirs of Samuel Foote, Esq.*, by William Cooke, 1805

Samuel Foote (died 1777), comic actor, playwright and wit, was famous in his day. Several collections allegedly containing his jests were rushed out when he died, including one called *Wit for the Ton!* Most of the jokes, as usual, are stolen.

2. Friars, Priests and Nuns

65 OF THE GREY FRIAR Merry 1526

Coffee J. picks this up and expands it a little:

... 'In a soft bed,' says he.
'How long?' says the friar.
'Why, all night long,' says he, 'and each of us had brought in the morning an excellent caudle wherein was ambergris.'
'By Saint Francis,' says the friar, 'thou wast well at ease!'

Priests were topical again in the Restoration period.

66 OF THE FRIAR THAT SAID OUR LORD FED FIVE THOUSAND Merry 1526

See Nos. 74, 79.

67 OF THE PRIEST THAT SAID OUR LADY Merry 1526

This Botley may have been the hamlet in Warwickshire, as Merry 1526 has a number of stories from that region.

68 OF THE TWO NUNS Merry 1526

69 OF THE FRANKLIN'S SON Merry 1526

A widespread story. It is in the French scholar Henri Estienne's reformist book with a harmless-seeming title, *L'Introduction au traité de la conformité des merveilles anciennes avec les modernes*, 1560. In the English translation, *A World of Wonders*, 1607, it is in a chapter entitled 'Of the gross and blockish ignorance of the Popish clergy'. The question that stumps the would-be priest is 'Who was father to the four sons of Aymond?'

His father told him that he was a very ass.... 'See, I pray thee,' quoth he, 'yonder is great John the smith, who hath four sons. If a man should ask thee who is their father, would thou not say that it were great John the smith?' 'Yes,' quoth he, 'now I understand it well. . . .'

In Scoggin there is yet another variation: 'How the scholar said Tom Miller of Osney was Jacob's father.'

70 OF THE PRIEST THAT WOULD SAY TWO GOSPELS Merry 1526

71 OF THE COURTIER Merry 1526

73 OF THE PARSON Merry 1526

73 OF HIM THAT PREACHED Merry 1526

A grim joke on these lines is credited to Braxfield, a Scottish hanging judge (1722–99), in Lord Cockburn's *Memorials of his Time*, 1856, page 117. Joseph Gerrald, on trial before Braxfield in 1794 for sedition, as a member of a group with revolutionary ideas, said all great men were reformers, 'even our Saviour himself'. 'Muckle he made o' that,' chuckled Braxfield in an under voice, 'he was hanget.'

(Gerrald was transported to Australia, and died soon after arriving there.)

74 OF THE CURATE Merry 1535

75 OF HIM THAT HAD HIS GOOSE STOLE Merry 1535

In *Mensa Philosophica*; originally from the East. *The Persian Moonshee* has an emir who undertakes to discover who is guilty of stealing a large quantity of cotton. He invites all the men of the city to a feast—

> and looking every man in the face, said, 'What ill-born, impudent blockheads these men are, who, having stolen the cotton, are come to my feast with it sticking in their beards!' Some persons instantly put their hands to their beards. . . .

The Arabs have a similar story about Solomon catching an egg thief by saying one man has feathers in his hair.

76 A PENITENT WIFE Schoolmaster

A later translation of *Mensa Philosophica—The Philosophers Banquet*, 1609— changes the ending:

> . . . her husband . . . said, 'Good sir, she is very tender, let me receive it for her.' When the wife, being prostrate there, said, 'I will suffer for myself. Strike hard, for I am a grievous sinner.'

Amusing, but there is a loss of verisimilitude.

NOTES

77 THE PENITENT NUNS Schoolmaster

78 A GOOD MARKET Schoolmaster

79 THE HUNGRY NOVICES Schoolmaster

80 BROTHERS IN CHRIST Wits

In the Spanish original, a Portuguese monk is preaching. He says, 'Moors are our neighbours, Jews are our neighbours, and even Castilians. . . .'

81 LEAVE THAT TO GOD L'Estrange

It adds to the comicality of this chaplain's scruple if one remembers that he was being most permissive in allowing Lord Brooke to play bowls, a game condemned by Puritans not only as a time waster but also because it was the occasion of heavy betting, and of other upper-class dissipations in the houses of pleasure around the bowling-greens.

82 THE SLEEPING LORD L'Estrange

83 NEVER AGAIN L'Estrange

84 LADIES IN BREECHES L'Estrange

Women still wore nothing beneath their skirts (see also No. 174). L'Estrange does not tell us whether these bold Suffolk ladies also rode astride—as women had in the Middle Ages, until the side-saddle style began to come in towards the end of the fourteenth century (see J. J. Jusserand, *English Wayfaring Life in the Middle Ages*, 1950, page 50). In the late Victorian and Edwardian periods, ladies rode side-saddle in breeches *with skirts over them*, which might have placated Mr Zephory. It was only after the 1914–18 war that riding astride began to be socially acceptable.

Sir Thomas Lewknor was a member of a powerful East Anglian family (note that he protects a silenced minister). L'Estrange's wife Ann was the daughter of another Lewknor, Sir Edward, of Denham, Suffolk. Rob Heigham was of an old family of Lavenham.

85 A FOOLISH QUESTION Oxford J.

This is straight out of Bebel.

86 OF A FACTIOUS MINISTER MS Sloane 1757

NOTES

87 OF A CURATE MS Sloane 1757

88 A CONTRARY WIND Jolly J.

3. From Marcolf to Scoggin

89 THE DIALOGUE OF SOLOMON *The dyalogus or communyng betwyxt Salomon and Marcolphus*, printed by Gerard Leeu, Antwerp, about 1492 (unique copy in Bodleian)

90 HOW MARCOLF WAS BANISHED as above

The man who cannot find a tree to suit him is in de Vitry (lxii in Crane's edition). The brief story ends: . . . '*Placet tibi arbor ista?*' *Ait ille:* '*Non placet mihi, in ista nolo suspendi.*' *Et cum per omnes transisset nunquam invenire potuit quam acceptoret.*

Tenali Rama, when sentenced to death (for the fourth time) is told by his king to choose how he shall die. 'I choose death by old age,' he says. The king laughs, and pardons him. Another time, Tenali is ordered not to show his face at the court again. He comes with a water-pot over his head.

91 HOW THE PARSON SOLD HIS WINE *The storie of the parson of Kalenborowe*, printed by Jan van Doesborch, Antwerp, about 1520 (unique copy in Bodleian)

Perhaps people were not excessively gullible to be taken in by mockers who announced they were going to fly. They were constantly faced with representations of winged angels. A woodcut with the Kalenborow story shows his wings exactly like an angel's. To sceptical minds, the message could be, 'Angels are a mockery too.'

Poggio has a story of a comedian who mocks the people of Milan with a promise to fly from their cathedral. In the end he *culum populo ostentavit* (bared his arse to the people). Poggio uses the story as a parable of the great promises made by Gregory XII (1406–15) to heal the papal schism, and his failure to perform.

Eulenspiegel tells the people of Magdeburg he will fly from their councilhouse. A great crowd assembles in the marketplace. 'He laughed and said to the people, "I thought there had been no more fools but myself, but I see well that here is a whole town full." ' The people go, 'some blaming him, and some laughing, saying, "He is a shrewd fool, for he telleth us the truth." ' He has held up his mirror to the owls.

See Scoggin, No. 102.

92 HOW HOWLEGLAS DECEIVED A WINEDRAWER Howleglas I

The trick with the two wine-pots appears in 'Les Repues franches' (free meals), the fifteenth-century French verse tales about the tricks used by Villon and his friends to get food and drink. See *Oeuvres de Maistre François Villon*, ed. J. H. R. Prompsault, Paris, 1832, page 382.

The hanging story appears to be derived from *Mensa Philosophica*; in its Schoolmaster version, the ending goes like this:

'When I am hanged, I beseech you to come unto me three days after, with a fasting stomach every morning, and kiss my bare tail with your mouth.'

'Now the devil hang thee and kiss thy tail!' quod the lord, and went away in a rage; and so he escaped.

Thirty years before that version, the story is used in Merry 1535. It is told of 'a merry fellow in High Almain (Germany)', which suggests an Eulenspiegel influence. The merry fellow says, 'I desire you, my lord, that after I am hanged, to come three mornings, fresh and fasting. . . .'

93 HOW HOWLEGLAS LAY SICK Howleglas II, III

Eulenspiegel spent his unrepentant dying days in 'an hospital of the Holy Ghost' at Mölln, about twenty miles east of Hamburg. A gravestone to his memory with the date 1350 was erected there—but apparently not until more than a century later.

One touch of his agnostic harshness is missing in the English version. In the Lower Saxon, when the beguine urges him to die well, he says, '. . . *das geschieht nit, das ich süss sterb, wan der tod ist bitter*' (That I die sweetly—that won't be, when death is bitter).

His regret about the knife—'that I had not shitten on the end of it'—is truer to the ordure-loving Eulenspiegel in the English, oddly enough, than in the original, where he regrets instead that he did not strike the man with the knife in the throat.

In the original his remedy for ageing women is not wedging but sewing up—'*ir ersz zŭ flicken*'—because '*die seint niemans nutz me uf Erden*' (they are no more use to anyone on earth).

94 HOW HOWLEGLAS DECEIVED HIS GHOSTLY FATHER Howleglas II, III, IV

The reformist message here is very strong. Dying men with bad consciences were a good source of money. Rich men would endow chapels devoted to the perpetual singing of masses for their salvation.

The dying Eulenspiegel prepared a heavily laden chest to be opened for the people of Mölln after his death. It was full of stones. Even at his burial he was rebellious: his coffin fell on end into his grave. They let him have his way, and dug him in bolt upright.

95 HOW JACK MADE HIS MASTER PAY Scoggin

At the time of this incident Scoggin was living 'at St Barthelmewes by Oxford'—that is, just beyond the village of Cowley.

96 HOW SCOGGIN SOLD POWDER TO KILL FLEAS Scoggin

In a book that probably dates from before 1600, *A Pleasant History of the Life and Death of Will Summers* (Bodleian; edition of 1676), the flea-powder trick is perpetrated by Summers. His victims are dimmer:

> 'Ay, but,' said Will Summers, 'you should have had a little stick in one hand, and with the other hand have caught them by the nape of the neck, and so have thrust it down their throats, and that will so torment them that they will never trouble you again.' So they bought more of the same powder, and went home, and thanked him heartily, without any suspicion of his knavery and deceit therein.

The joke is found in China. H. A. Giles has a story of a pedlar with a notice saying, 'First-class flea medicine sold here.' When asked for directions, he says, 'You hold the flea tight and wash out its mouth with the medicine. This will kill the flea at once.'

97 HOW SCOGGIN TOLD THOSE THAT MOCKED HIM Scoggin

A variation on a *Merry* 1526 story; see No. 163. The courtiers call Scoggin 'Tom' because that was a traditional name for a fool.

98 HOW SCOGGIN GREASED A FAT SOW Scoggin

In *Mensa Philosophica*, the same social message is directed against the Church. The Schoolmaster version reads:

> A certain merry fellow, being sick, was admonished by the priest to make his will. 'Marry, gladly,' quoth he. 'And I have none other goods but only two horses, which I bequeath to the kings and princes of the earth.' But the priest demanded why he would not rather give them unto the poor. He answered, 'You preach that we should imitate God, and He hath given all the riches of the earth unto them, and not unto the poor, and therefore I would fain do as like unto Him as I could.'

99 HOW SCOGGIN DESIRED THE KING Scoggin

De Bourbon tells of a courier who has given the king long service. When asked how he wishes to be rewarded, he obtains permission to whisper a *Pater Noster* in the king's ear when he is giving audience. The result is the same. But the story goes even further back. In a version current in the Kashmir in the 11th century (see Penzer, *Ocean of Story*, V, 186–8) a rogue persuades a king to take him aside every day for a few private words. The rogue pays the king 500 dinars a day, and amasses a fortune.

NOTES

100 HOW SCOGGIN DESIRED OF THE QUEEN Scoggin

Borrowed from *Le buffonerie del Gonnella*—the tales about, or attached to, Pietro Gonnella, a mid-fourteenth-century Florentine jester who served the court in Ferrara. It is the Duchess of Ferrara whom he tempts to sell herself.

The Scoggin book borrows another Gonnella story: Of how the duchess, to punish him, orders her ladies-in-waiting to form two lines, each lady holding a napkin with a stone in it, to beat him as he runs the gauntlet. She warns them not to let Gonnella talk them out of beating him. He begs one favour—that the first lady to strike him shall be the one he has kissed most often and who is the greatest whore among them. Or, as Scoggin puts it: 'I come, and the strongest whore of you all strike the first stroke.' The ladies fall into a great contention. In the Gonnella version, he seizes the chance to flee. Scoggin is coolly impudent. He says to the queen, 'Madam, and it like Your Grace, will you command me any more service?'

The trick echoes one used by the thirteenth-century priest Pfaff Amis. He displays a fabricated relic and calls for contributions from the congregation; but those who have not lived virtuous lives must not give. All press forward to give.

Scoggin plays another trick on the queen (again taken from Gonnella). He persuades the queen to let his wife have an audience of her. He tells the queen that his wife is deaf; he tells his wife the queen is deaf; the two women have a shouting-match. For this and other mad pranks, Scoggin is banished from England. 'I charge thee upon pain of thy death,' says the king, 'to go out of my realm and to tread upon none of my ground here in England.'

101 HOW SCOGGIN IN THE FRENCH KING'S COURT Scoggin

102 HOW SCOGGIN TOLD THE FRENCHMEN Scoggin

See No. 91.

103 HOW THE FRENCH KING HAD SCOGGIN INTO HIS HOUSE OF OFFICE Scoggin

Before Scoggin got himself banished from France, he carried out a number of Eulenspiegel-type deceptions on a poulterer, a tapster, a shoemaker and so forth.

'And he came into England again.' He had a trick for that, too. 'He filled his shoes full of French earth' and when the king saw him, he showed that he was obeying the king's order to tread upon none of his ground. (Eulenspiegel had a more extreme ruse when caught on the domain of a lord who had banished him with similar words. He killed his horse, disembowelled it, and stood in the horse's carcase at the roadside as the lord passed.) Scoggin's trick was an ancient one. In a manuscript of about 1300, Harl. 2851, there is a story about a man who claims his neighbour's land. A jury is brought to the scene to decide. The man stands in his neighbour's land with some of his own soil in his shoes, and swears he is on his own ground.

Scoggin's French earth did not restore him to the English court. The king said, 'I charge thee never to look me more in the face,' and Scoggin retreated to Cambridge and 'through one Master Everid that was his friend, he got him a chamber in Jesus College'.

104 HOW SCOGGIN CAME TO THE COURT Scoggin

See No. 90. Borde's humorous treatment more than justifies the repetition.

In the last paragraph, 'to our king' is the reading in a Scoggin fragment surviving from the 16th century; preferable to 'your king' in the 1626 version.

SCOGGIN'S END

Although Scoggin is something of an Eulenspiegel, he is not so malicious, violent and anarchic. He has bourgeois values. (When he is in favour at court, he gets what he can out of it, as many historical jesters did. The king gives him a house in Cheapside. Scoggin gets a promise that it is his to do what he will with, and then blackmails a good sum of money out of the house's tenant and the next-door neighbours by threatening to burn it down.)

After escaping hanging, Scoggin makes a shift to live away from court for a time; but that is where his heart is. One day, when the king and queen are in progress through the country, he finds out their route, and feigns to be lying dead beside the road. The king and queen stop. Scoggin's servant says, as instructed, that before Scoggin died he prayed that they should forgive him all his wickedness.

'Now,' said the king and queen, 'God forgive him, and we do.'

Scoggin start up, and said, 'I do thank both Your Graces, and hereafter I will no more displease you. For I see it is more harder to keep a friend than to get one.'

It is a line good kings find hard to resist. He is forgiven.

Dying later in earnest, Scoggin is shriven and receives the sacrament devoutly. He is no blasphemer to the end, like Eulenspiegel, and his last touch of merriment is genial, not satirical:

'Good Lord, I do thank thee for all thy benefits. But masters, I tell you all that stand about me, if I might live to eat a Christmas pie, I care not then if I die by-and-by after: for Christmas pies be good meat.'

His story ends:

'I pray you that I may be buried at the east side of Westminster, under one of the spouts of the leads, for I have ever loved good drink all the days of my life.' And there was he buried: whereas now the most ancient and sapient King Henry the Seventh did build the most sumptuous chapel in the world. . . .

If that is true, he was buried where several kings now lie.

4. Quips, Retorts, Tricks and Blunders

105 DEMANDS JOYOUS *The Demaundes Joyous*, 'enprynted at London in Flete strete at the sygne of the sonn (sun) by me Wynkyn de Worde. In the yere of our lorde a M.CCCCC. and xi' (unique copy, Cambridge University Library).

I give a selection from the fifty-three riddles in this six-page booklet. It is partly a translation from the French. Twenty-seven of the fifty-three are in *Demandes joyeuses en manière de quolibets*, an undated early sixteenth-century collection of eighty-seven *demandes*, of which there is a copy in the British Museum.

The French reply about hens on church steeples is not so funny: *Parce que si la geline [hen] pondait, les oeufs se casseraient*. (The English version reminds one of a clever insight of Hodja Nasreddin: 'Praise Allah for not creating camels with wings, for if he had, they would alight on your houses and your roofs would collapse.')

Instead of the horse/mare riddle, the French has: *Qu'est-ce que mieux ressemble à un chat en une fenêtre? —C'est une chatte.*

Instead of the goose/gander riddle, the French has a human one: *En quel temps est une femme plus douce? —Quand elle laisse l'homme monter sur elle.*

A more indelicate riddle missing from the English version is: *Qu'est-ce que plus on quiert [seeks] et moins on le trouve? —C'est le fond d'un con.*

One that looks pointless in the English (Who was he that let the first fart at Rome? —That was the arse.) is made clear in the French: *Qui fit le premier pet à Rome? —Le cul du pape.*

The riddle about the cleanliest occupation is not in the French. It seems to have come straight from Italy, for it is in the collection of stories ascribed to the Florentine priest and merchant Arlotto Mainardi (Piovano Arlotto), 1395–1484. Arlotto travelled to England as well as Flanders in the wool trade, and is on record as having amused Edward IV. In the Arlotto story, he and his friends are discussing who is the cleanest craftsman. He says their various reasonable suggestions are all wrong: the cleanest are *li fornacai* (workers in brick-and-tile kilns) *perchè non vanno mai a cacare che non si lavi no prima le mani* (because they never go to shit without first washing their hands).

For the jester Will Sommers' use of this riddle, see No. 177.

106 PENNING THE CUCKOO Gotham

Bar-Hebraeus, in his chapter on fools, has, 'Another fool whose hawk had escaped asked the governor to shut the gates of the city until he had caught him.'

Fool-stories like this were widespread in medieval times, and seem to have been localized at Gotham in Nottinghamshire only in the sixteenth century. Most of them come from the Arab world. For example:

In Gotham, twelve men go fishing, and before they start home again they count themselves to see that no one has been drowned, 'and every man did tell eleven, and the twelfth man did never tell himself'. A passing courtier counts all twelve by giving each man a thump, and they give him thanks 'that you have found out our neighbour'. Hodja (and also one of Bar-Hebraeus's fools) mounts one of a string of donkeys, counts the rest and is sure he has lost one.

Both Hodja and a fool of Gotham feel sorry for a donkey (or horse) they are riding when it is already heavy-laden, so they kindly take one sack from the animal's load and carry it on their own shoulders.

There is a more complex story in which Gotham follows Hodja. Two noodles argue over a hypothetical question (in the Hodja version, one says, 'I wish Allah would give me a thousand sheep' and the other says, 'I wish Allah would give me a thousand wolves to devour your sheep'; in Gotham, they quarrel over whether some sheep that one man has not yet bought shall pass over a certain bridge.) They come to blows. Hodja is so moved by their idiocy that he pours out some honey he is carrying and says, 'May my blood be spilled like this honey if you are not two consummate idiots.' In Gotham, a third fool pours a sack of flour over the bridge into the river and says, 'Even as much wit there is in your two heads, to strive for that thing you have not.'

Some of these fool-stories are found in Poggio—evidence once again of the joke trade-route. In Germany they are given to the village of Schildburg.

107 OF THE COURTIER THAT BADE THE BOY HOLD HIS HORSE Merry 1535

This was put into verse in the seventeenth century (No. 349 in my *Love and Drollery*).

108 OF HIM THAT WOULD GIVE A SONG Merry 1535

Poggio cclix; he gives the 'pay the host' line in Italian: *Metti mano alla borsa e pega l'oste.*

Diners did not always outwit their hosts. In *La Gibecière de Mome*, 1644, there is a nice story, *D'un gourmand attrapé par un hôte*, in which a traveller sits down at an inn table, orders soup, and says he does not want any meat in it. The innkeeper (I translate)—

> The innkeeper, noting the traveller's parsimony, made him cabbage soup, in the bottom of which he concealed a nice piece of meat. When the traveller had eaten the cabbage he found the meat and said 'Ha-ha!'—assuming that the innkeeper had put it there without thinking. But when he came to pay, the innkeeper reckoned so much for bread, so much for wine, and added, 'And three sous for the ha-ha.'
> 'What ha-ha?' said the traveller.
> The host replied, 'My friend, if you had eaten the meat without saying ha-ha, you would not be paying for it now.'

109 OF THE SCOFFER Merry 1535

Poggio clxv and clxvi. The merry scoffing fellow is Gonnella (see notes to No. 100). He has two methods of making a man a soothsayer. In the other one, the man is told to lie in a bed with Gonnella, who then farts and tells the man to put his head between the sheets. The man says, *Crepitum ventris edidisti, ut video* (You have broken wind, I believe).

Pellets of turd were a frequent source of fun. Long before Poggio there is a French *fabliau* in which a wife in merry mood hands her husband such a pellet (of her own providing) and bets him a measure of wine that he cannot guess in three guesses what it is. He studies it, feels it, suggests *pâte* and *cire*. And then (I quote Courde de Montaiglon's *fabliau* collection, vol. 3, 46–8):

> *Et cil en sa bouche dedanz*
> *La met et masche entre ses denz,*
> *Que paor a que il ne perde.*
> *'Par le cuer dieu,' fet-il, 'c'est merde!*
> *Je m'en puis bien apercevoir.'*
> *'Par mon chief, vous avez dit voir,'*
> *Fet la dame tout à estrous.*
> *'Jamès ne gagerai à vous.*
> *Déables vous ont fait devin.*
> *J'ai perdue denrée de vin.'*

A rough translation:

> And he, afraid that he will lose,
> Puts into his mouth and chews
> The pellet—grinds it every bit.
> 'By God's heart,' says he, 'that's shit!
> I can tell that well enough.'
> Then his dame cries in a huff,
> 'By my head, you have said true.
> I'll never bet again with you.
> Devils have taught you to divine.
> And I have lost my drink of wine.'

Eulenspiegel is generous with turds in many forms, including pellets; I have probably given an unbalanced picture of him by including only one such story of his, No. 94.

Scoggin was ill once and was given some nasty medicines by an apothecary. 'Some were bitter, and some were sour, and some sweet.' Wanting revenge, he found 'a white dog's turd', dried it, and took it to several apothecaries, 'and they could not tell what powder it should be'.

At last he came to an old apothecary and said, 'Sir, I pray you tell me what powder this is.'

The old apothecary tasted it, and spit it out again, and said, 'Fie! Cock's bodykins! That is a turd.'

'Oh, good lord,' said Scoggin, 'cunning is worth much money! You fellows here in the City have good mouths to taste lamp-oil, and you have judged right. . . .'

NOTES

110 OF THE DOCTOR Merry 1535

Poggio clxxix; he tells it of a Milanese doctor, *indoctus, atque insulsus* (unlearned, a ninny indeed). In *Floresta Española* the game becomes rabbits, and it continues so in *Wits* and in later English jestbooks. The foolish one shouts, *Ecce cuniculi multi!* and when rebuked he says, 'Who the devil would have thought that coneys understood Latin?'

In Borrow's version of the Hodja stories, Hodja is visiting Kurdistan, and is invited to a feast. He belches (it seems it was not a polite gesture to belch there). He is told, 'You do wrong to belch.' He says, 'I am among Kurds. How should they know a Turkish belch, even though they hear it?'

111 AUGUSTUS OUTJESTED Schoolmaster

From Macrobius (II, iv) by way of *Mensa Philosophica*. In the original the dialogue goes: '*Dic mihi, adulescens, fuit aliquando mater tua Romae?*' Negavit ille nec contentus adjecit: '*Sed pater meus saepe.*'

Freud, in his *Jokes and the Unconscious*, pages 68–9, quotes a version of the story told in the 1880's of 'Serenissimus' (the German satirists' term for their emperor). On a provincial tour Serenissimus noticed 'a man in the crowd who bore a striking resemblance to his own exalted person, and asked him, "Was your mother at one time in service in the palace?" "No, Your Highness," was the reply, "but my father was." '

Freud defines the technique of repartee as 'establishing an unexpected unity between attack and counter-attack.' He seems to have been unaware how old the joke is.

112 THE HORSELESS CART Wits

Bar-Hebraeus tells of a simpleton who says, when told his ass has been stolen, 'Blessed be God that I was not on him!'

Mrs. Pilkington's *Jests* has these verses:

> Giles Jolt as sleeping in his cart he lay,
> Some pilf'ring villain stole his team away.
> Giles waking cries, 'What's here, a-dicken, what?
> Why how now—am I Giles or am I not?
> If he, I've lost six geldings, to my smart;
> If not, Ods buddikins, I've found a cart.'

113 A MAN-MADE SQUIRREL Wits

114 NO MORE NOW Wits

See No. 129.

115 HOLD THE SHIP Wits

116 MAN OF FEW WORDS Wits

Wits is nearly always wordier than its Spanish original. This is so even in this joke. In *Floresta Española*, instead of the last paragraph there are two words: *Respondio, 'Supito.'*

Earlier, in Domenichi, there is a more complex version. A party of young men order partridges to be cooked. Meanwhile they have other things brought, intending that one of them, a Florentine, will eat so much that when the partridges come he will not be hungry. He eats; the rest pass the time recounting the misfortunes of their fathers. By the time the partridges come, it is the Florentine's turn to tell about his father; but he devours partridges. He is pressed to tell about his father. He says, 'He dropped dead.'

A related idea is in the earlier stories of Arlotto. At a merry gathering of priests, a chicken is put on the table between Arlotto and another man. While Arlotto is busy telling a funny story in his jovial way, the other eats up the chicken. Nothing is left but *l'ossa senza carne* (bare bones). Arlotto says, '*Tu faresti buon disciplinatore, tu hai in modo concio costui, che se ci veniscino il padre e la madre che l'acquistorono non lo conoscerebbano*' (You would make a good disciplinarian; you've dealt with that one so well that the father and mother that begot it wouldn't know it).

As so often, it looks as if the Arabs were first. In Basset, vol. 1, p. 390, we find:

> *Un chretien nestorien et un Arabe s'assirent pour manger ensemble. Le chrétien dit à l'Arabe, pour le distraire du repas par des paroles, 'Comment est mort ton père?'*—'*Il a été atteint de telle et telle maladie.*' *Et il commença un long récit pendant que le chrétien mangaiti. Puis l'Arabe lui dit, 'Et toi, comment est mort ton père?'*—'*Il a eu une indigestion et il en est mort.*'

Even if the Arabs borrowed the story from Europe, the 'indigestion' is a nice touch. Basset does not name or date his source.

The 1613 *Scoggins Jestes* has Scoggin at dinner once with an old priest, who—

> began to ask Scoggin many questions, thinking thereby to hinder the busy filling of his belly, but Scoggin, because he would not lose much time, answered the old man very briefly altogether in syllables. The questions and answers were these:
>
> 'What garment do ye wear?'
> 'Strange.'
> 'What wine do ye drink?'
> 'Red.'
> 'What flesh do you eat?'
> 'Beef.'
> 'How like you this wine?'
> 'Good.'
> 'You drink none such at home?'
> 'No.'
> 'What eat you upon Fridays?'
> 'Eggs.'
>
> —And such-like; but all this while he lost not one mouthful of meat, for his mouth was still going. . . .

117 FIRST AND LAST Wits

Again, *Floresta Española* excels with a laconic ending, simply: *Y aqui tambien* (And here too).

118 TOO MANY SPANIARDS Wits

This Spaniard-mocking joke is from *Floresta*, but seems to originate in Italy. In the facetiae of Giovanni Pontano (1426–1503), who was at the court of King Alfonso of Aragon in Naples, there is a story of a Gascon (traditionally wily fellows) who is served a duck at an inn. A Spaniard arrives and says he is sure the Gascon can welcome a friend to his table. Asked his name, the Spaniard says haughtily, 'My name is Alopanzio Ausimarchide Hibereneo Alorchide.' The Gascon, feigning amazement: 'How do you expect this little duckling to be enough for four such important persons—and Spaniards, too?'

119 NO MARVEL Wits

In Marguerite de Navarre's *Heptameron*—part of the eleventh *nouvelle* that was substituted in the first full French edition, 1559, for a much coarser piece. A comical Franciscan says in an Easter sermon:

> '*Je m'étonne fort de vous, qui vous scandalisez pour moins que rien, et sans propos, et tenez vos comptes de moi partout, en disant, "C'est un grand cas! Mais qui l'eût cuidé* [who would have thought it], *que le beau père eût engrossi la fille de son hôtesse?"*
> '*Vraiement,*' dit-il, '*voilà bien de quoi s'ébahir* [that's truly something to be amazed at], *qu'un moine ait engrossi une fille! Mais venez ça, belles dames: ne devriez-vous pas bien vous étonner davantage, si la fille avait engrossi le moine?*'

It is quite possible, of course, that the joke was in general circulation, and was picked up independently for the *Heptameron* and for Wits. The first English edition of the *Heptameron* appeared two years after Wits. However, the compiler of Wits could easily have had a French edition.

120 THE COLEWORT-LIAR Wits

There are many variations on this, among the Arabs and elsewhere. H. A. Giles gives a Chinese version. Some men are bragging about their native villages. One says his village has a temple in which there is a drum thirty-three miles round. Another describes an incredibly large ox. The first man refuses to believe in it. The ox-liar says, 'If there is no ox as big as that, where do they get a skin to cover your great drum?'

121 NO FOOL HE Wits

Fools could look after themselves. Another in the same collection was bitten by a dog. He found it asleep the next day, knocked out its brains, and said, 'He that hath enemies, let him take heed how and where he sleeps.'

NOTES

122 HANGMAN'S ADVANTAGE Wits

123 IF THE SHOE FITS Wits

This is picked up in 1800 by the *New Joe Miller*. Lord North, 'feeling some symptoms of an approaching fit of the gout, ordered his large gouty shoes'. His servant, unable to find them, decided they had been stolen and began to curse the thief. 'Poh, John!' said his lordship, 'how can you be so ill-natured? All the harm I wish the poor rogue is that my shoes may fit him.'

124 THE ANSWER OF A GENTLEMAN'S MAN Pasquil

Developed from a story in Wits:

> A servingman by mischance shed broth on his master's board, and his master said, 'Sirrah, I could have done so myself.' He answered, 'No marvel, sir, for your worship hath seen me do it first.'

125 TWO GOOD LEGS Wits 1614

This was put into verse: see No. 323 in my *Love and Drollery*.

126 VALUE FOR MONEY Taylor

127 BARGAIN IN OYSTERS Taylor

128 A MAN ON THE GALLOWS Banquet 1630

129 A DRUNKEN MAN'S MISTAKE Banquet 1633

A version that is probably older than this is in *The Sack-full of Newes*, 1673— the earliest surviving edition of a book first recorded in 1557. It is told of a priest who, going home drunk after a christening party, 'laid him down by a ditchside so that his feet did hang in the water, and lying on his back, the moon shined in his face'. When his companions find him, he says, 'Do not meddle with me, for I lie very well and will not stir hence before morning. But I pray lay some more clothes on my feet, and blow out the candle, and let me lie and take my rest.'

130 OF A TILER Gratiae

131 A FOOLISH RESOLVE Gratiae

132 A WITTY INSCRIPTION Gratiae

133 I'LL DIE FIRST L'Estrange

NOTES

134 ROOM AT THE INN L'Estrange

In Banquet 1630; but L'Estrange tells it better.

Arlotto figures in a similar story. He arrives cold and wet at an inn and finds a group of peasants monopolizing the fire. He pretends to discover that a sum of money has leaked from a hole in his bag along the road. One after another the peasants make excuses and go out into the wet night. The story ends: *Il Piovano rimase al fuoco alla larga, e trionfo, e i contadini trovorno i denari in sogno* (The priest stayed by the fire at his ease, and exulted, and the peasants found the money in their dreams).

But a closer version of the English story is found in the tales of Tenali Rama. During a hunting expedition he comes in wet through and finds the courtiers huddled round a fire eating mutton chops. He says, 'Can I have a few mutton chops to give my horse? He is starving.'—'What! Will your horse eat mutton?'—'Go and see for yourselves,' he said. . . .

L'Estrange got the story from 'Brother Roger'—the future Sir Roger L'Estrange. Part of the Banquet 1630 version is worth quoting: 'No?' saith he. 'Will not the sullen jade fall to? Is not his stomach come to him? Well, ostler, take away your oysters and give him so many oats, and bring that he scorns to eat hither to me, and see what I can do with them. . . .'

135 A FAIR OFFER L'Estrange

In Timoneda's *Sobremesa*. Velasquillo, a sort of Spanish Scoggin, is sentenced to death. Allowed to choose how he shall die, he says he will throw himself from a high window. The queen and all the court come to watch. Seven or eight times he runs forward and turns back. To an impatient caballero he says, 'If you're so eager, you do it and I'll let you have twenty tries.' The queen is so taken with his quip that she pardons him.

Gladwin's *Persian Moonshee* has a poet sentenced to die. A courtier mocks him for trembling. 'If you think it is so easy, take my place,' says the poet. He too is pardoned.

In the *Recueil des Bons Contes et des Bons Mots*, Paris 1693, the Velasquillo story is transferred to a soldier in a captured castle, condemned by the Baron des Adrets (d. 1587), a formidable Huguenot general, to jump from a tower.

136 I'LL TRY THEE L'Estrange

There were three Sir Dru Drurys in Norfolk during L'Estrange's time.

In Wits there is a story (from the Spanish) about a tight-fisted gentleman being released from prison and tipping the doorkeeper 'a common prisoner's fee, viz., threepence'. The doorkeeper demands sixpence. The gentleman answers, 'I am content thou take me for a peasant for this once.'

137 THAT WAS A BULL L'Estrange

This Trevor is presumably the judge Sir Thomas Trevor (1586–1656), who married a Blennerhasset of Norfolk. (See No. 143.)

NOTES

138 A WITTY ANSWER OF A LADY Mercurius Jocosus or the Merry Mercurie (a news-sheet), 14–21 July 1654

A similar joke, long popular, goes back to Arlotto—'The priest's reply to a woman more impudent than prudent':

> Arlotto: *Guardate che bella giovana e questa.*
> Donna: *Cosi non poss'io dir di voi.*
> Arlotto: *Si, potresti bene se voi dicessi le bugie, come ho detto io.*

(Look at that beautiful girl.—One couldn't say the same of you.—Yes, one certainly could if one told lies, as I have done.)

139 MORE RIDDLES *Wit Revived*, by Asdryasdust Tossoffacan, 1655

The first of these is almost the same as the French riddle quoted above (notes to No. 105); the second is like the one in No. 105 of the animal with its tail between its eyes.

And here I can fit in a thirteenth-century riddle from Bar-Hebraeus:

> When a cock wakes in the morning, why does he hold one foot in the air?—If he lifted both he would fall down.

140 PROVERBS WITH COMMENTARIES *The Mysteries of Love and Eloquence* 1658, by Edward Phillips, John Milton's nephew.

The point of 'A gentle shepherd makes the wolf shite wool' (an elegant pentameter line, by the way) is that if he does not guard the sheep aggressively enough, they will be eaten. Or, 'Don't be soft with your enemies.' Among the sayings of Marcolf in his dialogue with Solomon is: 'The shepherd that waketh well, there shall the wolf no wool shite.'

'Grass grows not in hot ovens' is also an ancient proverb; it is found, for example, in the Solomon-Marcolf rhyming versions cited on page 76.

141 ON A TAPSTER AND GENTLEMAN MS Sloane 384

142 HALF MEASURES Coffee J

143 NO BULL Oxford J.

A neat development of a story of the Sieur Gaulard, perhaps the begetter of the term 'bull' (see page 96). He was travelling through the Charrolais region, noted in the sixteenth century as now for its cattle.

> *Il vit une paysante qui était montée sur un boeuf, jambe deçà, jambe delà. Lors il cria à ceux de la compagnie, 'Venez voir, je vous prie, une femme qui est à cheval sur un boeuf.'*

144 THE NEW WAY Oxford J.

NOTES

145 ALL THE PRISONS Oxford J.

146 OFF WITH HIS LEG Oxford J.
Tenali Rama has this story, graced with a build-up in which various nobles brag of their exploits. One led a handful of men and routed a battalion: one held a pass alone against fifty picked men; one cut off the tail of the enemy's leading elephant. 'What's all that beside what I did?' says Tenali. 'I cut off the leg of the commander of the enemy on the battlefield itself.' He causes a great sensation. The *dénouement* is the same: 'Some fellow had done it already.'

147 THE IMPORTED HOUSE Cambridge J.
Gaulard again. He admires a cardinal's house and says it looks more Italian than French: 'Was it built in this town?' The doorkeeper says, 'No, sir, two men brought it from Florence.' Gaulard turns complacently to his friends and says, '*Pardieu, je m'en doutais bien*' (By God, I thought as much).

148 HAVE A CARE Cambridge J.

149 NOTABLE BULLS *England's Jests Refin'd and Improv'd*, second edition, 1687

150 THE BULL-SPEAKER *Apollo's Feast: or, Wits Entertainment* 1703
This famous bull-speaker was Ralph Amner, musician, who was appointed a Gentleman of the Chapel Royal in 1623, and died 1664. According to Cambridge J., when he was at the point of death, he said to his friends, 'Well, when I am dead, write only this on my tomb for my epitaph: Here lies honest Ralph, as dead as any man living.'

151 ESCAPE ROUTE *Apollo's Feast*, as above
William Lilly predicted the world's end for March 29, 1652.

152 POOR PATTY Miller 1740

153 WARY TEAGUE Pilkington

154 TAKING HIS MEASURE Complete J.

155 A LYING DOG Complete J.
In *Wits Museum*—and again in *Tegg's Prime Jest Book*, 1811—this is told of an Irish sailor and his English friend. When Paddy is told that the man has lost his

head, he flings down the body, looks at it 'very attentively', and says, 'By my shoul, he told me it was his leg.'

156 A GREAT SLAUGHTER Complete J.

This was stolen for *Quin's Jests* a year later. The retort is made to come from Charles Churchill, the satirical poet, and 'son of a bitch of a fellow' is improved to 'son of a bitch of an Irish officer'.

157 THE YELLOW PEAS Wits Museum

Non-English readers may wish to know that if one journeys west through Hammersmith one is on the way to Turnham Green.

158 GUINEA TOOTHPICKS Wits Museum

In some Hodja Nasreddin collections, a great man on tour stops for a meal, is charged a huge price for an omelette, and is given a similar excuse.

159 SIXPENCE EXTRA *Garrick's Jests: or, Genius in High Glee. Containing all the JOKES of the WITS of the Present Age* .... (About 1780: mainly old jokes, many of which are put in Garrick's mouth)

The fat peer was the 2nd Lord Holland (died 1774); his brother, Charles James Fox (1749–1806), the politician. The Thatched House Tavern, St. James's Street, was frequented by politicians.

160 A GOOD JOKE *The Witty and Humorous Jester* 1789

The witless Fellow should have been able to get the joke right, for it had been going round at least since the early seventeenth century.

'Tom Brown' is presumably meant to be the wit and miscellaneous writer (a Christ Church man), who died in 1704.

5. Men and Manners

161 OF A PROUD FRENCHMAN Caxton

Poggio ccii. In Merry 1535, 'Of the Frenchman that strove with the Janway [Genoese] for his arms', with this moral: 'By this tale ye perceive how nicely the vain bragging of the Frenchman was derided.'

162 OF THE GENTLEMAN THAT TAUGHT HIS COOK Merry 1526

This sounds like an actual incident. It is not in other books. The relationship between master and man is interesting: a hundred years later, the cook would be much less likely to call the gentleman 'mocking churl', even in anger.

NOTES

163 OF THE COURTIER AND THE CARTER Merry 1526

The retort is in the tradition of one in de Bourbon. A fat, wealthy Parisian sees a tattered, emaciated clerk in the street and says, 'You look as if you had come from hell.' The clerk: 'You look as if you were going there.'

164 OF SAINT PETER Merry 1526

The story is referred to by L'Estrange near the end of his manuscript, with this comment: 'But I believe our Englishmen would run as fast into hell, if one were there to cry a pipe of tobacco.'

165 OF THE TWO MEN THAT DRANK A PINT Merry 1535

166 OF HIM THAT SAID HE WAS THE DEVIL'S MAN Merry 1567

A parallel tale of a battered underdog is told of a ghetto Jew in Poland in the Tsarist days. He is carrying a chicken. A Cossack stops him and asks what he feeds it. Grain, he says. 'You feed it grain when Russian children are starving?' And the Cossack beats him. He goes on and meets another Cossack; the same question. Potatoes, he says, 'Potatoes, when Russian children are starving?' Again he is beaten. He goes on—an even bigger Cossack—the same question. He says, 'I give her a penny and she gets what she likes.'

167 A HIGH HAT Wits

The phrase 'do off' is the source of 'doff'.

168 BEARING THE SHAME Wits

169 A SPANIARD'S BRAG Wits

170 I HAVE NO BRAINS Wits

An earlier version in Domenichi, which also turns up in English jestbooks, has a similar bitter remark made by a man wounded to the brain trying to part two men who were fighting.

Developments of the Wits version turn up several times in the late eighteenth century, applied to the 4th Viscount Townshend. *The Witty and Humorous Jester* 1789, says that when Townshend was aide-de-camp to the Duke of Cumberland, the duke 'availed himself of many occasions to give him that uneasiness which is inflicted by the severity of remarks from our superiors'. In a battle against the French in Flanders, an English soldier was killed by a cannonball

—and the blood and filth flew from his shattered head over the face of Lord Townshend, who, lifting his hand to his eyes, endeavoured to clear them from the disagreeable matter that covered them. 'What!' exclaimed

His Highness, 'is the gallant Townshend afraid?' 'No, sir,' answered his lordship, 'I am not frightened. I am only surprised that a fellow with so much brains should have enlisted in your regiment.'

In *Wit for the Ton!* (1778?), General John Lee, who was colonel of the 54th Foot from 1743 to 1751, is said to have been given a similar retort:

> As the balls whistled about in abundance, he observed one of his aides-de-camp, a very young man, shrink every now and then. . . . ''Sdeath, sir!' cried Lee. 'What do you mean? Do you dodge? Do you know that the King of Prussia lost above a hundred aides-de-camp in one campaign?' 'So I understand, sir,' replied the young officer, 'but I did not think you could spare so many.'

171 TILING FOR TOMORROW Wits

172 CHANGE OF DIET Wits

This reappears in *Amusements Serious and Comical* 1719 (Bodleian). A lord's footman gets nothing but cheese and radishes. When the steward is called—

> 'What!' says milord in a passion, 'is it true what these men say, that you give them every night cheese and radishes to their supper?' 'Yes, milord,' answered the poor man, quaking for fear. . . .

At the end is the comment: *Perhaps it was then Lent.*

173 CONFESS AND BE HANGED Wits

This may seem too cruel to be funny, but it is crueller in the *Floresta Española* original, which uses forty-six words against a hundred and five in the English. When the *alcalde* halts the torture, he simply says, '*A fe de hidalgo hiziste esto que te piden?*' (On the word of a gentleman, tell us if you did it). Then come two words and no more: '*Respondio, Si.*' To a Castilian, the joke was simply that the Biscayan did a witless thing. The English version at least shows some awareness of the psychology of torture and confession.

174 DID YOU EVER SEE THE LIKE? Wits

A woman's innermost garment was her smock.
   In Tarlton, the story is borrowed almost verbatim. He is given an amusing offbeat reply: 'No, in good sooth, never but once, in London.'

175 I'LL BREAK YOUR ARROW Wits

A similar story of a man responding feebly to an injury is in Domenichi. A knight seizes a man's beloved young wife and drags her off into the woods, leaving his horse and his cloak at the roadside with the husband. When it is all over and the knight has ridden away, the ravished wife scolds the husband for having done nothing. 'Be quiet,' he says. 'I didn't stand here idle. I tore his cloak in several places.'

176 GOODNIGHT Wits

In *Floresta* this is told of a Portuguese. We are to laugh at his foreign remark, '*Fica a boas noytes, fidalgos*' (I wish you goodnight, sirs). At least in the English there is a hint of compassion.

In Taylor the story is told of a Spaniard in England; he says '*Buenas noches*'— so we are back where we started.

177 HOW THIS MERRY FOOL WILL SOMMERS *A Nest of Ninnies*, by Robert Armin 1608 (Bodleian)

The book is a slight revision of *Foole upon Foole, or Sixe sortes of Sottes*, which Armin published under the whimsical pseudonym 'Clonnico de mondo Snuffe' (Snuff, clown of the Globe Theatre). A 1605 edition is in the Folger Library, Washington. The book is thought to date from 1600.

Armin, from King's Lynn, Norfolk, was apprenticed to a London goldsmith in 1581. He became acquainted with Richard Tarlton, then at the height of his fame as a comedian, who got him on to the stage. Armin seems to have succeeded Will Kemp as the leading comic actor in Shakespeare's company, the Lord Chamberlain's, about 1599. He apparently played Dogberry in *Much Ado* and no doubt he was the Fool in *Lear*. His book gives a genial account of six sixteenth-century fools in action—not actors, but domestic fools in private houses. As one who became a royal jester, Will Sommers (or Summers) is an exception. The others are Jack Oates, Jemmy Camber, Lean Leonard, Jack Miller and Blue John. Some of them are true natural fools—a little mad. People were not squeamish then about laughing at comic infirmities.

Armin makes clear he wrote about men he had either seen himself or learned about from eyewitnesses. Sommers died in 1560, so in 1600 Armin would easily be able to write 'some will affirm it now living in Greenwich' (where the royal palace was).

The answer to the second riddle is imperfect (see No. 105). It is impossible to say now whether Armin, or his informant, or Sommers himself is to blame. Perhaps Armin felt he ought to censor the joke. It is unlikely that Sommers needed to with Henry VIII.

In the 1605 edition, the phrase 'to grace the jest the better' is followed by '(for he was in that humour to grace goodwill the excellentest prince on the earth)'. When Armin deleted it in 1608, perhaps he was thinking it might be taken to reflect on James I.

Sommers is said to have come from Shropshire (like Tarlton a generation later), and to have been the jester of Richard Farmer, a Northamptonshire wool merchant, before he went to the king.

Armin describes him:

> Lean he was, hollow-eyed, as all report,
> And stoop he did too; yet in all the court
> Few men were more beloved than was this fool
> Whose merry prate kept with the king much rule.
> When he was sad, the king and he would rhyme. . . .

Sommers and his jests were several times 'for mirth inserted into stage plays'. He was in a lost play, *The Rising of Cardinal Wolsey*, for 'Will Sommers' coat for *The Rising*' is listed in the properties of the Admiral's Men in 1602. In Samuel Rowley's *When You See Me You Know Me* (performed before 1605, printed 1613) Sommers has a good role. Charles Brandon, Duke of Suffolk, is shown urging him to get Henry VIII out of an angry mood:

Will   No, by'r lady. . . . His fist is too heavy for a fool to stand under. I went to him last night, after you had left him, seeing him chafe so at Charles here, to make him merry. And he gave me such a box on the ear that struck me clean through three chambers, down four pair of stairs—fell o'er five barrels into the bottom of the cellar—and if I had not well liquored myself there, I had never lived after it.

Suffolk   Faith, Will, I'll give thee a velvet coat and [if] thou canst but make him merry.

Will   Will ye, my lord? And I'll venture another box on the ear, but I'll do it.

Later, Sommers exchanges extempore rhymes with Wolsey, the king and others:

Wolsey   The bells hang high, and loud they cry.
    What do they speak?

Will   If you should die, there's none would cry,
    Though your neck should break.

Wolsey   You are something bitter, William. But come on, once more I am for ye:
    A rod in school, a whip for a fool,
    Is always in season.

Will   A halter and a rope for him that would be pope
    Against all right and reason. . . .

King   The bud is spread, the rose is red,
    The leaf is green.

Will   A wench, 'tis said, was found in your bed,
    Besides the queen.

Queen [Catherine Parr]   Godamercy for that, Will! There's two angels [coins] for thee. I'faith, my lord, I am glad I know it!

King   God's mother, Kate! Wilt thou believe the fool? He lies, he lies!. . . . Have at you once more:
    In yonder tower there is a flower
    That hath my heart.

Will   Within this hour she pissed full sour
    And let a fart.

It is incongruous that the king is given the 'in yonder tower' lines to speak in his court and in the presence of the queen. It looks as if Rowley gaily lifted them from *A Pleasant History of the Life and Death of Will Summers*, where the verse-capping bout takes place while Henry was 'riding upon a progress with his nobles' and they 'passed by a place where, it seemeth, he had a mistress, which Will Summers well knew'. The book also has the 'rod in school' exchange with

NOTES

Wolsey. It adds: 'These homely jests might pass in those days, though the refinedness of these our times will neither admit such coarseness of language, nor such boldness with princes.'

178 A JEST OF A FELON Pasquil

The felon's devil-may-care last words are from Wits: 'A felon being to be thrown off the ladder said to the people, "Have at yonder daisy." '

179 HOW A MADMAN IN GLOUCESTERSHIRE ANSWERED Pasquil

Poggio ii—where the story is set in Milan. I have passed over the rather wordy Caxton and Merry 1535 versions. The latter adds a moral: 'This tale toucheth such young gentlemen that dispend overmuch good [goods] on hawks, hounds and other trifles.'

180 A GENTLEMAN AND A BARBER Banquet 1630

From Timoneda's *Sobremesa*. The Spanish gentleman replies more tellingly in one word, '*Callando*' (silently).

181 GENTLEMEN AT AN ORDINARY Banquet 1630

182 PAY LIKE A GENTLEMAN Banquet 1639

183 A BRAGGART Banquet 1639

The first brag is a development of one in Wits: 'A gallant threatened one, saying, "If thou offend me, I'll throw thee so high into the element that rather mayst thou fear famishing than falling." '

184 OF ONE THAT DELIVERED A MESSAGE Banquet 1639

Many stories of farts in mixed company could be given. One is of a jester who farts at table, then whispers loudly to a lady who dislikes him, 'I'll say it was I.'

185 OF A CHEESEMONGER Banquet 1639

A gossips' or groaning cheese was bought for a wife's woman friends to eat as they kept her company in her childbed labour.

186 TWO ANCIENT COMPANIONS Banquet 1640

In Cambridge J. a seaman is drinking from a bottle of brandy during a sea battle when a bullet through a porthole kills him. His friend says, 'A pox light on you for a rogue, to spill all the brandy.' Miller 1745 has a sailor lad 'running

189

along the gunwale of a ship with a can of flip in his hand, of which he was to have a part himself, when a cannonball came suddenly and took off one of his legs. "Look you there now, damn it!" said he. "All the flip's spilt." '

187 A BUSH AND NO WINE L'Estrange

Cornwallis, remembered as an essayist, died 1614. Wotton (1568–1639) was a diplomat and then provost of Eton. In his manuscript L'Estrange has an alternative phrase for the wench: 'had nothing but hair'.

188 GOOD FOR AN OLD WOMAN L'Estrange

L'Estrange got the story from his mother. Banquet 1630 has a variant, 'Of a deaf hostess,' in which a young gentleman 'used to put many jests upon her . . . thinking to make his friends merry'. He says, 'I will drink to you and to all your friends, namely, the bawds and whores of Turnbull Street' [Turnmill Street in Clerkenwell, then notorious for its whores]. She replies innocently, 'I thank you, sir, even with all my heart. I know you remember your mother, your aunt and those good gentlewomen your sisters.'

There was a Sir Henry Sidney at Walsingham, Norfolk.

189 A GENEROUS SERVANT L'Estrange

190 ZOUNDS! L'Estrange

191 I HAVE ONE QUALITY L'Estrange

In a manuscript of about 1612, Corpus Christi 169 (Bodleian), the story is told of 'one Woodrofe that lived about London'. In Banquet 1630, of 'a young gentleman late come out of the country'. He says, 'If any man offer to touch the bread that I cut and lay by my trencher, I presently stab.' The reply is, 'When I perceive any man begin to stab, I stab again,' and the challenger, 'looking him in the face, snatched his bread and ate it'.

192 THE DOOMED OYSTER L'Estrange

Bell was a descendant of an Elizabethan judge of that name, a great-grandfather of L'Estrange.

In Banquet 1633 there is 'A hungry jest':

> A piece of stinking meat coming to the table, one that was hungry said, 'Nay, it is not your stinking shall serve your turn. I will be on the bones of you sure.'

193 BLESS HER HEART L'Estrange

Sir Martin Stuteville was sheriff of Suffolk in 1612.

NOTES

194 PAPER AFTER SHOT L'Estrange

Berkley told L'Estrange the story himself.

195 HEAR MY PRAYER L'Estrange

196 SPRINKLING THE TABLE L'Estrange

This story, told to L'Estrange by his cousin John Spelman, is a slander on poor Climme Hoe, for the same story is told of a Hungarian by Poggio (cclxvi). However, it is revealing that L'Estrange accepted it as likely at a Norfolk supper-feast.

L'Estrange tells another story—from his brother-in-law Sir William Spring—of a member of the Crofts family of Suffolk:

> Sir —— Crofts came in a little tipped [tipsy] one night to supper, and fell to a coney in the dish next him, and would needs carve of it to a lady there, and as he reached it to her, swore, 'By God, this hand had a raw one [coney = cunny] in it within this half-hour; but you must eat it, madam, for all that.'

In Andrew Borde's *Introduction of Knowledge*, 1547, there are striking glimpses of sixteenth-century table manners. In Holland, 'right many of the men . . . will quaff till they be drunk, and will piss under the table whereas they sit. They be gentle people. . . .' In the Rhine valley they are sometimes a little better provided:

> The people be gentle and kindhearted. The worst fault that they have: many will be drunken, and when they fall to quaffing, they will have in divers places a tub or a great vessel standing under the board, to piss in; or else they will defile all the house, for they will piss as they do sit; and other-while the one will piss in another's shoes.

For Serjeant Atthow's wife, see No. 203.

197 WIGGETT IN PERIL L'Estrange

Wiggett was the resident fool in the Hunstanton mansion in the time of L'Estrange's grandfather Sir Nicholas, who died in 1591. This Sir John Heydon is presumably the one mentioned by John Chamberlain in a letter of October 1600 as being almost killed in a duel, and in February 1614 as quarrelling violently with the Earl of Essex. Wiggett was indeed in great danger. What saved him was the combination of his comical remark and an instinctive animal reaction; an appeasement signal by a creature in danger. See Desmond Morris, *The Naked Ape*, 1967, p. 158: 'Regardless of sex . . . it may suddenly assume the female rump-presentation posture.' In discussing the same instinct among humans (page 167) he says, 'the adoption of the female rump-presentation posture as an appeasement gesture has virtually vanished, along with the disappearance of the original sexual posture itself.'

198 WIGGETT INGRATIATES HIMSELF L'Estrange

NOTES

199 A FAIR EXCHANGE L'Estrange

In Banquet 1630, a Welsh servant of the gentleman cuts off the thief's ear, and the story ends with the Welshman saying, 'No harm done, good friend, no harm done. Give hur master hur purse, and I will give hur hur ear.'

200 HAVE IT FOR FIVE L'Estrange

201 ADVICE AT THE GALLOWS L'Estrange

Having the knot behind the ear gave a quick death with a broken neck instead of a slow one by strangling.

202 DRUNKEN MUSIC L'Estrange

203 A NAUGHTY NICKNAME L'Estrange

Serjeant[-at-law] Atthow seems to have been a distant relation of L'Estrange; in the sixteenth century one Joan Athow married a L'Estrange.

Elsewhere in his manuscript L'Estrange describes Atthow as 'the most ungraceful pleader that ever stood at the bar, in regard of his oratory and some wringing and distortions in his face', and adds, 'Sir John Pooly used to say of him that when he was pleading he looked like a dog fleaing of his ballocks.'

204 ONE PUSH MORE L'Estrange

205 NO NOSE FOR ME L'Estrange

Tom Brewer (born 1611) was a noted performer on the viol. Some of his song settings are in manuscripts and songbooks of the time.

206 A WAGGISH WENCH Conceits, Clinches, Flashes and Whimzies, 1639

'Crack me that nut' was a multi-purpose catch-phrase, originating presumably in a play on the sound.

207 FRUITFUL WALES Mirth

208 THE WAY TO SALISBURY Mirth

209 HARD AT THE BOTTOM Mirth

210 THE GLORY OF THE WEST Mirth

211 A VOMIT WITHOUT PHYSIC MS Sloane 1925

NOTES

212 A CURE BY A HUMOUR MS Sloane 1925

213 OF A BARBER MS Sloane 1957

214 NO FORENOONS Oxford J.

215 A CARPENTER! Cambridge J.

216 A PASSIONATE GAMESTER Cambridge J.

217 A POOR SCHOLAR Cambridge J.

A different poor-scholar joke is in Banquet 1633:

> A soldier came to beg of a poor scholar. The scholar asked him by what authority he went thus a-begging. 'Sir,' said the soldier, 'I have a licence.' The scholar replied, 'Well, thou mayst have lice, but thou hast no sense to beg of a poor scholar.'

218 A BUTCHER'S BARGAIN Coffee J.

(By this tale a man may learn the price of a shoulder of mutton in Oxford three hundred years ago.)

The story is from the French. In Tabourot's *Les Escraignes dijonnoises, recueillies par le sieur des Accords*, 1608 (a companion work to *Les Bigarrures*), I find:

> En la boutique d'un cordonnier, un passant demanda combien lui coûterait une paire de bottes. 'Cinquante sous,' dit le maître.
> 'Mais cinquante pets!' dit l'autre.
> 'Vraiement,' dit le maître, 'si tu les peux faire de suite, je te les donnerai pour rien.'
> Ce compagnon, bien aise, se va asseoir sur le bout d'une table à demi fesse, et commença à dire au cordonnier qu'il contât. Puis, sans tirer ni reprendre haleine, il fit si bien qu'il gagna les bottes, qui lui furent librement laissées. Ce que voyant, les serviteurs de boutique dirent, 'Monsieur, donnez le vin aux compagnons.'
> 'Oui,' dit-il, 'vous serez payer de même monnaie,' et leur lacha encore trois gros pets, qu'ils partirent egalement les uns avec les autres.

Substantially the same story appears in *Le Courrier Facétieux*, 1668, beginning' 'Un certain Normand étant à la foire à Rouen—' which is Coffee J.'s probable source.

Stories of irrepressible wenches appealed to the compiler of Coffee J. In his 1688 edition, a servant-maid washing 'a very large tripe' is told by her mistress to use some hot water.

> Then the pretty heart pissed upon it very plentifully, and rubbed it in with great care. Says her dame, 'I bid you use some hot water about it.'

NOTES

'So I did,' says she, 'all that I could make, for I can do no more than I can.'

219 SOME PROBABLE STORIES Coffee J.

I give three out of about a dozen of these tall tales. This one is outdone by an earlier version in Banquet 1640:

> One commended the goodness of his blade, 'For,' saith he, 'going to cut a hard barley loaf . . . and summoning all my strength together, ere I could be aware I sliced through the loaf, myself, and two behind me. As sure as I live,' quoth he, 'quite through myself and two men behind me.'

220 ANOTHER PROBABLE STORY Coffee J.

221 AND ANOTHER Coffee J.

222 HOW TO CATCH A HARE Coffee J.

223 I KNOW IT London J.

224 WHERE I STARVE Pinkethman

225 HOT CUSTARD Pinkethman

This is a modernized, weakened version of one of the three stories that are found in the mutilated British Museum copy of *A Hundred Merry Tales* (two hundred years before Pinkethman). Part of the right-hand side of the page is missing in the original. The two eating together are a merchant and a courtier, which gives a social point to the story. The courtier, 'somewhat homely of manner', eats first. His explanation of his tears is that he had 'a brother which did a certain offence wherefore he was hanged', and he had chanced to 'think now upon his death'. When the merchant burns his tongue and weeps, the courtier says, 'Why do ye weep now?' The ending is sharper than Pinkethman: 'The merchant perceived how he had [been beguiled], and said, "Marry," quod he, "I weep because thou wast not hanged [when thy bro]ther was hanged." '

A parallel is in Borrow's Hodja collection. Hodja's wife, to plague him, puts some very hot broth on the table. Then she stupidly puts some in her own mouth first. Tears spring to her eyes. 'O wife,' says Hodja, 'what is the matter? Is the broth hot?' She says her mother always loved broth very hot, and eating this, she thought of her mother, and wept. Hodja, typically, burns his tongue despite the warning. His final words are, 'You cry because your mother is gone, but I cry because her daughter is here.'

Miller 1739, borrowing from Pinkethman, makes the custard apple-pie and the father a grandmother.

NOTES

226 GOD BLESS TADLOE Polly

The weighty doctor was Charles Tadloe (D. Med., Oxon, 1693), who died in 1716, aged 56. Joe Miller, having lifted the story in 1739, also prints a Tadloe couplet in 1742:

> On Dr Tadloe, a very fat man
> When Tadloe walks the streets, the paviours cry,
> 'God bless you, sir!'—and lay their rammers by.

227 NO ROOM AT THE TOP Miller 1739

228 DEAF OLD CROSS Miller 1742

229 WATCH AND WATCH ABOUT The Irish Miscellany, or Teagueland Jests, 1749

There are not many laughs in this collection of alleged Irish humour. Another of about 1700, *Bog-witticisms*, is no better.

230 A DESERVING CASE Pilkington

231 A LOUD HINT Quin's Jests: or, the Facetious Man's Pocket Companion, 1766

The jestbook was published together with *The Life of Mr James Quin*—rushed out in the year of the famous comedian's death. David Garrick wrote an epitaph on him, which may be found in MS Add. 21508:

> That tongue *which set the table on a roar*
> And charm'd the public ear, is heard no more;
> Clos'd are those eyes, the harbingers of wit,
> Which spake before the tongue, what Shakespeare writ;
> Cold is that hand, which living was stretch'd forth,
> At friendship's call, to succour modest worth;
> Here lies James Quin. . . .

If this story of Quin, and the next one, seem unedifying, what of the ones that are lost? The introduction to *Quin's Jests* says:

> . . . Many of his jokes and impromptus were indelicate and indecent. . . . They might have swelled this work to a much greater size, and of course increased the editor's profit. . . . The following sheets contain nothing but what may be called the quintessence and refinement of Mr Quin's wit and humour, divested of every gross and indecent idea that might offend the chastest or most delicate ear.

Theatrical historians may be interested in a story reflecting on Garrick. The jestbook says that when Garrick married he asked Quin 'to stand godfather to his first child'. After a time, Quin asked

> when he might think of preparing himself for the solemn occasion; to which David answered, 'All in good time.' 'Indeed,' said Quin, 'it must be a *very good* and a *very fruitful* time, when *you* become a father.'

[Garrick left no children.]

232 QUIN INCONVENIENCED Quin, as above

A lesson on the eternally unsolved problem of euphemisms.

About thirty years later, in *The Theatrical Jester, or Green-room Witticisms*, there is a politer story about the actor John Quick (he played Tony Lumpkin in the first run of *She Stoops to Conquer*, 1773) going by appointment to a friend's house and being told by a maid-servant, 'He is gone out, sir.'

'Then your mistress will do,' said Quick.
'She,' said the girl, 'is gone out too.'
'My business is of consequence,' returned he. 'Is your master's son at home?'
'No, sir,' returned the girl, 'he is gone out.'
'That's unlucky indeed,' replied he, 'but perhaps it may not be long before they return. I'll step in and sit by your fire a bit.'
'Oh, sir,' said the girl, 'the fire is just gone out too!'

233 THE COST OF LIVING *The Macaroni Jester*, 1773

The Covent Garden Magazine of the same date, which gives the names, addresses and prices of whores, mentions half-a-guinea as 'the price for a night' and five shillings and threepence 'for a temporary favour'. This was for girls to be found in taverns or behind shop-counters; yet labourers were then earning less than two shillings a day.

234 UP WITH THE TIDE Macaroni, as above

This definition of a buoyant Irishman is similar to the modern one of a Hungarian: He'll follow you into a revolving door, and come out first.

235 MY BEST RAZOR! Miller 1780

236 HARD AT WORK Jolly J.

237 GENUINE BRITISH Jolly J.

238 A POLITE HINT *New Joe Miller; or, The Tickler. Containing five hundred good things*, 1800

239 POOR DOG Tickler, as above

240 PAID IN ADVANCE Tickler, as above

Henry Home, Lord Kames (1696–1782) was a formidable character on the Scottish Bench. Lord Cockburn, *Memorials of His Time*, 1856, page 117, says, 'When Lord Kames, an indefatigable and speculative but coarse man, tried Matthew Hay, with whom he used to play at chess, for murder at Ayr in September 1780, he exclaimed, when the verdict of guilty was returned, "That's checkmate to you, Matthew!" '

The Dictionary of National Biography records Kames's last public words, a few days before he died: 'On the day the court rose for the Christmas vacation, 1782, he took an affectionate farewell of each of his brethren, and on leaving the courtroom cried in his usual familiar tone, "Fare ye a' weel, ye bitches!" '

241 A NICE CORNER Tickler, as above

The full story of this eccentric miser, John Elwes (1714–89) may be found in *The Life of Mr Elwes*, 1790, by Major Edward Topham. Elwes inherited a fortune from his uncle, Sir Hervey Elwes, in 1763; and left about £500,000.

242 WHITE MAN'S JUSTICE *The Cabinet of Mirth*, about 1805

243 WAR AND PEACE *The Cabinet*, as above

244 WHAT'S BECOME OF WILKES? *The Comical Jester*, 1808

APPENDIX

BORDE AND SCOGGIN

Despite the direct attribution of the Scoggin book to Andrew Borde, scholars of the eighteenth and nineteenth centuries questioned or denied his authorship. As their view has tended to be accepted, some discussion of the question will be useful.

The earliest surviving copy of the book is the one in the British Museum, printed by Francis Williams in 1626 with the title *The First and best Part of Scoggins Jests, gathered by Andrew Boord, Doctor of Physicke*. It is called 'first and best' because a rival *Scoggins Jestes* had been put out towards the end of the sixteenth century. A 1613 edition of this interloper is in the Bodleian. It is a rather flavourless collection of borrowed stories, of which twelve are from the *Nouvelles Recreations* of Bonaventure des Periers (1558), two from *Mery Tales, Wittie Questions, and Quicke Answeres*, and eight from Howleglas.

The earliest record of the original Scoggin book is in the Stationers' Register of 1566, when Thomas Colwell paid fourpence for the right to print 'the geystes of skoggyn'. Colwell was in a good position to acquire a book by Borde, having served his apprenticeship with one of Borde's printers, William Powell, and taken over the business of another of them, Robert Wyer, in 1560. The Stationers' Register begins only in 1557, so it is impossible to say whether the book came into print in Borde's lifetime. It may well be that it was left in manuscript when Borde died in prison in 1549, and that Colwell was the first to print it; but that would not make it any the less Borde's.

Popular books were read to destruction. Of all the copies printed before 1626, only odd pages survive. They too are in the British Museum (items 210, 328, 331–2 in Harl. 5995, part of the John Bagford typographical collection). The running title is *The Jestes of Skogyn*, and Colwell was quite possibly the printer. The fragments contain parts of eight stories; a comparison with the 1626 copy shows very few changes of wording. Moneymaking books like this were passed on from printer to printer. Colwell's widow married another printer, Hugh Jackson, and Scoggin is recorded in Jackson's list when he died in 1616.

Now for the scholars. The usually reliable Professor Frederick Furnivall, in his introduction to *Andrew Borde's Introduction and Dyetary* (1870), says he doubts that Borde wrote the Scoggin book, and this verdict is perpetuated in Furnivall's article on Borde in the *Dictionary of National Biography*. In his 1870 introduction Furnivall supports his opinion by saying that the Oxford antiquarian Anthony à Wood described *Scoggin's Jests* in *Athenae Oxonienses* as 'an idle thing unjustly fathered upon Dr Borde'. Here Furnivall erred. In Wood's article on Borde in *Athenae Oxonienses* (1692, vol. 1, column 60), the only jest-book mentioned is *The Merry Tales of the Mad-Men of Gottam, gathered together by A. B. of Physicke Doctor*. Wood says of this book that it was 'printed at London in the time of King Henry 8; in whose reign and after it was accounted a book full of wit and mirth by scholars and gentlemen. Afterwards, being often printed, is now sold only on the stalls of ballad-mongers.' It is in fact a slighter book than Scoggin; but Wood accepts it as Borde's.

The phrase about 'an idle thing' comes not from Wood but from another Oxford antiquarian writing even longer after the event: Thomas Hearne. Furnivall was quoting a 19th-century edition of *Athenae Oxonienses* in which something that Hearne wrote about Borde in 1735 was inserted. The passage in question reads:

> There were other books of mirth ascribed to Dr Borde, on purpose to promote a sale of them, one of which is that call'd Scogan's Jests, which tho' an idle thing (and therefore unjustly fathered upon Dr Borde) hath been often printed in Duck Lane, and much bought up by those that to their collections of books of the first class aim at adding little pieces that tend to promote mirth.

Dismiss the book as 'an idle thing', and it is 'therefore' not Borde's! And yet it is sought after by eighteenth-century gentlemen. This tangle of snobbery ought not to have influenced Furnivall. He might have reminded himself that in Henry VIII's days (and later too), men from university would not only write about merry japes, but sometimes perform them as well. For example, in *Athenae Oxonienses* (I, 28) Wood says, 'I find one John Pace who from Eton School was elected scholar of King's Coll. in Cambridge, 1539 or thereabouts, went away Fellow, became jester to K. Hen. 8 for a time, and afterwards to the Duke of Norfolk.'

A century after Furnivall, when universities are once again not ashamed to produce jesters, it is possible to give Borde his due, guided by his own words: 'Divers times in my writings I do write words of mirth.'

BIBLIOGRAPHY

ALFONSI, PETRUS, For an English version, see Hulme. There are a few Alfonsi stories in Caxton's and other early editions of *Aesop*.

AMRAIN, KARL, *Deutsche Schwankerzähler des XV bis XVIII Jahrhunderts*, Leipzig, 1907. Jest collections of Heinrich Bebel and others, in German, with extensive background material.

ARLOTTO, PIOVANO (ARLOTTO MAINARDI), *Motti e facetie*, Florence, ?1515 (first edition). Eight other editions before 1600, with varying titles, in British Museum. *Le facezie del piovano Arlotto*, edited by G. Baccini, Florence, 1884. *Les Contes et Facéties d'Arlotto*, Paris, 1873.

ARMIN, see Collier and Grosart.

ASH'AB, see Rosenthal.

BAR-HEBRAEUS, see Budge.

BASKERVILL, C. R., *The Elizabethan Jig*, University of Chicago, 1929 (English paperback edition, 1965).

BASSET, RÉNE, *Mille et un Contes, Récits et Légendes Arabes*, 2 vol., Paris, 1924–6. Contains many Djoh'a stories.

BEBEL, HEINRICH, *Heinrich Bebels Facetien*, ed. Gustav Bebermayer, Leipzig, 1931 A number of sixteenth-century Latin editions of the *facetiae* of Bebel (died 1518) survive. He borrowed heavily from Poggio.

BENZ, RICHARD, *Deutsche Volksbücher*, Heidelberg, 1956 (includes full version of Eulenspiegel with weighty introduction).

BOBERTAG, FELIX, *Narrenbuch* (vol. 2 of *Deutsche National-Litteratur*), Berlin and Stuttgart, 1884. Includes the Parson of Kalenberg and Solomon and Marcolf in their original old German verse.

BOHUN, EDMUND, *The Character of Queen Elizabeth*, 1693.

BORDE, ANDREW, *The Brevyary of helth*, 1552 (first published ?1547). A *compendyous Regyment or a dyetary of Helth*, 1542. *The Introduction of Knowledge*, 1547. (And see Furnivall.)

BIBLIOGRAPHY

BRACCIOLINI, see Poggio.

BREWER, THOMAS, *The Life and Death of the merry Devill of Edmonton*, 1631 (from 1600 or earlier). Merry tales about Oliver Smug the smith. One, based on Chaucer's *Miller's Tale*, begins, 'As honest Smug loved (as he loved his life) the society of his bearded associates, so in like manner loved he sometimes to be mad merry amongst a mad company of his barechinned boon companions, his little wanton wagtails, his sweet-and-twenties. . . .'

BUDGE, E. A. WALLIS, *Oriental Wit and Wisdom, or the 'Laughable Stories' collected by Mar Gregory John Bar-Hebraeus*, 1899. Translated from Syriac.

CAMDEN, WILLIAM, *Remains*, 1605.

CHAMBERLAIN, JOHN, *The Letters of John Chamberlain*, ed. Norman McClure, Philadelphia, 1939; cut version, ed. Elizabeth McClure Thomson, 1966.

CHAMBERS, SIR EDMUND, *The Elizabethan Stage*, 4 vols., Oxford, 1923; *The Medieval Stage*, 2 vols., Oxford, 1954 (1903). These works together provide a finely documented history of the theatre and of all entertainers from the Dark Ages to the seventeenth century.

CLOUSTON, W. A., *The Book of Noodles*, 1888; *The Book of Sindibad*, 1884; *Flowers from a Persian Garden*, 1890; *Popular Tales and Fictions*, 1887. Much information on the spread of stories from the east.

COCKBURN, LORD, *Memorials of his Time*, 1856.

COLLIER, JOHN PAYNE, *Fools and Jesters*, 1842. Reprint of Robert Armin's *A Nest of Ninnies*, 1608.

COURDE DE MONTAIGLON, ANATOLE, *Recueil Général des Fabliaux des XIII et XIV Siècles*, 6 vols., Paris, 1872–90.

CRANE, T. F., *The Exempla of Jacques de Vitry*, 1890. Latin text with introduction. *Italian Popular Tales*, 1885.

Demandes joyeuses en manière de quolibets, ?1500.

Les dictz de Salomon: avecques les responces de Marcon / Fort joyeuses, ?1500.

DJOH'A, SI, see Basset and Mouliéras.

DOMENICHI, LODOVICO. His jest collections were revised and expanded more than once after the publication of the first, *Facetie, et Motti arguti*, Florence, 1548. The later title was *Facetie, motti, et burle*. The British Museum has thirteen editions of between 1548 and 1609. There is also an edition of the 1548 version with parallel text in French, *Facécies et motz subtils*, Lyons, 1559.

DORAN, JOHN, *The History of Court Fools*, 1858.

DUFF, E. GORDON, *The Dialogue of Solomon and Marcolphus*, 1892. Facsimile reprint of the Bodleian copy of 1492.

DUNN, THOMAS F., *The Facetiae of the Mensa Philosophica*, Washington University Studies, 1934.

BIBLIOGRAPHY

Eulenspiegel, see BENZ and KNUST.

FREUD, SIGMUND, *Jokes and their Relation to the Unconscious*, 1960 (Routledge paperback 1966); paper on 'Humour', vol. xxi of standard edition of Freud's works, 1961.

FULLER, THOMAS *The History of the Worthies of England*, 1662.

FURNIVALL, FREDERICK J., *Andrew Boorde's Introduction and Dyetary*, Early English Text Society, 1870.

Gaulard, see TABOUROT.

GIBB, E. J. W., *The History of the Forty Vezirs*, 1886. Turkish tales, from the Arabic.

Gibecière de Mome, La, Paris, 1644. One of the best seventeenth-century French jestbooks. Others (in British Museum and Douce Collection, Bodleian) are: *Le courrier facétieux, Les divertissements curieux, Le facétieux réveille-matin, Les récréations françoises, Recueil des Bons Contes et des Bons Mots*.

GILES, H. A., *Quips from a Chinese Jest-book*, Shanghai, 1925.

GLADWIN, FRANCIS, *The Persian Moonshee*, Calcutta, 1795. Translations of tales and jests; no sources given.

GOMME, G. L., *The History of the Seven Wise Masters of Rome*, 1885. Reprint of Wynkyn de Worde's edition of popular medieval tale collection.

GONNELLA, PIETRO, A group of Gonnella stories is contained in *Facezie, Motti, Buffonerie, et Burle del Piovano Arlotto, del Gonnella & del Barlacchia* (Florence 1565 and various other editions). Gonnella's pranks were put into verse as early as 1506 (reprinted by Ferdinando Gabotto in *La Epopea del Buffone*, Bra, 1893).

GROSART, A. B., *The Works of Robert Armin*, 1880. Includes *Foole upon Foole*, or *Sixe sortes of Sottes*, 1605 (now in the Folger Library, Washington).

HALLIWELL, J. O. (later Halliwell-Phillips), *Nugae Poeticae*, 1844.

HAZLITT, W. CAREW, *Shakespeare Jest-Books*, 3 vols., 1864. Reprints of fifteen jestbooks and related books, including *A Hundred Merry Tales* (the British Museum copy), the 1535/67 *Tales and quicke answeres*, Scoggin, Tarlton, Gotham, Pasquil and Taylor. The others are: *The Merie Tales of Skelton, The Sack-Full of Newes, XII Mery Jests of the Wydow Edith, The Merrie Conceited Jests of George Peele, Jack of Dover, The Pleasant Conceites of Old Hobson, Certaine Conceyts & Jeasts* (from *The Philosophers' Banquet*), and *Conceits, Clinches, Flashes, and Whimzies*.

— *A Hundred Merry Tales*, 1887. Photolithographic reproduction of the unique 1526 copy at Göttingen.

HEILAND, CARL, *Pfaffe Amis*, Munich, 1912. Reprint of thirteenth/fourteenth-century verse tale of priest-rogue.

BIBLIOGRAPHY

HERFORD, C. H., *Studies in the Literary Relations of England and Germany in the Sixteenth Century*, Cambridge, 1886. Herford takes a superior line on Eulenspiegel: 'All his jests together would scarcely yield a grain of Attic salt; we could not read the book but for the light which it throws upon a society which could and did.'

HERRTAGE, S. J. H., *Gesta Romanorum*, 1879. Early English version of popular medieval collection of tales, edited for Early English Text Society.

HULME, W. H., *Peter Alphonse's Disciplina Clericalis from the Fifteenth-Century Worcester Cathedral MS. F.172*, Western Reserve University Bulletin, vol. 22, no. 3, Cleveland, 1919.

JUSSERAND, J. J., *English Wayfaring Life in the Middle Ages*, 1950. This book, first published in 1889, provides valuable information on popular entertainers.

KAO, GEORGE, *Chinese Wit and Humour*, New York, 1946.

KEMBLE, J. M., *The Dialogue of Salomon and Saturnus*, 1848.

KNUST, HERMANN, *Dyl Ulenspiegel*, reprint of 1515 edition in British Museum, *Neudrucke deutscher Litteraturwerke des XVI under VII Jahrhunderts*, Nos. 55 and 56, Halle, 1884.

LA TOUR LANDRY, CHEVALIER GEOFFROY DE, *The Booke of Thenseygnementes and Techynge that the Knight of the Towre made to his Doughters*, edited by Gertrude Rawlings, 1902, from Caxton's edition of 1484; *The Book of the Knight of La Tour-Landry*, edited by Thomas Wright, Early English Text Society, 1868, from MS. Harl. 1764 (time of Henry VI); *The Book of the Knight of La Tour Landry*, ed. G. S. Taylor, 1930.

LECOY DE LA MARCHE, A., *Anecdotes historiques*, Paris, 1877 (Etienne de Bourbon's exempla); *L'Esprit de nos aïeux*, Paris, 1889 (selections from de Bourbon, Jacques de Vitry and others).

MENNER, R. J., *The Poetical Dialogues of Solomon and Saturn*, Modern Language Association of America, Monograph Series, XIII, 1941.

Mensa Philosophica, see WAY.

MOULIÉRAS, AUGUSTE, *Les Fourberies de Si Djeh'a*. Vol. 1, text in the Berber tongue, Oran, 1891; vol. 2, French translation, notes, etc., by René Basset, Paris, 1892.

NASREDDIN, HODJA. A few versions in English:

    ARRATOON, NICHOLAS, *Gems of Oriental Wit and Humour* (from Persian), Calcutta, 1894.
    BORROW, GEORGE, *The Turkish Jester*, Ipswich, 1884 (150 copies only).
    DOWNING, CHARLES, *Tales of the Hodja*, Oxford, 1964.
    SHAH, IDRIES, *The Exploits of the Incomparable Mulla Nasrudin*, 1966; *The Pleasantries of the Incredible Mulla Nasrudin*, 1968.

OUVRY, FREDERIC, *Howleglas*, 1867. Reprint from British Museum and Bodleian copies of Copland editions.

OWST, G. R. *Literature and Pulpit in Medieval England*, Oxford, 1966 (first

BIBLIOGRAPHY

published 1933); *Preaching in Medieval England*, Oxford, 1930. Two illuminating studies.

PAINTER, WILLIAM, *Delectable demaundes*, 1566. Question-and-answer on love.

PANCHAPAKESA AYYAR, A. S., *Tenali Rama*, Madras, 1957.

PENZER, N. M., *The Ocean of Story*, 10 vols., 1924–8. Translation of 11th-century Kashmir cycle of tales, with copious annotation.

A Pleasant History of the Life and Death of Will Summers, 1676 (Bodleian). The book probably dates from before 1600.

POGGIO (BRACCIOLINI), *Liber facetiarum*. Many early editions; in British Museum alone there are eleven printed in Italy, France, Germany and Switzerland between 1470 and 1488. British Museum has several early MS. copies, including Harl. 1456 and Harl. 3333. *The Facetiae or Jocose Tales of Poggio*, Paris, 1879, gives Latin text (273 stories) with English translation of all but a few passages. A similar Latin-and-French edition also appeared in 1879, and a new French translation by Pierre des Brandes, *Les Facéties de Pogge Florentin*, in 1900.

PONET, JOHN, *An Apologie fully answering . . . a blasphemose Book . . . against the godly mariadge of priests*, Strasbourg, 1556.

PROMPSAULT, J. H. R., *Oeuvres de Maistre François Villon*, Paris, 1832. For '*Les repues franches*'.

REED, A. W., *Early Tudor Drama*, 1926. For John Rastell and his time.

ROWLEY, SAMUEL, *When You See Me You Know Me*, 1613. Will Summers on stage.

The Sack-full of Newes, 1673 (licensed 1557). Mainly borrowed jests.

Scoggins Jestes, 1613 (Bodleian). The inferior collection in Scoggin's name.

SPERONI, CHARLES, *Wit and Wisdom of the Italian Renaissance*, University of California Press, 1964. Selections from a dozen creators or compilers of facetiae, including Arlotto, Angelo Poliziano, Giovanni Pontano, Lodovico Domenichi and Gonnella, with useful introduction.

STORER, EDWARD, *The Facetiae of Poggio and other Medieval Story-tellers*, 1928. A cautious selection. *Il Novellino*, 1925. Expurgated translation of *Le Cento Novelle Antiche*, pre-Boccaccian collection.

TABOUROT, ETIENNE. Under the pseudonym '*Le Seigneur des Accords*' he published *Les Apophthegmes du Sieur Gaulard, Gentil-Homme de la Franche-Comte Bourgignotte* in 1585, and *Les Escraignes dijonnoises* in 1588. Both are rich, delightful collections of anecdotes and stories (some of them derived from Italy). Other works of Tabourot are *Les Touches du Seigneur des Accords* (verses) and *Les Bigarrures* (a treasury of verse-techniques, word-games, etc.). Many editions survive from Tabourot's lifetime and from the generation after his death in 1590. A study of the man, with bibliography, is Georges Choptrayanovitch's *Etienne Tabourot des Accords*, Dijon, 1935. An incomplete translation of the Gaulard stories, in a seventeenth-century manuscript which I have been unable to trace, was published by Alexander Smith (Glasgow, 1884) with the title *Bigarrures, or the Pleasant and witlesse and simple Speeches of The Lord Gaulard of Burgundy.*

Tegg's Prime Jest Book, Bang up to the Mark!! Published by Thomas Tegg, 1811 (Bodleian). One of many jestbooks with new-style lively titles, and some new jokes, published in the Napoleonic and Regency period. The Francis Douce Collection in the Bodleian has a good selection (as well as numerous earlier English and French jestbooks). A few from after 1800 are: *The New Fun Box Broke Open*, by Johnny O'Daisy; *The Care-Killer*, by Jonathan Jolly; *Jests of the Camp*; *The Female Jester: or, Wit for the Ladies*; *Fun for the Fireside, or, Joe Miller Alive Again*; *Grineology*; *The Sprightly Jester.*

Tenali Rama, see PANCHAPAKESA AYYAR.

The Theatrical Jester, or Green-Room Witticisms, ?1795.

THOMPSON, STITH, *Motif-Index of Folk-Literature*, 6 vols., Copenhagen, 1955–8. *The Types of the Folktale*, Helsinki, 1961–4. Folklorists' guides, the product of forty years' labour begun by Antti Aarne of Helsinki and completed by Professor Thompson of Indiana University, Bloomington. Coverage of jestbooks, however, by no means comprehensive.

THOMS, W. J., *Anecdotes and Traditions Illustrative of Early English History and Literature*, 1839. Prints 141 of the stories in Sir Nicholas L'Estrange's collection, MS. Harl. 6395, with introduction and notes. *Early Prose Romances*, 1828.

TIMONEDA, JUAN, *Obras*, vol. 1, Madrid, 1947 (*El Patranuelo, El Sobremesa, El Buen aviso y portacuentos*).

TOPHAM, MAJOR EDWARD, *The Life of Mr Elwes*, 1790.

WARDROPER, JOHN, *Love and Drollery*, 1969. Amatory, merry and satirical verse, 1600–70 (including some versified jests).

WAY, A. S., *The Science of Dining*, 1936. Translation of *Mensa Philosophica.*

WELLDON, SIR ANTHONY, *The Court and Character of King James*, 1650 (reprinted with other memoirs of the time in *The Secret History of the Court of King James* by Sir Walter Scott, Edinburgh, 1811).

WELSFORD, ENID, *The Fool*, 1935, reprinted 1968. Comprehensive study.

Wit for the Ton! The Convivial Jester; or, Sam Foote's Last Budget Opened, ?1778. Claimed to be from the mouth of the actor Foote (died 1777), 'that immortal Child of Humour, the English Aristophanes', the stories are nearly all stolen from earlier collections.

INDEX

Aesop, 1, 20
Agrippa, 160
Albigensians, 18
ale, 50, 142–3, 154
alehouse, 56, 142–3 see also inn, tavern
Alfonsi, Petrus, 16–17
Alfonso of Aragon, 179
Amis, Pfaff, 78, 79, 172
Amner, Ralph, 112, 183
anarchists, 148
angels, 169
Anthropophyteia, 25
Antwerp, 77, 79, 152
apothecaries, 44, 176
apricots, in Hodja Nasreddin's sleeves, 15
Arabs, 16, 17, 74, 167, 174–5, 178, 179
arbour, 31–2, 64–5
Arlotto, Piovano, 174, 181, 182
Armin, Robert, 187
arms, challenge over, 116–17
Armstrong, Archie, 10, 23–4, 151
arrow, Hodja Nasreddin's, 15; pierces brain, 121; in nose, 123; in arse, 143
arse, Marcolf's proverbs on, 80–1; Marcolf bares, 82; Howleglas tells lords to kiss, 85; Howleglas would wedge old women's, 86; Scoggin greases fat sow's, 90; Scoggin bares, 94; cat's, 97; and holly leaves, 97; left behind, 110; kissing woman's, 135; arrow in, 143; lord told to kiss, 170
Arsehole, Mrs, 135

Ash'ab, 14–15
Ashmodai (Asmodeus), 74
Athenae Oxonienses, 199
Atthow, Serjeant, 192; his wife, 131, 135
Augustinian friar, 3
Augustus, young man like, 100; his daughter Julia, 160
Ave Maria, Scoggin says in king's ear, 91

backgammon, 140
bacon, wife eats, 41
bailiff of Colchester, 134
Banquet of Jests, 9–11, 27, 97
barber, 126, 139
Barcelona, siege of, 121
Bar-Hebraeus, 17–18, 162, 174–5, 177, 182
Baskervill, Colonel, 135
Bath, 59, 146
bawdy-house, 128
beast, Marcolf as a marvellous, 81–2; Scoggin as a monstrous, 94–5
beasts, women no, 44
beds, maids asleep in, 133; for Irishmen, 145
beer, 109, 128
Beggar's Opera, 12, 165
beggars, 98, 107, 140, 145
belch, 146, 177
Bell, Sir Robert, 130
bellows-blower, 134
Berkley, Sir Henry 131
Berthelet, Thomas, 153
betrothal, broken, 40

INDEX

birds, frightened by Latin, 100
Biscayan, 122
bishop, 65–6
Black Monday, 112
Boccaccio, Giovanni, 17
Bohun, Edmund, 22
Bonaparte, Napoleon, 150
boot, Climme Hoe's, 131
Borde, Andrew, 1, 5–8, 27, 191, 198–9
Botley, 64
bowls, 71, 168
boy answers friar, 63; answers courtier, 98; answers ship's master, 148
braggart, 36–7, 113–14, 127, 129
brains, 121, 185
brandy, 148, 189
Braxfield, Lord, 167
bread, for novices, 70; for hound, 80; by trencher, 130; sliced through, 141, 194
breeches, ladies in, 72, 168
Brentford, 73
Brevyary of Helth, 7
Brewer, Tom, 135, 192
bride, and Ash'ab, 15; disappointed, 29–30; experienced, 54, 163–4; Chinese, 157
bridge, narrow, 98, 124
Briefe and necessary Instruction, 20
Brooke, 2nd Lord, 71
Brown, Tom, 115
Bruges, young man of, 40
Buckingham, 1st Duke of, 24
bugiale, 2
bulls, 96–7, 107, 110, 111, 112, 182
Burbage, Richard, 4
Burton, Robert, 151, 152
Bury St Edmunds, 11, 72, 107
butcher, 141
buttocks, pillows under, 3; Marcolf's, 82; Wiggett's, 132

calves' tails, 97
Cambridge: St Mary's Church, 71; Corpus Christi MSS., 75; Trinity MS., 76; Scoggin weary of, 94; no forenoons in, 139; Scoggin at Jesus, 173; John Pace at King's, 199

Camden, William, 158
camels, if they had wings, 174
candle, husband told to eat, 35; verse on, 157
capon, and two travellers, 101; on floor, 104
captain loses leg, 139–40
Carmarthen, Marquis of, 114
Carmelite, 63
carpenter, 111, 112, 139–40
carter cuckolds Yeoman of Guard, 34; mocks courtier, 118
Castilian, 122, 168, 186
cat, Marcolf's proverbs on, 80–1; with tail between eyes, 97; in a hole, 108
Catherine (Parr), Queen, 188
cauldron, 103
Cavaliers, 62, 110–11
Caxton, William, 1–2, 3, 26–7
chair (sedan), 115
Chamberlain, John, 10, 23, 191
chamber-pot, 136
Chambers, Sir Edmund, 20
Charles I, 9, 10, 24
Charles II, 110
Charrolais, 182
chastity belts, 109
chat, riddle on, 174
Chaucer, Geoffrey, 19, 26
Cheapside, Scoggin's house in, 173
checkmate, 197
cheese, 119, 122, 128, 186
chicken, thief, 161; Arlotto's, 178; Jew's, 185
chickens, found in kite's belly, 143
child, wench had a very little one, 51
China, 157, 161, 171, 179
Christ, feeding the five thousand, 63, 68, 70; riding on a Sunday, 68; all men brothers in, 70; curate and, 73; and Saturn, 75
Christmas carol, 45–6; pie, 46, 173
Churchill, Charles, 184
Cibber, Colley, 13
cleanliest leaf, 97; trade, 98, 124, 174
Clerkenwell, 190
Clive, Mrs Kitty, 59, 165
cock, on church steeples, 97; one foot in air, 182
Cock and Leather Breeches, 58

208

INDEX

cockney, 101
coition, 3
Colchester, 134
colewort, huge, 103
collier, 126, 157
Colwell, Thomas, 198
Compendyous Regyment, see *Dyetary of Helth*
con, *le fond d'un*, 174
Conceits, Clinches, Flashes and Whimzies, 96
Condover, Shropshire, 21
coney, a raw one, 191
confession, 63, 64, 69, 72, 158
cook with toothache, 117–18
Coombe, Harvey, 150
Copland, William, 79, 152–3
Copley, Anthony, 8–9
cork, 142–3
Cornwallis, Sir William, 128
Cossack, 185
cotton, stolen, 167
Courde de Montaiglon, Anatole, 17, 176
courtier lies with braggart's wife, 36–7; drowns friar, 67; and horse, 98; mocked by carter, 118; and hot custard, 194
Covent Garden, 145; Magazine, 196
Coventry, 4
cow, a-horseback on, 97, 110; in flock of sheep, 97; why does it lie, 98
Crofts, Sir —, 191
Cromwell, Oliver, 62, 110
Cromwell, Thomas, 5
Cross, actor, 145
Croydon, 100, 157
Crusades, 14, 18
cuckold, 31–2, 34, 36–7, 39, 42–3, 45, 49, 52, 53–4, 57, 157, 158, 162, 163
cuckolds, why so many, 108
cuckoo, penning the, 98; time, 46
cuff, and Tarlton, 161
Cumberland, 151
Cumberland, Duke of, 185
Cumberland, 3rd Earl of, 8
curate and miller's daughter, 64; says Christ fed five hundred, 68; and stolen goose, 68; and Day of Judgment, 73
cure for melancholy, 139

custard, hot, 144
cutpurse, 133, 192

dauber, cleanliest occupation, 97, 124
daughter told to break off betrothal, 40
deaf, woman, 129; old Cross, 145; Scoggin says wife and queen are, 172
death, pretended, 41–2, 48–9
de Bourbon, Etienne, 18, 165, 171, 185
debts, 15
Decameron, 156
defecation, 3, 79
Demandes joyeuses, 174
des Adrets, Baron, 181
des Periers, Bonaventure, 198
devil, his cure for cuckoldom, 39–40; best master, 120
de Vitry, Jacques, 18–19, 165, 169
Disciplina Clericalis, 16–17
Djoh'a, Si, 14–15, 16
doctor and birds, 100
dog, how to scare wild, 17; gull pretends to be, 47; Scoggin pretends to be, 92; with three whelps, 66; hungry, 109; fool kills, 179
Domenichi, Lodovico, 15, 178, 185, 186
Dominic, St, 18
Dominican, 70
donkey, 3, 30, 175
Donne, John, 4, 19
Downes, Andrew, 71
dreams, 24, 25, 39–40
Droman, David, 23
drum, huge, 179
drunkard, 101, 105, 134, 180
Drury, Sir Dru, 107
Drury Lane Theatre, 12, 59
duck, 179
duel, 106, 116–17
Dyetary of Helth, 5, 6, 7

ear, cutpurse loses, 133, 192
Edgehill, battle of, 73
Edinburgh, 149
Edward IV, 6, 120, 174
Edward VI, 7

INDEX

eels stolen by parson, 67
eggs, in Si Djoh'a's sleeves, 15;
  hens on steeples would lay, 97
Elizabeth, Queen, 21-2, 27
Elwes, John, 149, 197
Ely, 134
enema, 131
engagement dissolved by contrary
  lovemaking, 159
Erasmus, 4, 22
Essex, 117
Essex, Earl of, 191
Estienne, Henri, 166
Eulenspiegel, 6, 74, 78-80, 169,
  170, 173, 176 see also Howleglas
exempla, 18-19
eye struck out, 123

fabliaux, 17, 176
Farmer, Richard, 187
Farquhar, George, 59
fart, Howleglas's advice on, 86;
  Sommers's riddle on, 124; in
  lady's chamber, 127; in street,
  136; in bed, 176; at table, 189
farts, to be let, 106; for shoulder
  of mutton, 141; under Quin's
  table, 146; for pair of boots, 193
fat lady, to make her lean, 108
father, and twelve sons, 42-3; and
  foolish scholar, 65-6; died
  suddenly, 101-2; excuse for
  tears, 144
felon, 125, 189
femme, plus douce, 174
fencing, 123, 137
fenny-countries unhealthy, 112
Ferrara, Duchess of, 172
fiddler loses wager, 54-5
Filelfo, Francesco, 159
Finet, Sir John, 23
finger in mouth and breech, 138-9
Finsbury, 4
fire, Old John for, 38; gone out
  too, 196
fleas, powder to kill, 89-90; in
  China, 171
Fleet Prison, 5, 8
Fleet Street, 140, 145, 148
Florence, Poggio in, 2; house from,
  183
Floresta Española, 8-9, 177, 178,
  179, 186, 187

flying, pretence of, by Parson of
  Kalenborow, 82-3; by Scoggin,
  93; at Milan, 169; by Eulenspiegel, 169
fool, 103, 174-5, 179, 187;
  Wiggett, 132-3
Fool, King Lear's, 24, 187
football, 137
Foote, Samuel, 13, 61, 166
fowler, 100
Fox, Charles James, 115
foxtail for punishing nuns, 69
Franciscan, 63, 179
Frankfurt, siege of, 128
Frenchman, tricked by Scoggin,
  92; tries to fly, 93; challenges
  Genoese, 116-17
Frenchwoman loves Scoggin, 92
Freud, Sidmund, 24-5, 177
friar, left in wife's bed, 36; an
  amiable confessor, 63, 166;
  glutton and niggard, 63; sins
  with nun, 65; drowned, 67;
  preaches against riding on
  Sunday, 68
friars, 19, 62
froth blown off beer, 109
fruit first and last, 102
Fudasa, 77
Fuller, Thomas, 21
funeral, Ash'ab at, 15; widow at,
  33; a pleasure, 56
Furnivall, Professor Frederick, 198-
  199

Galician, 121
gallant, 36, 64, 102, 130, 136, 137,
  189
gallows, 44, 85, 103, 105, 125, 134,
  160
gamester, 140
gardener, 44
Gardiner, Stephen (Bishop of
  Winchester), 7
Gargantua, 77, 79
Garrick, David, 13, 195-6
Gascon, 179
Gaulard, 97, 182, 183
Gay, John, 12
Genoese mocks Frenchman, 116-
  117
Gerrald, Joseph, 167
gipsies, 163

INDEX

girl, who told her mother, 40, 159; not ruined yet, 60 *see also* maid, wench
Globe Theatre, 187
Gloucestershire, 125
gloves, flapped like dog's ears, 47-8
gluttony, 63-4
Gonnella, Pietro, 172, 175-6
goose, stolen, 68; bearing most feathers, 98; barefoot, proverb on, 157
Goring, Sir George, 23
Gotham, fools of, 20, 42, 98, 174-5
gown, too short, 115
grass, not in hot ovens, 109, 182
Greece, 15
Greeks, jokes of, 16
Greenwich, 123
Gregory XII, Pope, 169
Guicciardini, Lodovico, 160
gulls, 46-8
guts, soldier's, 135

ha-ha, three sous for, 175
Hammersmith, 114, 184
hanging, 44, 85, 103, 105, 110, 125, 134, 160, 170; choosing tree for, 82, 94-5
hangman, 103
hard at the bottom, 137
hare, 143
hat, at play, 120; to catch hare, 143
hawking, pun on, 96
Hay, Matthew, 197
head, enemy's, 111; blown off, 113, 128, 185
Hearne, Thomas, 199
heaven, 33, 119
Heigham, Rob, 72
hen, or egg first, 98; and church steeples, 174
Henley, John, 13
Henry VI, 120
Henry VIII, 3, 4, 7, 22, 42, 123-4, 187-9, 199
Heptameron, 179
heretics, 18
herrings, Scoggin goes without, 88-89
Heydon, Sir John, 132, 191
Heywood, John, 4, 22
Hicks, Captain William, 154

Hitopadesa, 16
Hodja, *see* Nasreddin
Hoe, Climme, 131, 191
hogs, 161
holes, how to stop three, 108
Holland, 2nd Lord, 115
holly leaves, cleanliest, 97
horse, priest's, 69; what is most like a, 97; courtier's, 98; oysters for, 106; in Wales, 136; stuck in mud, 137; West-Countryman's, 137-8; flayed, 142; heavy-laden, 175
hound, Marcolf's proverbs on, 80-81
house, from Venice, 111; from Florence, 183
Howleglas, 20, 79-80, 84-8, 170, 198
Hundred Merry Tales, 3-4, 19, 27, 194
Hungarian, 191, 196
Hunstanton, 11, 191
hunter, 125
husband, one-eyed, 16; seeks wife upstream, 18; demonstrates his sufficiency, 30; beaten by prentice, 31-2; rejected by St Peter, 33; dreams he is a cuckold, 34; tries to get the mastery, 35; leaves friar with wife, 36; cries 'bleh' under bed, 36-7; agrees with wife, 37; called cuckold, 39; dreams of devil, 39-40; plays dead, 41-2; loses wager, 42; and wanton wife, 42-3; breaks wife's head, 43-4; hanged, 44, 160; believes wife, 45; breaks wife's neck, 48-9; impotent, 55; early to rise, 57; complains of wife's cost, 60; follows wife to confession, 69; returns after three-month absence, 163; tastes wife's pellet, 176; feeble, 186
husbands and pillows, 3

India, 16
Indians, their undoing, 108
inn, 101, 102, 106, 144-5, 175
Introduction of Knowledge, 5, 7, 191
Irishmen, 97, 112, 113, 115, 145, 147, 183

INDEX

Jackson, Hugh, 198
jakes, 106
Jamaica, 150
James I, 10, 23, 187
Japhet's father, 65–6
Jehā, see Djoh'a
Jenkins, Elijah, 12
jesters, 5, 19–24, 189
Jews, 16, 17, 185
Joe Miller's Jests, 12–14, 165
John, Old, 38
John XXIII, Pope (deposed 1415), 2
John-a-Nokes, 100
Jokes and Their Relation to the Unconscious, 24
Jonson, Ben, 79–80
justice, for wench, 52

Kalenberg, Pfarrer von, 78, 79
Kalenborow, Parson of, 78, 82–3
Kames, Lord, 149, 197
Kashmir, 171
Kemble, John M., 75
Kemp, Will, 187
king, and Scoggin, 91, 94–5, 172, 173; of France and Scoggin, 92, 93–4; well trimmed, 139; and Pater Noster, 171; and rogue, 171
King's Lynn, 11, 187
King's Place, 60
kiss, demanded by Howleglas, 85; where you like, 108; without ruffling woman's ruff, 135; demanded of lord, 170
kite, killed by ale cork, 143
knife, 141
Kraus, Dr Friedrich, 25
Kurdistan, 177

ladies in breeches, 72, 168
lady, hates tobacco, 53; questions maid with child, 54; embarrassed by sign, 58; wanton, 59; with amazing memory, 61
La Fontaine, Jean de, 156, 159
lapdog, 148
Latin, 67, 100, 125
La Tour Landry, Chevalier de, 165
Laud, Archbishop, 24
lechery, 64–5
Lee, General John, 186
leg, enemy's, 111; wooden, 140
legacy, pun on, 96

legs, asunder, 50; twins, 104
Leicester, Earl of, 22
L'Estrange, Sir Nicholas (1603–56), 11, 27, 185; his grandfather Sir Nicholas (d. 1591), 132–3, 191
L'Estrange, Sir Roger, 11, 159
Lewknor, Sir Thomas, 72
Liber facetiarum (of Poggio), 2–3
Lilly, William, 112, 183
Lob, 22–3
Lodge, Thomas, 21
London, 4, 8, 10, 34, 36, 42, 44, 53, 64, 104
lord, asleep, 71; and a meaner man, 108; told to kiss arse, 170
lords of Lübeck, 84–5
love, 51, 81, 108, 109
lover, hidden, 158, 161
Lübeck, 84–5, 88
Luther, Martin, 3, 4, 22, 78–9
Lyons, 3, 70

Macho, Julien, 3
Macrobius, 155, 157, 160, 177
madman, 125
Magdeburg, 169
maid, of widow, 38–9; with child, 54, 102; thrown by mare, 122; cuts throat, 147
maiden of Bruges, 40
maids, bared by Wiggett, 133
Marcham, Berkshire, 149
Marcolf, 74–8, 80–2, 182
Margate, 114
Marguerite de Navarre, 179
Marryat, Captain Frederick, 162
Mary, Princess (later Queen Mary I), 7
Matthias, Dr, 52
Medina, 14
Menner, R. J., 75
Mensa Philosophica, 155, 167, 170, 171, 177
merchant, 54, 120, 194
Mery tales, wittie questions and quicke answeres, 8, 198
Midshipman Easy, 162
Milan, 169
miles, argument over, 134
miller, and experienced bride, 54, 164; of Botley, 64; parson steals eels of, 67; horse flayed, 142
Miller, Joe, 12–13, 145

INDEX

minister, Puritan, 72, 72–3
mirror, Hodja Nasreddin finds, 16
Mitchener's Coffee-room, 114
Mölln, 170
Montpelier, University of, 5
More, Sir Thomas, 4, 158
Morris, Desmond, 191
Moslem culture, 14; jests, 14–17, 174–5
mother, and betrothed daughter, 40; of twelve sons, 42–3; excuse for tears, 194
Mother Bunch, 154
mothers-in-law, 28–9
Mottley, John, 12–13
Much Ado About Nothing, 3
mutton, 141

Naples, 179
Nasreddin, Hodja, 14–16, 174, 175, 177, 184, 194
negro, 150
Neville, Sir Henry, 51
nightingale, Hodja Nasreddin pretends to be, 15
Noah, his three sons, 65–6
Norfolk, 11
Norfolk, 3rd Duke of, 5, 7, 199
North, Lord, 180
North-Countryman, 137–8
Northamptonshire, 187
Norwich, 52
nose, arrow in, 123; Tom Brewer's, 135
novices, Dominican, 70
Nugae Poeticae, 22
nuns, confess lechery, 64–5; whipped with foxtails, 69; with child, 162

organist, 134
Ostend, siege of, 141
ostler, 106, 144
ox, huge, 179
Oxford, 58, 88–9, 125, 139, 141, 144, 171, 193
oysters, 105, 106, 130

Pace, John, 199
Painter, William, 20
Palace of Pleasure, 20
Pantagruel, 159

pape, le cul du, 174
Paris, 93
parson steals miller's eels, 67; prays for rain, 73; of Kalenborow, 78, 82–3 *see also* curate, minister, preachers, priest
partridges, 178
Pasquil's Jests, 27
paviours, 144, 195
peas, 114
Persia, 15
Persian Moonshee, 165, 167, 181
Peters, Hugh, 62
Piccadilly, 58
Pinkethman, Will, 12
Pinkethman's Jests, 12–13
piss, 132, 149, 188; in Holland and Rhineland, 191; servantmaid's, 193
play, 53, 120, 133
Poggio (Bracciolini), 2–3, 8, 17, 28, 29
politician, 150, 157
Polly Peachum's Jests, 12
Ponet, John (Bishop of Winchester), 7–8
Pontano, Giovanni, 179
Pooly, Sir John, 135, 192
Pope, Alexander, 13
Portuguese, 121, 187
posset, 132
pottage poured on husband, 35
Powell, William, 198
pox, biggest, 104
prayer, 72, 73, 131
preachers, 3, 18–19, 64, 68, 70, 71, 72, 168
precipice, man condemned to leap from, 107
prentice cuckolds husband, 31–2; replaces Old John, 38–9
priapismus, cures for, 7
priest and miller's daughter, 64; and two nuns, 64–5; and dogcheap mass, 66; steals miller's eels, 67; and horse-thief, 69; called old fool, 72; and Howleglas, 87–8; and dying man, 171; and Scoggin, 178; drunk, 180
Prior, Matthew, 159
prisons, 110
privy, 93

INDEX

proverbs, 80–1, 109
Publilius Syrus, 157
puddings, dirty, 109
puns, 96
punster, 114
Puritans, 20, 72, 128
purse, 53, 133
Pynson, Richard, 76

Quaker, 150
queen and Scoggin, 91–2, 172, 173; Elizabeth, 21–2, 27
Queensberry, 4th Duke of, 60
Quick, John, 196
Quin, James, 13, 27, 146, 147, 148, 195, 196

Rabelais, François, 5, 77, 79, 159
rain through roof, 149
Raleigh, Sir Walter, 22
rape, 50, 51, 162, see also ravish, ravished
rapier, 132
Rastell, John, 4, 27, 153
raven, 200-year test of, 16
ravish, impossible to, 108
ravished 20 times, 50; in wood, 186
razor, 147
Read, T., 13
Reformation, 19, 62, 74
Richard III, 1, 26
Richardson, Lord Chief Justice, 129
riddles, 97–8, 108, 174, 182
ring, Ash'ab refuses to give, 15
rogue and king, 171
Rome, 2, 100; le premier pet à, 174
Romeo and Juliet, 20
Rowley, Samuel, 188

sack (drink), all in the bottom, 97; and old woman, 129; and Tom Brewer, 135
sack, lover in, 161
Sack-full of Newes, 180
sailor, 19, 112, 113, 189-90
St Peter, 33, 119
salads and cheese, 122
Salisbury, 136
Sancroft, Archbishop, 19
Santa Cruz, Melchor de, 8
Saturn, 75–6
Saxony, Lower, 78, 170

Schildburg, 175
scholar, and dying wife, 55; and bishop, 65–6; and felon, 125; at Cambridge, 139; poor, 140, 193; in burning house, 164
scholars, foolish, 106
Scoggin, Jests of, 1, 6, 27, 198–9
Scoggin, John, 6, 88–95, 171–3, 176, 198–9
Scot, Scotchman, preaching, 70; in sea battle, 109–10; and Welshman, 136
seasick traveller, 101
sempstress, verses on, 13
servant, 31–2, 55, 63, 103, 104, 122, 123, 146, 180, 196
Shakespeare, 187
sheep, skins for flayed horse, 142; fools argue over, 175
shepherd, gentle, 109, 182
ship, 101, 109, 112–13, 139–40, 144, 189–90
shoes, stump-footed fellow's, 103; filled with earth, 172
Shottery, 66
shout, Hodja Nasreddin pursues his, 16
shrew, 43, 48–9, 158
Shropshire, 21, 187
Si Djoh'a, see Djoh'a
Sidney, Sir Henry, 129
skirts, 28
slaughter, 113
slaves, 121, 150
Sluis, siege of, 135
smell, filthy, 126
smell-smock, 109
smith, pragmatical, 96; with four sons, 166
Smithfield, 144
smock, 51–2
socks, 126
soldiers, 121, 128, 135, 141, 143, 145, 149, 185, 193
Solomon, 74–8, 80–2
Sommers, Will, 22, 123–4, 171, 187–9
song for dinner, 99
Songs and Sonnets, 20
soothsayer, man taught to be, 99, 175–6
soup, 175
sow, Scoggin roasts, 90

214

INDEX

Spaniard, 8, 102, 121, 179, 187
Spelman, John, 191
Spring, Sir William, 11, 191
squirrel, 101
Stationers' Register, 198
statue, 38, 158
steeple, of Kalenborow, 82–3;
  why not hens on, 97, 174
stockings, 104
Strange, *see* L'Estrange
Stratford upon Avon, 66
Stuteville, Sir Martin, 130
Suffolk, 11, 52, 190, 191
Suffolk, Duke of, 188
Summers, *see* Sommers
surgeons, 44
sword, 36

Tabourot, Etienne, 162, 193
Tadloe, Dr Charles, 144, 195
Tales, and quicke answeres, 3, 8
tapster, 109
Tarlton, Richard, 21–2, 44–5, 160–161, 186, 187
tavern, 84, 99, 112, 114, 119, 129
Taylor, John, 96, 155, 160, 164, 187
tears, before judge, 81; with hot custard, 144, 194
Tenali Rama, 169, 183
thief and goose, 68; and priest, 69; loses ear, 133, 192; and chickens, 161–2
Thoms, William J., 11
tiler, 105, 121
Timms, Colonel, 149
Timoneda, Juan, 160, 164, 181, 189
tobacco, to preserve chastity, 53; shop, 126; Englishmen and, 185
toothache, medicine for, 117–18
toothpicks, 114
torture, 122
Tower of London, 4, 110
Townshend, 4th Viscount, 185
traveller, 101, 103, 175
Trevor, Baron, 107
tripe, 193
tunic, Christian keeps, 17
turds, 87–8, 99, 176
Turkey, 15, 17
Turnbull (Turnmill) Street, 190
Twine, Thomas, 155
twins, 16; legs, 104

usurer, 108

vaginismus, 165
Vane, Sir Francis, 130
Velasquillo, 181
Venice, house from, 111
Villon, François, 170
vomit, 138

wager, by Gotham man, 42; by fiddler, 54
Wales, 136
wall-eye, Scoggin's, 90; carter's, 118
Wapping, 144
Warwick, Countess of, 135
water, Howleglas trick with, 84–5; served to countrymen, 119
wedge, for women's arses, 86
Welldon, Sir Anthony, 23
Welshmen, 119, 136, 192
wench, 50, 51, 52, 58, 59, 64, 128, 136
West-Countryman, 137–8
Westminster Abbey, 1–2, 173
Westminster Hall, 129
When You See Me You Know Me, 188
whore, 51, 57–8; price, 196
widow, excuse of, 31; wooer too late, 33; and second husband, 37; and statue, 38–9; who did not desire the nice play, 40–1; and gull, 46–7; remembering husbands, 50; weeping, 156–7
wife kisses one-eyed husband, 16; falls in river, 18; of sailor, 19; and prentice, 31–2; tells husband to eat candle, 35; pours pottage over husband, 35; in bed with friar, 36; with courtier, 36–7; swears husband is cuckold, 39; had done it 100 times, 40; whose husband played dead, 41–42; wins wager, 42; names her sons' fathers, 42–3; shrewish, 43; will see husband hanged, 44, 160; Tarlton's, 44–5; whose husband believed her, 45; and gull, 47–8; pretends to be dead, 48–9; a loose fit, 52; loses purse, 53; hates tobacco, 53; prays God it be John, 56; dead enough, 56;

INDEX

sends smart answer, 57; sick, 60; at husband's service, 60; a great sinner, 69; good, 80; Thomas More's, 158; French, 163; and gipsies, 163; and her pellet, 176; ravished, 186; Hodja Nas-reddin's, 194
Wiggett, 132–3, 191
Wildair, Sir Harry, 59
Wilkes, John, 147, 150
Williams, Francis, 198
Winchester, Borde's scandal at, 7–8
windfall, 51
Windsor, Forest of, 95
wine, Parson of Kalenborow's, 82–83; Howleglas's trick with, 84–5; countrymen order, 119; wife's bet for, 176
wine-drawer, 84–5, 119
Wit and Mirth, 96
Wits, Fits and Fancies, 8–9
Wits Miserie, 21

wives, and pillows, 3; faithless, 16; have the mastery, 45–6; fashion-mad, 64; and flea-powder, 89–90
Woffington, Peg, 59
wolf, 81, 182
Wolsey, Cardinal, 188–9
women no beasts, 44
Wood, Anthony à, 199
Woodward, Harry, 145
wool, wolf shites, 109, 182
World of Wonders, 166
Wotton, Sir Henry, 128
wrestling, 137
Wyer, Robert, 198
Wykes, Henry, 154

Yeoman of Guard, 34
Yorkshire, 60, 144

Zephory, Mr, 72
Zouche, Sir Edward, 23